Nick Rosen is a documentary-maker, journalist and broadcaster. He devoted the early years of his career to a study of the power of global corporations. In 1995 he founded one of the UK's first Internet companies, and discovered the joys of life off-grid when he bought a shack in Majorca. After a decade of living in city squats and unlicensed warehouses in London, he now has a proper house in the city but gets away whenever he can. In 2005, he launched a website on the subject of this book: www.off-grid.net.

D1331511

www.**rbooks**.co.uk

how to live
off-grid

journeys outside the system

nick rosen

BANTAM BOOKS

LONDON • TORONTO • SYDNEY • AUCKLAND • JOHANNESBURG

TRANSWORLD PUBLISHERS
61–63 Uxbridge Road, London W5 5SA
a division of The Random House Group Ltd
www.booksattransworld.co.uk

HOW TO LIVE OFF-GRID
A BANTAM BOOK: 9780553818192

First published in Great Britain
in 2007 by Doubleday,
a division of Transworld Publishers

The Random House Group Limited supports The Forest Stewardship Council (FSC), the
leading international forest certification organisation. All our titles that are printed on
Greenpeace approved FSC certified paper carry the FSC logo.
Our paper procurement policy can be found at www.rbooks.co.uk/environment

Typeset in Daily News by
Falcon Oast Graphic Art Ltd.

Printed in the UK by CPI Cox & Wyman, Reading, RG1 8EX

6 8 10 9 7 5

Mixed Sources
Product group from well-managed
forests and other controlled sources
www.fsc.org Cert no. TT-COC-2139
© 1996 Forest Stewardship Council

To Fiona and Caitlin Jett – the journey continues.

Contents

1

Looking for Something

*I should not talk as much about myself if there was anybody else
I knew as well.*

from *Walden, or Life in the Woods* by Henry D. Thoreau, 1854

I WAS SEARCHING FOR something different when I found the off-grid way of life, but I didn't know what.

I was a journalist, specialising in environmental stories. But this was in the 1990s and mainstream media had little or no time for subjects like pollution caused by transport, or the dangers of pesticides. 'Why don't you, just for once, bring us a story about a kidnapped baby, or something simple?' an embittered news editor once snarled as he spiked my carefully researched and potentially libellous article about pollution from a factory making a well-known brand of photographic film.

Things are better now. Global warming gets plenty of press these days – partly because you can't pin the blame on any one organisation. But newspapers and TV current affairs programmes still fight shy of anything that might accuse a specific business or product of damaging the environment. And in the perfect storm of climate change articles and documentaries that tell us how to turn off lights, turn down thermostats and prepare for the bad times ahead, there is still little or no mention of any need to radically change our lives, or rethink our habitual over-consumption; it is still all about maintaining what we've got but with just a little belt-tightening.

Back in the 1990s, I was out of step with mainstream concerns but didn't let this bring me down (I still don't). I lived in a squat in central London, so overheads were low. Freebies, from sample products and launch parties to foreign junkets, rain down on journalists. Had I really put my mind to it, I could have lived completely for free. As it was, I walked from my Holborn squat to the parties, and wrote my stories. Some of them were even published. Each winter I escaped the freezing flat by writing travel articles.

Then my focus shifted. I started a relationship with a fashion designer who had a holiday home in northern Majorca. This was long before leisure flights were identified as eco-sinful because of the carbon in jet fuel, so we flew off for weekend breaks with not the slightest cloud over our conscience. Our favourite village was Deia, international summer playground for writers, actors, models, businessmen and artists. The parade of vain people was a comical backdrop, but not the main attraction. I loved the area for the same reason they did: it's one of the most beautiful places in the world. The Majorcans wrecked the other side of the island with uncontrolled high-rise hotels, but over here the rule was strict: you could only build in the local style with local materials. Even superstar Michael Douglas was ordered to tear down a brand-new $1 million granny house on his huge estate near neighbouring Valdemossa. Beyond a ridiculous number of restaurants in Deia itself, there was little development. You went to the area to swim in the tiny coves, and wander the hills in the company of a few sheep.

My relationship with the fashion designer lasted slightly longer than a vapour trail, and after it ended the thing I missed was the soft air tinged with the scent of orange blossom and the sweep of the mountains down to the Mediterranean. I wanted my own home there. But I couldn't afford it. This was 1995 and my savings were just £10,000, from my first TV documentary. Staying on the sofa beds of friends, I searched fruitlessly around the outskirts of the village. These days there's a German estate agency every 500 metres, but before the local government tunnelled a fast road through the mountains, property deals were rarer.

I was getting nowhere until a friend introduced me to Señor Bisbal, known to us all as Baseball. Among his many activities, which included farming and antique dealing, Baseball was a registered real estate broker. A wizened seventy-year-old for whom no deal was too small, for weeks he drove me around the area, his narrow, tanned face showing no emotion as I rejected one option after the other. We shuttled between Deia and the richer and less ostentatious neighbouring village of Fornalutx, viewing a range of shepherd's huts, some built of dry stone wall, others hewn from the granite of the mountains, or made of olive wood. They had certain features in common: at least a century old, they were perched on ancient rights of way, had one room, no water, no electricity, and were inaccessible except in the tiniest of cars, or by motorbike (or on foot – though that was never an option I attempted). But none of them matched my fantasy.

I was considering applying for a mortgage to buy a sensible house in a lower-priced area, or waiting until I was old and grey and presumably had more money, when Baseball contacted me again. He was still set on helping me catch my dream, and the latest place was the most inaccessible of the lot, inconceivably high up a ridiculously rutted mountain track. But with each hairpin bend my heart leapt higher, and as we hit 700 metres above sea level, before I had even seen the place, I had decided to buy it.

'It' turned out to be a tiny structure built of dry stone wall on three sides, the fourth being the face of the mountain cliff that towered over it. That's right, the wall actually was the side of the cliff. To this day, as I drive my tortured hire car up the winding lane I still wonder why I bought it. Did I really need a twenty-minute hair-raising drive up and down the mountain every time I wanted supplies or company? The answer was 'yes'. It was exactly what I needed, and it still is. My ability to spend time on my own, just relaxing, had taken a real beating with all those launch parties back home. Here was a place where I could raise the virtual drawbridge, chill out and be alone – somewhere hard to enter, and therefore hard to leave. You were never going to get any writers and artists up here! International or otherwise.

There used to be a sixties phrase, 'only connect'. Get stoned, talk all night, and merge your mind with the collective unconscious. Then in the 1980s science fiction writer William Gibson had his *Neuromancer* characters 'jacking into the matrix'. For a while we were entranced by the idea that we could be connected to the world all the time, having one-on-one conversations with everybody on a twenty-four-hour basis, always and for ever. Now the ever-growing Internet is no longer the object of infinite possibility, it's just another resource for our lives and a tool for our work, albeit one that has made it possible to be at your desk on top of a distant mountain. The twenty-first-century challenge is how to *dis*connect, how to pull back mentally and physically from the endless merry-go-round that is modern life. I wasn't looking for a simpler, eco-way of living. I wanted to grab back what social change has stolen from us, or rather what we have stolen from ourselves – a sense of place, of being here and now.

The Majorcan hut was my way of disconnecting, and it seemed to suit my needs perfectly. No utility bills or maintenance charges or

Where it all started – outside the hut.

mortgages. No sense of obligation to go there regularly. The smallholding had survived for a thousand years; it would continue on its humble way whether I was there or not. There were hundreds of trees on the mountain: gnarled olives, statuesque pines and reassuring figs and tamarinds, as well as unidentifiable species that one day I plan to categorise. Each winter the wind blew hard, and one or two fallen pines would fulfil my heating requirements for the following year. Below ground level, the hut sat on top of an amphora – not a natural spring, but a rainwater receptacle the size of another room. The water ran down the mountain onto the roof of the hut, through the gutter and into the amphora.

Because there was no source of fresh water, the price was right: £7,000. These days it would cost £7,000 just to rebuild the amphora, and £20,000 to replant the olive trees, never mind the hundreds of metres of dry stone walling it was now my duty to maintain. The vendor was notorious locally – as I would discover later, long after two of his many brothers had retiled the tiny roof, stuffed cement into the gaps in the dry stone walling, and erected two telegraph poles like giant sentinels looking along the gulf of the valley towards the sea. I planned to hitch a yacht sail to the poles and attach it to the hut, increasing the amount of covered space, but I forgot to creosote the poles and within a year they had rotted away.

It is harder work, for sure, than just turning up at a luxury villa and flopping down by the side of the pool, but more of a change and a break for that. Admittedly there have been trips when I have arrived late at night in springtime, after the winter rains have finished but before the summer has dried out my encampment, and have not been able to face scrambling down the hillside from the road at the top of my land to the damp hut. On these occasions I have slept in the hire car for the first day, or even two, and have woken up to find families of locals out on a weekend walk through the hills peering in horror through the dusty window. Once, when I was lying naked in the sun outside my hut, a nextdoor neighbour suddenly appeared high up on a crest and began yelling at me in Spanish. I could only understand part of his rant, but it was to do with my habit of sleeping in the car upsetting his mother. (I discovered, by the way, that the Ford Ka is the best for sleeping in. The back seat folds down flatter than others, allowing one to sleep until well past sunrise.)

Only the smallest class of hire car can pass easily between the olive trees lining the road, but again, that was all I could afford. Sometimes I walk up the mountain when I first arrive and use the mobylette (the olive picker's motor scooter of choice) for shopping trips. But when I have to bring up supplies, the car is the modern mule. I am guiltily aware that an old-fashioned, real-life, four-legged mule would be better for the environment. The plane ride and the hire car alone spew far more hydrocarbon back into the atmosphere than any minor savings I might be making through my unconventional retreat, but at the time that was not an issue. A decade later, and I have become adept at living this way – at least for a few weeks or months at a time. I have a fully fitted outdoor kitchen, with butane fridge and cooker, as well as a built-in barbecue. Some of the rainwater is pumped up to a tank on the roof of the kitchen, so I even have running water of sorts. There are drawers full of torches, camping lights, candles and candlesticks of every type and size. There's even a wind-up record player and a stack of old 78s. And if I want The Libertines or Blondie, there's always the hire-car stereo.

On occasion I stay up the mountain for days at a time, just thinking and dreaming, and watching the tiny dots of cars driving along the seafront far below. The longer I'm there, the less I want to listen to music, and the less I want to make shopping trips down to the town. It was at times like these that I learned to value edible plants, especially the wild asparagus that sprouts at various times of the year like a succulent grass.

I now have the ability to disconnect, but also the ability to re-connect. This is not a retirement home. When I am there for longer stays, I have to work to pay my Easyjet bills. I can use a fold-up solar panel to power the laptop, and the latest twist is the Vodafone 3G card which allows me high-speed Internet access at the top of the mountain. That 3G card is a trade-off and a contradiction I embrace willingly. It may be hypocrisy or self-delusion, but I think it's something else: it's a solution to a problem, one we all face if we live in cities and go to work yet want something more.

Nine years after I bought the hut I married Fiona, an artist who was just as captivated by the romance of the mountains. When I first took her there she told me I had to be completely crazy to have such a mad second home, and that she loved me for it. Then she asked if we could go down to the local town and buy some new sheets and a duvet. 'When you told me you had a bit of a shack I thought you were just being cool and modest,' she said to me later. 'I never thought that it would be just, like, a bit of a shack.' On each visit, while I wanted to flake out and watch the surrounding peaks change colour through the day, she faithfully ferried up a carload of trees and potted herbs, and wrestled with the stony ground to plant things that would either be promptly eaten or be dried out and dead by the time we returned.

More improvements were carried out with the help of our second nearest neighbour, Toni the village plumber. Toni's primary residence is in the nearby town, but he inherited hundreds of acres of what was near-worthless land fifteen years ago. Changing fashions and improving technology have reversed his fortunes, and he spends all his free time prowling the peaks and valleys in his tiny Suzuki 4WD. Toni Baloney, as Fiona affectionately calls him, is fifty but has jet black hair and healthy teeth, albeit blackened through years of pipe-smoking. He is learning English so he can lure other foreign purchasers on to the mountain he has loved since he was a boy.

It was Toni who talked me into a series of madly expensive build-ing projects. One can never have enough water, so now I have a huge stone water tank as big as a house, at a cost of €20,000, which gathers

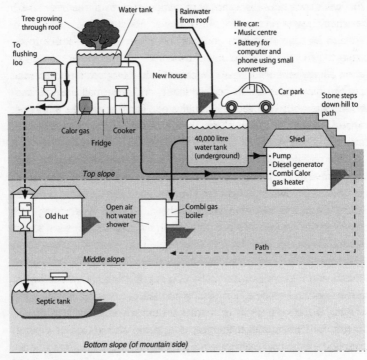

My mountain haven.

rainwater from the roof of another building I have acquired, higher up the mountain. Toni then installed a combi boiler powered by butane gas bottles. Hot water now gushes from the tank via a butane-powered overhead shower with the click of a battery-operated switch (after a few minutes spent lighting the boiler each time we arrive). I have also added a gazebo on the site of an old ruin, and Toni's greatest triumph, a net-work of grandiose, millionaire-style stone steps around my crumbling mountainside. Much as I moaned at the expense, the steps do mean I use the land more, especially in winter when it would be tempting to huddle in the hut and light the fire. The other major innovation is a flushing loo, using rainwater from the privy roof, and a view over the mountains down to the sea. A second loo lower down is sheltered beneath an overhanging rock. Toni dug a kind of septic tank (a '*forca negra*') at the bottom of my hill.

Toni's own house is a model of what a mountain building should be when there is no mains water or power. Solidly built and airtight, it is warm in winter yet cool and airy in summer. It has an industrial-strength generator, housed in its own little room, which comes on automatically whenever he so much as flicks a light switch or opens a tap. His olive trees are in perfect shape, and the small area of land around the house is beautifully cultivated. There is also an amphora, topped off with a quaint shelter made of olive wood to house the bucket and chain.

As I said, Toni is not my only neighbour. On any Friday night, other locals arrive at the handful of nearby houses – each a kilometre apart, perched on its own outcrop – and start up their generators in order to watch TV soaps. My own generator is a Subaru, used mainly for powering the cement mixer and the chainsaw, and for pumping water around the land. I can also charge up batteries and run a twelve-volt light or two, but I prefer candles and fires. For the moment our neighbours are still locals, but it's unlikely to stay that way. We have heard rumours of weekenders from Palma arriving in a huge 4×4, its sides scraping the olive trees as it trundles up the mountain track. When I bought the land, it was at the very end of a road that has now been extended – whether legally or not I can't say. At least two cars a day go past, as well as the occasional hiker on what are becoming world-famous walking paths, helpfully signposted by the local council. Half an hour's walk from my land, one of the tiny paths that criss-cross the mountain now widens into the entrance to a six-star hotel. Ca's Xorc is much favoured by the heads of German multinationals. We go there to use the infinity pool (just until we get our own), but these new developments are unwelcome – to me, though not to Toni. Deia's property prices are steadily climbing the 700 metres to my little retreat, and I may have to consider selling out and beginning the whole process over again.

Plus, I am embarrassed to say, I made some rather basic errors in my choice of hut. This is a painful admission for a self-styled expert, but I hope others can at least learn from my mistakes. For one thing, any work on the building, or the land, is preceded by an epic journey to bring materials up the mountain. Having shelled out for quite a few improvements over the years, I know what Hannibal must have felt when he crossed the Alps. Or maybe Noah and his Ark is a better analogy. It is a good idea to buy a property above flood level, but the cost of being so inaccessible is high.

The bigger mistake was believing the guy who sold me the hut when he told me there was sun on the land all year round. That should mean solar panels will heat the place in winter, I naively thought. Had I looked more carefully – sorry, had I looked at all – I would have noticed my mountaintop was overshadowed by a far greater peak a few hundred metres away. By late October there are just a few patches of sunlight on my garden, and from mid-November, when the hunting season starts, until January, no winter sun at all on my land.

And the size of the holding, which had seemed such a bonus when I bought it, means I am permanently battling against the encroaching brambles, and I spend most of the time I am there tending the olive trees. As I am only an occasional visitor, I cannot cultivate the land. Anything we plant is eaten by the wild mountain goats, the *cabras*, during our long absences. Why should the *cabras* get all the best plants? I wondered. So I decided to leave the vegetation to look after itself. As a result, the only non-native species are a few clumps of heather which took hold and just one healthy jasmine bush climbing up the side of the shepherd's hut.

Less than a year after our wedding, Fiona and I were back in Majorca with our new daughter Caitlin, who was three months old by

Fi and Caitlin in one of our thousand-year-old olive trees.

then. Toni cooed and smiled at her, and we drew up careful plans for chicken-wire play areas to guard the tot from the twelve-foot drops between one *bancal* (terrace) and the next. After a decade of casual indoor camping I was suddenly confronted with the need to make the place warm, safe and child-friendly; arriving late at night and sleeping in a damp bedroom was no longer an option.

For years I had been wondering whether a small wind turbine attached directly to an electric fire would heat the hut in winter. When the wind blew the fire would come on, and when the wind did not blow, it would presumably not be that cold. It was an interesting theory, but one I had never had a chance to test – because I had never met anyone I could ask, preferably someone who also had the ability to mount and wire up a wind turbine. And someone who was willing to make the journey. I took to the Internet for help, and although I did find plenty of advice, I could not be sure how it applied to my particular situation.

I soon realised that the only way to educate myself was to go and meet people who were living this way. It's not that I wanted to become a full-timer; I just knew I could learn from them, and though I had come to accept that my little haven would never be the perfect retreat, I could at least make the best of it. Or perhaps just give it up, sell it and put my new knowledge to use finding a better place.

Another factor was also entering into my thinking. It was at just about this time that a new awareness was taking hold of the damage wreaked by unlimited tourism in general, and air travel in particular. I still can't accept that holiday flights are a sin, nor do I believe that I must cease all air travel, but it seems a tiny bit self-defeating to have an eco-home so far away that you damage the environment just getting there. I had stumbled on a neat idea when I bought this patch of Majorcan heaven, and I didn't want to leave it, but I decided I could only justify the journey if we stayed a decent length of time – a fortnight at least, preferably a month. Short breaks of a weekend or even a week were going out of style.

That left us with the question of what to do when we wanted to get out of London for a couple of days. We could stay with friends, sure, but we wanted somewhere to go whenever we could grab the time, even if it was just a short trip, arriving late one night and leaving the next. So the whole process of looking for a place to call our own started over again, this time in the UK, and preferably within walking distance of a train station as traffic gridlock worsened. I had one big advantage: I knew from my experience in Majorca that we could survive very well in a shack or even a camper van; we did not need a £250,000 cottage with walls of honeyed stone. Which was just as well, because Caitlin's arrival meant we would never again be able to afford one.

How to be Free

You won't find the phrase in the *Oxford English Dictionary* – yet – but what I was doing in the Majorcan mountains was 'going off-grid'. During my Internet search for that wind turbine to power a heater (and the solar panel for my laptop) I discovered that, literally, the word 'off-grid' refers to places, buildings or people without mains water, power or a phone-line. Until recently it has been largely an American phenomenon, and something of a subculture at that. In 2005 there were approximately 180,000 off-grid homes in the US according to *Home Power* magazine, and by 2006 this number had grown to 235,000 according to *USA Today*. The locations range from country houses and old farm huts to tree-houses, container dwellings, and tents and their ethnic variations, such as benders (shelters made by covering a framework of bent branches with canvas) and Mongolian yurts (circular tents of felt or skin). The people living there might be back-packers or right-wing survivalists, international business travellers with their own private islands or groups of friends who decided to start a commune; they move around in buses and four-wheel-drives, yachts and houseboats, caravans and Winnebagos. They are all outside, or in between, the criss-crossing lines of power, water, gas and phone that delineate the civilised world.

Reading about it online, I learned that pioneering didn't need to mean discomfort. Some of the cosiest-sounding places in the world are off-grid. And I detected that as well as this physical sense of off-grid, there also seemed to be another meaning – an off-grid attitude that you could take into the local park or your own back yard, a sense of feeling at ease in the world, of reclaiming your independence and individuality. A practical, freewheeling kind of self-sufficiency.

Back in Blighty I began to study books about building cob houses, and the skills of foraging for wild food. I read Richard Mabey, author of *Food for Free*, and Hugh Fearnley-Whittingstall. Although I have never shot an animal, I have thought about it, especially whenever one of the Majorcan *cabras* ate the tender stems of the jasmine. Alternatively, I thought, I may one day find some roadkill as I drive around town on my Honda 90, and bring that back for a barbecue. I had come across the philosophy of Freeganism, which advocates an existence completely free from shopping, cars and utility bills, but this amounts to a boycott of the economic system, whereas I want to drop in and out of 'the system', partly for ethical reasons, but also because I need the mental space.

Going off-grid is pro-environment and pro-consumer. It's a positive message, not oppositional.

Part of the attraction of going off-grid is enthusiasm for a bargain. I call it putting the 'free' into freedom. Not that I would advocate sacrificing comfort just to save a few pounds. It's a mistake to retreat from the on-grid world only to lead a hair-shirt existence. But the new trend towards buying cheap or second-hand goods is part of the off-grid philosophy. Partly thanks to the Internet, prices have been forced down, to zero in some cases. Forget Top Shop. Say hello to Oxfam, and Freecycle. The international Freecycle movement has a different website for each city and allows members to post up things they want to give away, from old railway sleepers to their ex-lover's entire wardrobe. Hundreds of thousands of items that would once have been thrown away or left to rot in cupboards are now being given away to anyone who is willing to collect them, even if that person is only going to sell them on at their local market. I used to rely on freebies from journalism; now I get them from Freecycle – and from nature.

We are entering a post-consumer era where owning stuff and being busy and working too hard will seem unfashionable. How we arrived at this point is something I will explore later, but it is not a new idea. *Walden, or Life in the Woods,* by Henry Thoreau, is a classic nineteenth-century text about downshifting. Thoreau repeatedly returns to the theme of our innate need to hoard and accrete belongings that make us unhappy. 'How many a poor immortal soul have I met well-nigh crushed and smothered under its load, creeping down the road of life, pushing before it a barn 75 feet by 40 and 100 acres of land,' he says as he plans his two-year stint in the wilderness. Better to own nothing and have no security than be harassed for a mortgage you cannot pay, or weighed down by a feeling of uselessness because you are not looking after your land properly (as I am not in Majorca).

For a newcomer to the off-grid world, the price can appear high. I knew from my time in Majorca that if I was to live this way, even part-time, I would suddenly have to think about things I had hitherto taken for granted. Where would the power and water come from? How much would I be using? Was I about to run out? On the other hand, once I had the basics of heat, light and water under control, the payback would be instant and valuable: greater peace of mind, a feeling that I had partly freed myself from the commercial world and gained the power – the ultimate power – of control over my own life.

I decided to visit as many types of off-grid dwellers as possible. Environmentalists, for sure – they are living the purest off-grid lives, and I wanted to seek their point of view – but also people who live that way because that is all they can afford, or because they value the freedom, or because they just want to dip into it for weekends or holidays. Because it is a movement with its roots in 1960s counterculture, there are already thousands in the UK who are living off-grid or who have incorporated off-grid into their lives in a combination of ancient wisdom and new technology. And the numbers are growing rapidly. By the time I finished my journey around the United Kingdom I had concluded that there are at least 25,000 households living off-grid all year round in the UK – perhaps 75,000 people. But this number certainly doubles and perhaps trebles in the summer months. I had also learned that thousands every year are going abroad to live off-grid in Spain, Portugal, Greece, Italy, India and South America. This is an important trend, and it is likely to continue unless we make it easier for those who want to live off-grid in this country to do so.

Many of those living off-grid in the UK are in conventional houses – conventional, that is, except for one thing: they are too remote to have their own power or water. There are 300 of these houses in Northumberland alone. We know that because there was an EU survey, but we have less to go on for the rest of the country. I came across remote old houses in almost every county, but more in the most rural corners of Scotland and Wales. So I will make a very conservative estimate of 5,000 off-grid homes that are houses. As with all my calculations and statements from now on, I am only talking about off-grid homes.

Next to stand up and be counted are the people living in static homes that are not conventional houses, in yurts, benders, tree-houses or caravans whose wheels have long since rusted over, as well as those living in tents or shacks of one sort or another. I met literally hundreds of people in this category on my trip around Britain, and my journey was not in the least exhaustive. So another 5,000 unconventional homeowners is surely an underestimate.

Then there are 3,000 homes on boats. About 22,000 boat owners have mains hook-ups on their moorings, but I am not talking about them. The official British Waterways figures are quite precise, so 3,000 off-grid boats on our waterways is an accurate figure, as far as it goes. In addition there are perhaps another thousand boat-dwellers on our coasts, people not living on canals or rivers but on the high seas, sailing down to the Med for the winter and coming back here for the summer.

And there is that other great class of off-gridders, mobile home and van dwellers. There are 130,000 camper vans in the UK, and many more parked overseas that are British-owned. I am not including foreign vans, but judging by the van-dwellers I met and talked to there are easily another 5,000 in the UK, perhaps far more. And that does not include the most feared of van dwellers, the gypsies. Despite the fact that I met some inspirational civil liberties campaigners and lawyers who spend their lives defending gypsies in court, I chose not to include them on my route. To be frank, I disapprove of them. I would not take issue with their refusal to join the society within which they live, nor their frequent use of the dole. That is up to them, and I am glad to live in a country that can sustain them. I just don't like the way gypsies so often despoil the sites they use, leaving broken fridges, old sinks and nameless pieces of metal in their wake. 'They sometimes ride roughshod over the law,' said Nigel Cant, a Gloucestershire planning consultant who has acted on their behalf in planning battles in the past, and who has also acted for the other side – the property owners who have found themselves involuntarily hosting a gypsy settlement.

The old image of gypsies in wagons pulled by carthorses is no more; these days they are as likely to have a Mercedes sprinter as their main vehicle and a Mitsubishi 4×4 as a runaround for the wife. But the carthorse-owning fraternity still exists. They refer to themselves as 'horse-drawn', and they are the least visible residents of the off-grid virtual city, hidden down green lanes and other ancient rights of way. A few are probably gypsies, but most are radical ex-squatters and road protesters, or simply the rural poor.

The final category is the present generation of homeless and squatters, living in empty industrial buildings, decaying flats or old farm buildings. Many of them care about the environment, contribute to the community in which they live and go to great trouble to leave no trace of themselves when they depart. There are 10,000 squatters in the UK and perhaps 3,000 completely homeless types who are not even kipping down on a friend's floor but are sleeping rough. Not all the squatters are off-grid, however, only perhaps 2,500 of them.

So, that's 5,000 conventional houses, 5,000 static non-houses, 3,000 boats, 5,000 vans, about 1,500 horse-drawn, 2,500 squatters and 3,000 rough sleepers. My quest was now to meet some of them.

Think of what follows as a guidebook. In sharing my own voyage of discovery I will recommend paths and point out byways into this burgeoning world. But first we must explore how we arrived where we are today and why there is such a pent-up desire among a wide swathe of the population to live with renewable energy and rainwater harvesting. The story starts long ago, before the grid was built.

2

We Were All Off-Grid Once

The London citizen of the year AD 2000 may have a choice of nearly all England and Wales south of Nottingham and east of Exeter as his suburb.

from *The Anticipation of the Reaction of Mechanical and Scientific Progress Upon Human Life and Thought* by H. G. Wells, 1902

THE GRID SILENTLY and invisibly underpins modern life. I'm talking about the simple, literal grids of the power and water networks, roads as well. These physical networks are also a metaphor for all the big, impersonal systems and organisations that circumscribe our lives. Fuzzier grids include government computers and ID cards; cellphones, Internet and satellite TV; plane routes and the delivery routes of supermarket lorries, as well as retail outlets; brands; and even schools and universities. They are more subtle, less escapable than the simple, physical tentacles of power and water, sewage and roads. We can rarely get away from these metaphorical grids for long – unless we completely step away from society.

But the grid doesn't extend to every part of our lives. There are still vast areas of human experience it can't touch, from meditating in a city park to roaming the wilderness; from making your own music or poetry and performing it among friends, to illegal workers in the black economy or surviving and thriving in a yurt, or perhaps in a field with a solar panel and a vegetable patch.

In this book I'm using the word 'off-grid' to mean independent of the basic power and water grids only (the trend in the US is to use the phrase 'off the grid' to mean dropping out of sight of the system altogether). The phone grid is a less clear-cut issue now that a mobile signal can be found pretty much everywhere. You could argue that the wireless grid is all-pervasive, but I prefer to see the glass half full. The wireless phone allows you to get off the grid and still earn a living. I see its liberating rather than its enslaving effects. As I said, we can get away from all grids some of the time and some of them all the time, but to take yourself completely off the grid for good would be an extreme experiment. You can imagine the TV reality show, *How to Disappear*, with contestants cashing in all their assets, closing their bank accounts, shredding their credit cards, losing their social security numbers, and bribing homeless people to buy them a pay-as-you-go phone so as to avoid the CCTV cameras on the way into Woolworths . . .

There is a charming convention some top academics still observe: if members of the public contact them with a question they find interesting, they will discuss it. I phoned Avner Offer, Chichele Professor of Economic History at All Souls College, Oxford, seeking his reaction to the idea of going off-grid. 'Maybe we just end up exchanging one grid for another' was his reply. He has a point. Broadband Internet, mobile phones, a car to take you along a road to and from your off-grid haven . . . this is not the purest form of off-grid living. So sue me. I have no obligation to be consistent. I just like the idea of living out of sight of the nearest electricity pylon; far enough off the beaten track that the water pipes don't reach me; away from advertising, newspapers, and all the other bothersome distractions of modern living. What's more, I like the idea of dropping back into modern life whenever I fancy. At least I do at the moment.

James Lovelock, the scientist who devised the Gaia theory of the Earth as a self-regulating system, believes that before long the grid will start breaking down; that within our lifetime most of us will face rationing of water, food and energy. Power cuts and drought will be the norm for part of the year, then global warming will lead to global flooding. The things we all take for granted in the industrialised West won't work the same way any more. Individual countries, especially islands, will have to become self-sufficient for food and energy. A wartime mentality will prevail. It is not good enough just to ignore Lovelock's warning in the hope it won't happen. And you don't have to believe he is right to want to change the way you live right now. Wasting less energy is a good thing in itself. Embrace what that future may hold, acquaint yourself with the off-grid life, and you will fear the future less.

But the politics of going off-grid are more complex than they at first seem. It is a personal choice, but it also has repercussions for the big, powerful utility companies. In fact, virtually every aspect of modern life – planning permission, school inspections, transport, water, food, to name just a few – is surrounded by a well-developed set of regulations. In some countries the law goes so far as to prevent individuals from providing their own electricity. I want somehow to evade as many of these rules as I can and live my own life the way I want, without interfering with anyone else, and without them harming or bothering me; in the future, I don't want aspects of life such as work schedules and school holidays to delimit my off-grid life. Understanding how the grid came to be, and what its constituent parts are, was the first step in my journey to separate myself from it and discover how to claim back my individuality.

Imagine the grid did not exist. Imagine we had somehow segued from the era of candles and coal fires to one that featured home generators, gas canisters, solar power and fuel cells. Imagine if, in this rainy country, we all gathered our own water – or at least most of us did. How would life be different? Would we be less happy? Don't get me wrong, I'm not talking about returning to a time before electricity and gas and clean, safe drinking water; I am just asking whether power and water has to be delivered via a grid or whether there is another way. I am not harking back to the pre-grid days as some kind of utopia; I simply want to try to define what we lost when we gained the grid. We still hear the occasional story about a remote village that used to have to provide its own power but is now at last connected. I have filmed in such places myself. As the villagers blink into the cameras, and the electric power arrives, their own power is sapped away. Now there is a move in the opposite direction. Whole new villages are being planned off-grid.

It's time to question our assumptions about the naturalness of the grid. It's convenient, sure. We enter the room, flip the switch, and the light goes on. But we don't need the grid for that. Do we really need it at all?

Water sets the pattern

The supply of water has been organised on a commercial basis since the late eighteenth century. Setting a pattern they would follow down the centuries, the water companies started abusing their market dominance almost as soon as they received their licences to trade. One of their earliest customers was so irate that he published at his own expense an elegantly bound 1790 tract called 'A Bone to Pick . . .' They weren't afraid of long book titles in those days, and the full title, as found in the British Library catalogue (www.bl.uk), is worth quoting: 'A Bone to Pick; recommended to the several Water Companies of this Metropolis; or a check to avarice, tyranny and oppression . . . Being an . . . account of what steps the author hath taken to withstand the rapacity of a certain Water Company [viz. the Shadwell] . . . Also a friendly address to the public . . . stating the trifling expenses of the Water-Companies when compared with their excessive profits . . . Intended as an encouragement to a more public . . . inquiry into this matter, etc.' At one point John Robins, the author, describes his visit to the office of the Shadwell Water Company to complain about a 50 per cent price rise dropped on him with no warning. He is shown in to meet the manager and is about to say his piece when 'there was suddenly a shout of "turn him out, turn him out"' and Mr Robins found himself ejected onto the street.

I began my research with a preconceived idea that today's leaky remnants of the Victorian water system are a legacy of high-minded reforms at a time of growing urban pollution and deadly epidemics. As the industry began to form, one of the main sources of water was the Thames, and the new practice of letting cesspits overflow into the river meant that the Thames stank in summer. By 1805 all the fish had died, London had a population of over a million, and the water supply was overstretched. Water 'is impregnated with the foulest and most unwholesome substances,' London's Metropolitan Water Company told investors at its launch in 1833. It promised to change all that. But Christopher Hamlin, in his book *A Science of Impurity*, proves that the nineteenth-century water companies went on to behave in a way that is comparable with twentieth-century cigarette companies and twenty-first-century oil companies (though he does not put it in those terms), hiring scientists to present one-sided accounts that concealed evidence damaging to their position, and inflicting disease on the public through their refusal to apply the highest scientific standards. To take a few examples: a private water supplier in Newcastle-upon-Tyne caused a cholera epidemic in 1854 by taking water out of the Tyne; a cholera outbreak in east London in 1866 was traced back to the water company; and there was a waterborne typhoid epidemic in the Tees Valley in 1890.

Far from being motivated by public good, the reality was the familiar one of water companies maximising their profits at the expense of their customers. At the 1896 annual meeting of the East London Water Company, the self-righteous chairman told outraged shareholders that their management was being called 'grasping monopolists, and other hard names' by its customers. Between 1860 and 1914, the private water companies had such low standards and such high prices that local councils were granted the power to take them over for the public good, and towards the end of the nineteenth century those local councils took it upon themselves to start appointing medical officers of health and public analysts who produced far more stringent and reliable analyses of water quality than the water companies. All this would have happened sooner but for the close financial links between the water companies and dozens, perhaps hundreds, of MPs, according to historian W. M. Stern. The problems the new municipal owners inherited led to huge new pumping stations being built, and eventually a new sewage system. Water began to be chlorinated and steel water mains were installed as well as double filtration.

Calls for a national water grid first surfaced in the 1920s, initially from entrepreneurs and engineers. 'It would banish for all time the possibility of drought in even the remotest village,' an engineer wrote (inaccurately) to *The Times* in 1933. The idea was defeated on the grounds that there was no need for it if each area built its own reservoirs. A national water grid would simply 'put up water rates all over the country', Henry Brooke, the Tory minister for local government, told Parliament in 1959. But the movement of water from wetter parts of the country to drier parts continued to attract policymakers. By 1971 a massive underground tunnel had been built to carry winter water from Norfolk to Essex where a huge house-building programme was being held up because of a lack of water. In 1976 the Labour government was again talking of a national grid. That year torrential rain fell in Sussex at the same time as supplies to residents were cut off in a dozen towns in North Devon. Yorkshire County Council announced it was to put the beginnings of a regional grid in place.

Why did the British not take to capturing rainwater or digging boreholes? It was certainly an option, especially if a group of householders got together. And it still is an option. In fact, new houses in flood-prone areas may be forced to have rainwater harvesting systems to be granted planning permission. Private boreholes were first regulated under the

Water Act 1945 with further restrictions applied by the 1961 Rivers Acts. Anyone can still drill a hole without permission if it's for domestic use only. These days a domestic filter plus ultra-violet light would be more than adequate for anyone wishing to have a private supply of drinking water. In isolated areas where mains water still does not run, that is exactly what happens.

After decades of suggestions for regional water distribution, such as a trans-Pennine pipeline and a long-distance water pipe to Manchester, the system of multiple local water authorities ended in 1973 with the regionalisation of the water industry. In retrospect, the industry was being fattened up for privatisation in the 1980s. The bite-size local water companies were not tasty enough for the stock market.

At no point amid all this reorganisation and grandiose toys-for-the-boys engineering projects did any party to the debate seriously consider securing a reduction in water consumption, either by repairing leaks or limiting the amounts households used every year. Within a couple of years of regionalisation, the Great Drought of 1976 forced water shutdowns and standpipes in the street. The new regions were blamed, perhaps wrongly. Another was the Yorkshire drought of 1995 (so-called even though other parts of England received an even smaller propor-tion of their average rainfall that year), which marked a crisis of confidence in the privatised water industry. Yorkshire Water threatened shutdowns and standpipes in the street, yet its profits rose that year. It floated the idea of introducing water meters, raising suspicion that water companies were creating a false climate of scarcity in order to argue for compulsory metering.

Having read the papers and listened to ordinary consumers, the most persistent concerns today are that the privatised water companies are not spending enough on maintenance, especially the fixing of leaks, which account for the loss of an estimated 30 per cent of water from the system. Although some of this water runs into rivers and thus back into the system, some of it is just lost. So the first conclusion of my research is that far from our water system being shaped by altruism and public service, the present water industry is merely continuing a pattern of corporate greed and contempt for the customer set down from its inception.

With rainwater harvesting and community boreholes many of us could live without the water companies, as long as we acted responsibly about consuming and treating our own drinking water. We all take for granted the safety (if not the purity) of the water that gushes out of the kitchen tap. We would not be so carefree if we lived with drought. Most industrialised countries insist that if you have your own water supply it has to be tested by the public analyst at least once a year. If society's water was off-grid, we could not just assume that everyone would be a good citizen. But so what? Perhaps all this entails is travelling with a litre of Evian in a backpack – many already do – or carrying water purification tablets in a pocket. Dealing with our own sewage is another matter, but we could do it if we had to.

Gas to every home

The first gas company, the London Gaslight and Coke Company, was founded in 1812. It was followed by start-ups in Preston and Liverpool. In the early days gas was mainly used for street lighting, which made towns and cities safer at night, but the Victorians soon took to gas for home lighting, then for cooking and heating. By the mid nineteenth century there were 2,000 miles of privately owned gas mains in London alone, and accidents were common. An 1843 explosion in a pub was 'visited by crowds of persons of all classes', reported *The Times*. The risks were tolerated, and for decades there were reports of explosions which made the pavements 'heave' and caused 'great fissures' in the streets.

The arrival of electricity in the late nineteenth century slashed demand for gas. To compensate, the gas companies aggressively marketed cooker hire at loss-making prices, then hiked the cost once they had the user base. Immediately after the First World War, the Board of Trade investigated gas companies for 'profiteering' on gas appliance rental costs. There were nearly a thousand of these companies in the inter-war years, most of them quite small, but after the Second World War they were nationalised. By 1955 the beginning of the national gas grid had been firmly established. In 1965, the Ministry of Power decided to finance the exploitation of gas fields in the North Sea.

The 1967 Arab–Israeli war, followed by the shock OPEC oil price rises of the early 1970s, led the Labour government to switch the whole country to take advantage of North Sea gas. A huge natural gas conversion programme costing over a billion pounds at 1970s prices gave an extraordinary boost to the nation's plumbers and heating engineers. By 1977, 2,600 more miles of new pipe had been laid underground to create a national grid of gas, and it was no longer stored in the huge cylinders whose remains still adorn many an urban landscape. Although millions of houses already owned gas cookers thanks to the earlier marketing efforts, these did not run on 'natural gas' and had to be replaced or modified. Many households also switched to gas heating – a decision they may come to regret. As the UK's own reserves decline and world prices fluctuate, gas-connected households are facing sharp increases. At the very least consumers may be wise to make sure they have a wood-burning stove installed, in case prices rise to impossible levels, or the Russians simply cut off supplies to Europe for political reasons.

Nearly two centuries after gas was first piped into the nation's homes, what have we to show for it? Our vast gas reserves are running down. We have invested in a huge distribution system, a built-in dependence that will now act as a money-box for Russian despots. Although lights are no longer gas-powered, the legacy of those early gaslights is light pollution in every built-up area, and an almost pathological fear of complete darkness in our culture.

'Electricity for life'

The gas marketers' invention of 'natural gas' (as opposed to unnatural gas?) was mirrored by the electricity industry's equally preposterous slogan 'Electricity for Life'. In a 1980s TV ad for the Central Electricity Generating Board (CEGB), a couple were shown snoring in their idyllic cottage. 'Every night while you're asleep a miraculous power is at work in the land,' the voiceover intones, 'a power which is used for everything from printing your morning paper to baking your daily bread . . .' Images of domesticity and Englishness reinforce this 'miraculous' tale. 'Long before you wake, your electricity board is working for you,' the ad continues, 'drawing on its massive resources to serve you through the day.' Hardly surprising, then, that on some subliminal level we are convinced that the power supply and the way it is brought to us via the national grid are integral to the fabric of our existence.

This confidence trick began at the dawn of the age of electricity: slick salesmanship built the national grid, further marketing activity persuaded people to use as much power as possible, then came the PR coup of foisting nuclear power stations on the country rather than simple energy-saving measures.

In 1901, the scientist Lord Kelvin spoke at the opening of the new Neptune Bank power station in Newcastle. 'What I am seeing today is the dream of my life realised,' he said. 'I do not know the limits of electricity, but it will go beyond anything we can conceive of today.' The reality was less uplifting. Only 9 per cent of the country's tramways were electrified in 1897 compared to 88 per cent in the US; and although half the key inventions needed for the commercialisation of electricity were made in the UK, the major manufacturers of our equipment – Siemens, Westinghouse and General Electric – were all overseas.

Bill Luckin, Professor of Urban History at the Bolton Institute, coined the term 'electrical triumphalism' to characterise the dogmatic insistence by the pro-electricity lobby that electricity would solve all the country's problems – economic, physical and even spiritual. 'Electricity permeates all life and has been stored and harnessed by man for his joy and use,' stated a 1936 pamphlet from the Electrical Association for Women (EAW), one of a network of industry-funded pressure groups. Each electricity company was required to donate 2.5 per cent of revenues to the industry PR campaign, Luckin revealed in his book *Questions of Power*, and in 1925 this was raised to 10 per cent. The EAW's role was to win over the housewife. Its charismatic leader Caroline Haslett toured the country giving inspirational speeches about the glories of the electric vacuum cleaner. 'You can put your clean apron on and keep it clean, and you don't have to go down on all fours, like some monkey,' she told the Women's Institutes she visited.

Still, every local scheme from the New Forest in 1933 to the Lake District in 1949 met opposition. The grid builders' tactic was to divide and conquer. Whoever held out against the march of the pylons was derided as some sort of eccentric, or worse, selfishly impeding progress and harming the community. The Verderers of the New Forest, whose ancient duty to protect the forest was created by royal charter, were apologetic when they refused the power company a right of way in 1933. They were one of a handful of groups or individuals able to make a stand. The Central Electricity Board (CEB), supposedly impartial, co-ordinated lobby groups like the Electricity Development Association and the Overhead Lines Association, whose slogan was 'electricity without spoilation'. The technical press helped things along with attacks on reactionary anti-electrical elements in society who did not want to sacrifice local independence for the sake of this new energy source.

As happened in the gas industry, nearly a thousand electricity companies battled for a share of the market, which meant every area had at least one and usually several local firms. Legislation designed to centralise control of what was seen as a strategic industry forced many of them to amalgamate or go bust, with the result that what could have been a highly competitive industry made up of small companies serving local areas eventually became an uncompetitive monopoly 'in the national interest'. Privatisation in the Thatcher years transformed it into a profitable, some would say profiteering, oligopoly.

The centralisation of the electricity industry and the decision to create a national grid were the work of a cabal of engineers, politicians and financiers organised by the messianic Charles Merz, designer of the aforementioned Neptune Bank power station in Newcastle. When the CEB was established in 1926, its first act was to adopt Merz's idea of linking power stations through high-voltage lines carried on pylons. Seven self-contained areas around the country were 'gridded' – interconnected with a 132kV cable. To overcome opposition this was sold to the public as a means to transfer power between areas only in emergencies.

The arguments against the establishment of the grid were both ecological and local, i.e. based on a desire to keep power generation and distribution in local hands. In Keswick, in the heart of the Lake District, there was total opposition to the pylons on visual grounds, and a demand that the area be turned into a national park. The anti-pylon campaigners, Professor Luckin tells us, argued that Penrith and Keswick were 'non-industrial towns with populations of 8,000 and 4,000 respectively, both of which already have their own supplies of electricity' and did not need it brought in from outside.

But in the end money talked. In 1929, a year of intense anti-grid activity, the CEB won their right of way through a backdoor agreement with the National Trust which owned the land the townspeople were fighting to defend, and by early 1930 construction was underway on a gigantic line of pylons east to Penrith, through over ten miles of what is now the Lake District National Park. The unsuccessful campaign damaged personal relationships in the community for a generation.

Perhaps the decisive moment in the rise of the grid had come a few years earlier, however, in 1927, when Battersea power station in London was given the go-ahead despite huge opposition, largely on environmental grounds. The King himself, plus a former Archbishop of Canterbury and all the local residents, warned of the effects of burning 2,000 tons of coal per day. Battersea's owner, the London Power Company, reassured the electricity commissioners, who in turn re-assured residents of Chelsea, just across the Thames, 'we have evidence that there will be no emission here of gases which will be objectionable.' Nobody believed them.

By 1934, Parliament had approved plans to compulsorily purchase the rights of way needed for a national system of pylons. Nearly 20,000 compulsory orders were needed. Wherever they found opposition too intense to handle, the power companies simply buried the cable. But it was cheaper to build the pylons. An aesthetically pleasing pylon design was commissioned, and a distance calculated at which the curve of the cable would be reminiscent of the shape of the Bristol suspension bridge. Houses throughout the countryside were soon being wired up at the rate of 300 a week, and *The Times* reported triumphantly, though incorrectly, 'there is hardly a village in this country today which has not got electricity supply.'

Over a dozen power stations were under construction and there were more electric cookers in use in the UK than in the whole of the United States. However, those cookers were not all to the same standard. The infant days of mass electric power in Britain were a whirligig of madly divergent technologies, offering services at dozens of different voltages, some two-wire, some four-wire, some AC and some DC (alternating/direct current). In London alone, eighty-two power companies, subject to 243 different Acts of Parliament, offered seventeen different voltages, both DC and AC, with two-, three- and four-wire cables into the house.

The CEB was determined to stamp this out, and the decision was taken to standardise on AC. The advantage of AC that convinced Merz and others was its ability to carry electricity across long distances using much thinner and cheaper wires than DC. Once the AC standard was accepted, centralised power generation would be possible and relatively cheap, but if DC became the standard then power generation would have to take place much closer to the end user – in fact no more than a mile at most, using the technology of the time. The adoption of DC would have created a very different world, much closer to a series of micro-grids, than one national grid.

Electricity use doubled every ten years to 1970, and this consumption was spurred on by cross-subsidised consumer durables such as cookers and fridges, later supplemented by TVs, deep freezers, washing machines, tumble dryers, vacuum cleaners, blenders and the like, sold out of electricity and gas 'showrooms'. With the whole country being encouraged to use energy by what was now a nationalised industry, it is no surprise that the population took to these new toys, then became dependent on them.

In 2006, land campaigner Simon Fairlie reminded us in an article called 'Ecoburbia', published in *Building for a Future* magazine, that he grew up perfectly well without a fridge in the 1950s, but 'all the infrastructure for living decently without one has now gone. Houses don't have cellars or larders; daily deliveries by local milkmen, butchers, greengrocers and bakers have been swallowed up by centralised supermarkets; local market gardeners have been ousted for development; even the ice cream van doesn't call.'

The development of electric power could have been different. There was no compelling reason why we had to have a national grid. It is likely that we would have a smaller economy if not for the national grid, but whether our economic success has made us any happier as a nation is at least questionable in this age of rising binge-drinking and violent crime. Suppose we had muddled along with much smaller, more widely distributed power plants. They would have been less reliable, for sure, perhaps more expensive, but we would have learned to use less power as a result, which would have been a good thing. Many households might have felt it was worth installing their own back-up power for those times when the local grid was down. There would have been more community power, from rivers and windmills. But today we live with the legacy of an era of centralisation in UK politics: a series of high-polluting trophy projects from Drax to Sellafield and a population lulled into thinking it can be no other way.

Planning for roads

In the eighteenth century the British countryside was teeming with labourers who squatted tiny patches of land and made their living from that land. But the second great wave of enclosures in the early 1800s seized some fourteen million acres of land for the rich, causing a huge migration to the towns and the gradual emptying of the countryside.

In 1915, travelling showman Charles Neville spotted some derelict land near Brighton and bought it to launch a remarkable scheme. Planning permission as we know it today did not exist then; if you owned land, you had the right to do pretty much what you wanted with it. Through ads in national newspapers, Neville asked the public for a name for the new town he intended to build there. The top prize was a plot of land allegedly worth £100, and there were fifty prizes of plots worth £50. A fee of £3 would cover the administration costs of the winners. The competition was wildly popular: there were over 80,000 entries. Neville's South Coast Land & Resort Company increased the number of runner-up prizes to over 2,400.

The winning name was New Anzac-on-Sea. It lasted less than a year. Neville changed it to Peacehaven in 1917, a name that remains to this day. The *Daily Express* saw the scheme as a fraud and took Neville to court. He lost, but by then Peacehaven was famous, and 3,000 homes were built on what had been an empty, barren patch of land. The 2,400 runners-up paid for the land transfer, and the South Coast Land & Resort Company profitably supplied the new owners with either a house or the materials to build one.

Peacehaven showed that there was a huge pent-up demand for somewhere affordable to live in the country, even if it had no services. The 'town planning' community, to the extent that there was one, and government policymakers were appalled by the project. They saw Peacehaven as an 'anarchic mess', but there was nothing they could do other than prevent a repetition, so they began the process of framing laws that would not allow such a massively popular success story to recur.

But it would be a few decades before such a law was enacted, and in the meantime the idea of dividing rural land into plots took hold, and tens, perhaps hundreds of thousands of dwellings were built on what became known as 'Plotlands'. In *Arcadia for All*, Colin Ward and Dennis Hardy chart the rise and fall of Plotlands, with their strange dwellings made of redundant railway carriages and garden sheds – 'a motley collection of makeshift structures [which] carried dispersal (from town to suburb and country) to its limits'. Historian S. P. B. Mais in *Britain and the Beast* bemoaned one development on the North Downs, 'honeycombed with hidden shacks thrown haphazard like splodges of mud against a hillside once covered with trees. The hut-dwellers both get the view and spoil it.' Few of the Plotlands caused as much furore as Peacehaven, however, with the exception of a series of developments in the Thames Valley which attracted the full weight of establishment criticism. Residents of Eton, Windsor and Henley suddenly found 'greengrocers from Acton and printers from Fulham making free with their squalid little huts', wrote Ward and Hardy. 'The time has come,' Lady Cynthia Moseley informed the House of Commons in 1930, 'when we must choose between the end of laissez faire and the end of rural England.' Eventually other forces combined to destroy many of the Plotland houses. As soon as the Second World War started, the Ministry of Defence swept away thousands along the south coast, and the freak storm surge of 1953 reduced the shanty buildings along the east coast to rubble. Many more were simply forgotten and abandoned.

Then, in 1947, the Town and Country Planning Act removed the sole right of landowners to decide what could be built on their property. Planning permission was now required for land development; ownership alone no longer conferred the right. *The Times* called it 'the effective "nationalisation" of the right to develop land ... rights were appropriated by the state, to be released only at the political judgment of local authorities'.

The planning permission process was creaky from the start, and there was suddenly a scarcity of building land. Land prices for housing, which had hardly increased at all in the previous fifty years, rose tenfold over the next half century. As a result, houses were built ever closer together and to lower standards because so much had to be spent on the site. Selected villages became high-density, middle-class dormitories.

As farming land became more valuable, it made less and less economic sense to farm it when it could be used for building houses or factories, or simply sold as an investment. This led to a further decline in the rural population. It became almost impossible to create employment outside urban or industrial areas. In 1946 there were 976,000 agricultural workers in England and Wales; by 1989 there were 250,000.

And just as this change to Britain's basic property laws was making it more difficult for individuals to live close to the land, the last barriers to the construction of a national motorway network were falling.

Before the Second World War, Britain was among the most reluctant of European countries to build motorways, despite having the highest per capita car ownership. British policymakers believed that a national system of highways through the countryside was totally unnecessary, and private ventures in the 1920s to build motorways failed to win government approval, which contrasted strongly with the likes of Italy and Germany, where *autostrada/autobahn* construction was embraced with enthusiasm. After the war, UK policy was reversed; in fact, an officially endorsed outline of a national network had been developed for planning purposes by 1944. It was decided that there were, after all, immense benefits to be derived from building motorways, such as time-saving.

Some, like media guru Marshall McLuhan, saw roads as a medium of communication, just like TV or newspapers, and believed that wide straight roads were a sign of a strong centralised government, whereas random, disjointed roads implied the absence of control. More and more motorways were built over the succeeding three decades, but as we know, instead of speeding up traffic and alleviating jams, they simply created a greater demand for road travel and encouraged people to use their cars more. One consequence of the rise of roads is a smooth distribution network allowing chain-store groceries to send food almost any distance economically, with little consideration for locality or freshness. This has had the effect of destroying community deliveries by milkmen, butchers, bakers and the like. We are now moving swiftly towards a state of permanent gridlock.

Imagine if motorways had not been built, and at the same time a looser version of the 1947 Planning Act had been passed leading to lower land prices and more building in the countryside. There would be less open countryside, but fewer cars, and better public transport. Cars and lorries would have fewer, slower routes around the country, but the train network, which was decimated in the 1960s, would have grown instead. Meanwhile, if people wanted to live in the country they could have done so much more easily. Land and property prices would not have rocketed, so the gap between rich and poor (i.e. property haves and have-nots) would be narrower. The nation would have less overall wealth, but would the quality of life be any worse? Based on the numbers of people who appear to want to leave the city and live in the country, I think the level of overall happiness would be much higher.

But property prices exercise people's minds more than roads. Currently, less than 10 per cent of the UK is built on, and 89 per cent of the population live in densely packed towns and cities. Many on the left and right are calling for the scrapping of planning laws, 'the state's 60-year stranglehold on urban development' as the *Sunday Times* labelled them in an October 2006 article entitled 'Welcome to Superbia'. Sweeping away the planning laws would bring with it a slump in property prices, but too many voters have too much invested for that to be a believable political option. 'The entire system is designed to protect the kind of urban neighbourhoods in which [the advocates of the current planning system] live, and the country houses where they vacation, while the problems fall most heavily on other parts of the population,' says Robert Bruegmann, an American professor of urban planning and author of *Sprawl: A Compact History*. In 1966 Britain built 400,000 homes; in 2006 we built less than half that. Yet 500,000 people live in over-crowded homes and 95,000 households are in temporary accommodation. And the population is rising. According to one forecast another six and a half million people will be living in Britain by 2030. The Treasury economist Kate Barker condemns the planning system for inhibiting growth and wants it relaxed so that huge new suburbs can be built. Nick Hubble, head of Kingston University's Centre for Suburban Studies, comments that 'a combination of immigration and families wanting to move into more spacious surroundings will create such pressure that greenfield sites [will] have to be developed. It would be better to plan that now.'

I am no expert in these matters, but I do not want jerry-built homes in the middle of the countryside. If we are to keep what is attractive about the countryside then overdeveloping it is not the solution. I want to see the system altered to allow non-commercial, low-density, low-impact development of the countryside. It would not solve the housing shortage, but it would help. Following Simon Fairlie, I want to see the Department for Rural Affairs (DEFRA), the ministry responsible for the environment, fund half a dozen experimental off-grid developments. Each would have a few hundred inhabitants and each would be allowed to generate, say, 10 per cent of the energy used per capita in the rest of society. The government's 2006 energy review forecast that 18 per cent of homes will have some form of 'microgeneration' by 2030 and announced, 'we will be removing barriers, where viable, in planning, in selling electricity and in accessing the benefits of renewables obligations.' I'd like to see them go a bit further than just removing barriers, proactively creating conditions for successfully living with renewable energy. There would be no shortage of volunteers willing to live in these experimental communities. It would at the very least allow the concept of off-grid living to be tested.

Why should the government want to test it? Because it would be good for society, and it would help to solve some of the key problems confronting us in the twenty-first century. And because the trend towards off-grid living is not just a result of the ravings of a few back-to-the-landers. During research for this book I met many people who thought the idea of living off-grid was alien and unintelligible, but an equal number of all ages and backgrounds responded enthusiastically. This awakening of interest is happening for a reason. Or to be precise, several reasons.

Why Off-Grid?

Environmentalism

I cannot say which reason for off-grid living is playing loudest in people's minds, but clearly the environment is one reason, and it has been for many decades. Since the 1960s, when the hippies led a movement away from urban living and back to the land, we have always harboured a guilty knowledge that the way most of us live now is not healthy for the environment. We might have largely ignored it over the decades, but in our hearts we knew it to be true, even though huge and powerful forces argued against it. The environmental campaigner George Monbiot, in his 2006 book *Heat – How to Stop the Planet Burning*, showed how the giant energy companies deliberately spread misinformation, denying that our lifestyles were damaging the planet, in order to maintain sales of their products. But for a small minority, the knowledge that wealthy Westerners such as themselves were gobbling up global resources was a reason in itself to reduce their own consumption, without any thought of the effect it might have on them personally. For some of them, that entailed living off-grid.

There is also a more selfish but still purely ecological reason for living off-grid. Many feel that the health risks of living in modern society are not worth the potential benefits. Additives in paint, and the effects of other building and decorating materials; allergies to synthetic clothes or furnishings; the unknown dangers of genetically modified (GM) food – there is no shortage of reasons to justify turning away from society in terms of the personal benefits to us and our families.

You could take the view that the damage technology has caused, technology will also solve. New ways of limiting or dealing with carbon emissions, more efficient agriculture, even GM food could all limit or eradicate the threats posed by global growth. But there are other reasons for the rise of the 'downshifting' movement.

Post-consumerism

We live in a secular age, and the spiritual emptiness of modern life has led many to turn away from the obsession with consumption and material success and consider going back to the land, closer to nature. Indeed, the present decade may prove to be the high-water mark of our love affair with brands and products, and infatuation with celebrity.

The UK has some of the longest working hours in Europe, and many of us daily take long, expensive, polluting journeys to our jobs. The realisation that working less hard may not reduce our net earnings is another reason why living off-grid now seems more attractive. By cutting our consumption levels and growing a bit of food or fixing our own car or house, we may even be better off on a thirty-hour working week than the sixty-plus-hour week many endure that leaves us no time to do any of these things. I occasionally hear via the off-grid website from people who were living successful, high-stress lives until something went wrong. Their business might have gone bust, for example, forcing them to sell their house and move to a plot of land they bought when they were flush with cash. They universally say the change of circumstances made them happier, or at least no more miserable.

Survivalism

As well as ecological and spiritual reasons for living off-grid there is also an element of what the Americans call survivalism. Global warming, long predicted as a by-product of our overuse of resources, is a reality, and its arrival has acted as a tipping point for many who now believe it possible that normal life will become unsustainable as a result. Weird weather and changing crop patterns may cause food and energy shortages. As well as doing our bit to prevent such catastrophes, living off-grid could provide a fallback solution, offering shelter, food, fuel and a place to live for urbanites if city-based civilisation were to crumble, even if it did not break down completely. James Lovelock calls this approach 'Prepare and Survive'. On an individual level this may be a selfish response, but it has benefits for society as a whole, as I will go on to discuss.

Geopolitics

There are major geopolitical factors that militate in favour of off-grid living. The price of fuel is one. Oil from the Middle East and gas from Russia are both vital to our economy, and both could simply be turned off by the Kremlin or an Arab state in response to, say, our policy towards a foreign country. The fast-growing economies of China and India will simply add to the demand for fuel and other raw materials. And leaving aside economic growth, don't overlook the sheer scale of population growth both in Asia and many other parts of the world. The cost of installing renewable energy is still high – too high to be justified purely on the grounds of saving money if you live in a grid-connected home – but this equation may change.

And it is not the only consideration. The rise of terrorist attacks will do more than scare people out of city centres; they raise the real possibility of long-term dislocation in the event of a successful strike on a power station or the water supply. Internet viruses and spam have also been linked to anti-Western activists. If the network of global computer systems was brought down, even for a day, it could spark financial chaos. Wealthy people who work in the financial sector say they have taken to keeping thousands of pounds in cash in their homes because they know that in the event of a successful attack on global computer systems credit cards would be worthless pieces of plastic and there would be no way of withdrawing money from bank accounts. The same people also keep a string of gold sovereigns in a money belt, and a full tank of gas in their SUV.

The Need for Resilience

Each of the above reasons on its own might not be enough to justify a decision to drop out and live off-grid (or merely to move to a remote location and continue commuting or working via wireless Internet), but taken together they add up to quite a list. The possibility that more than one of these threats might happen simultaneously in several places has convinced some leading thinkers that there is a need to prepare for potential future catastrophes.

Canadian forecaster Thomas Homer-Dixon, director of the Trudeau Centre for Peace and Conflict Studies, is an authority on what he calls 'social adaptation to complex stress'. Professor Homer-Dixon believes there is a substantial possibility of multiple catastrophes occurring simultaneously, with consequences adding up to more than the sum of their parts. He calls this 'synchronous failure' and considers it, rather than any of the individual things that might go wrong, to be the real danger of the twenty-first century. He argues that limited off-grid living is part of the answer because society needs a diverse range of responses if we are to have the best chance of maintaining the best bits of our present system.

To the threats I've already listed, such as population growth and the forecast decline in energy resources, Homer-Dixon adds two 'multipliers' – factors which in certain circumstances can intensify the threat. The first is the increasing connectedness of everything, thanks to communications technology. This could cause 'cascade effects' as damage to one part of the world, 'whether caused by a new pathogen, a computer virus, or a financial shock . . . spreads rapidly to other parts of the network.' The second multiplier is the unprecedented power of our weapons systems, which could be turned against us: 'steadily fewer people could kill steadily larger numbers of people more quickly than ever before.' And the terrorists are sophisticated: they are also aware of the possibilities of using the cascade effect to increase the power of their actions. Suppose 2008 turns out to be an even hotter year than 2006 was, and there is a global crop failure, coupled with an Asian financial crisis and a series of terrorist attacks. It could happen. Homer-Dixon, who comes to his conclusion after studying events such as the French and Russian revolutions, puts the odds at perhaps 15 per cent in the next few decades. 'A breakdown of global institutional and social order might then happen very suddenly,' he warns.

It is up to governments, with our support and prompting, to try to ease some of these stresses in the system. As individuals, I believe one contribution we can make is live off-grid. If many millions of us were off-grid, the stresses on society would be far less acute. We would be consuming less, and depending less on global corporations and systems for our money, energy and entertainment. Fewer of us would be vulnerable targets in cities. Our lifestyle would be more like the lifestyles of those who currently envy and resent us. In *The Upside of Down*, Homer-Dixon talks at length about the need for 'resilience', in our economic infrastructure as well as in our personal and household systems. Being able to handle damage and shortages and being able to undergo lengthy privation is, he maintains, something that needs to become second nature to us all, as individuals and as a group. Societies, Homer-Dixon believes, become complex in order to deal with the everyday problems that arise, but over time they can become too complex, at which point they become highly vulnerable to any sudden change. In a phone conversation with me the Canadian writer confirmed that he is in favour of off-grid homes because a mixture of off-grid and grid-connected properties adds to resilience in society, and pioneers solutions others can adopt in times of crisis.

My own passion for the off-grid way stems from a feeling that modern society has stripped us of the power to manage our own lives sensibly. We can no longer grow enough to feed ourselves, or mend things that break, or even maintain things before they break. Many of us have allowed ourselves to be lulled into an age of obsolescence; we've forgotten what it's like to feel in control of our own destinies, both individually and as communities. At the beginning of the last century, community ties were still strong and many regarded having control over, for example, their own gas or electricity supply as something to be proud of. The fact that this was not efficient, in the sense of saving every last penny, was not the point. If each area had a gas company and a power station, it would be free to run its own affairs, make its own mistakes, and be insulated from the mistakes next door; and they would never be very big mistakes, because the power stations would never be as big as Drax or Windscale. *That's* the point.

Self-sufficiency gives you self-control.

Seven Reasons to Go Off-Grid

The power grid has existed in its present form for only eighty years and may prove a temporary phenomenon. The water grid has been around longer, but the reason for setting it up in the first place – the provision of clean, safe water – has been superseded by technology: anyone can now install their own water treatment system. Our water and energy grids ended up as large national entities, but it did not have to be that way. There are many advanced economies where that did not happen – the United States, for example. Nor do advanced or developing countries need it to be this way in the future. A large number of small power stations could work just as well as a small number of large power stations.

Just to recap before I start out on my off-grid odyssey, the immediate forces that are directly impelling us off-grid are as follows.

Environmentalism. Whether out of fear or a rational study of the evidence, large numbers of people are now convinced that we are damaging the planet, and many of them want to do their bit to stop damaging the planet. That means driving less, or not at all, instead using a bicycle and public transport; reducing energy and water consumption; recycling as much household waste as possible. Going off-grid is at the extreme end of the spectrum, but for some it is a logical choice.

Post-consumerism. A new kind of mentality is growing in the UK and other Western countries. Many of us feel we have too much stuff, too many gadgets, too many choices. We want to simplify our lives and adjust our work-life balance. There is also the related trend of anti-consumerism, a feeling that we are becoming slaves to big brands and big government.

Rising energy prices make it more cost-effective to install renewables, for some or all of your needs, and act as a reminder and warning that expensive energy may become scarce energy.

Water shortages. Recent dry winters and hot summers have made people think about rainwater harvesting and boreholes as never before.

Rising house prices. The rising price of property has been one of the major global trends of the last two decades, and the UK has become one of the world's most expensive countries in which to buy a house. The combination of mass economic immigration, safe haven status for investors, and a welcoming tax and visa regime for the super-rich has helped house prices in Britain soar out of the reach of many first-time buyers, especially those who live and work in rural areas. Low-paid workers and a growing army of students, fed up with the system, are now choosing to live in unconventional homes rather than put up with substandard housing at high rents. Perhaps they could scrimp and save, and buy a share of a house, but many do not see the point, so they move into vans or boats or barns or caravans in the corners of fields and become part of the off-grid population. It's a lifestyle that seems unnatural to us now, less desirable than the conventional British aspiration of a home you can call your own castle. But what's a poor man to do? And in any case, how much are these ideals our own and how much have they been moulded by advertising over the last fifty years?

Fear, whether of a synchronous failure or a more specific event like bird flu, a terrorist attack, a food shortage or an extended power cut. Chinese economic growth, terrorism and climate change are just three fear factors providing a context within which the off-grid movement is developing.

The availability of new technology. New technology means we now have access to smaller, more powerful batteries, more efficient solar panels, better wind turbines. Fuel cells will soon replace our century-old battery technology. Wireless broadband Internet and other innovations aimed at marine and camping communities have given us the means to live luxuriously in the middle of nowhere.

I hope that what follows will empower readers to find the off-grid solution that is best for them. Some will want to dive into the full off-grid life from day one, but many more will want to ease themselves into the life, and perhaps never put more than a couple of toes in the water. If the reason for going off-grid is to save money, then it will probably be an all or nothing decision, but if a general dissatisfaction with consumer society is the impulse, then an off-grid break might be the right answer, at least for now. It depends on existing commitments and, to a large extent, on how and where you earn a living. Everybody has different needs and priorities, and this book aims to provide at least a starting point for research.

3

A Home Away From Home

Small is the new big.

Portable Houses by Irene Rawlings and Mary Abel (2004)

I KNEW THE REASONS why I ought to consider living off-grid, but how practical was it? Could you live luxuriously in a bender in a wood in the Welsh valleys, or in a crofter's hut on moorland in north-west Scotland? How easy was it to dwell well in a camper van in town, or on a narrowboat in Oxfordshire? Was it even possible to take an urban house off the grid? And is there any point? Is going off-grid the natural next step for our civilisation, or is it merely rural nostalgia with a sprinkling of anti-globalisation? Is it any more ethical than its on-grid equivalent? And how do you go about getting planning permission?

When I first started asking such questions my interest, of course, was more than academic: I wanted to transform my Majorcan mountainside into a paradise of power and water. As my life changed with the birth of my daughter, and as the climate changed, making weekend flights seem questionable, the same interests and questions transferred themselves to a British context. I neither had nor have much prospect of buying a country house in the UK, but I wondered if it were possible to buy or rent a little patch of woodland where I could build a tree-house or erect a shed from B&Q. And if so, what would I do to stave off the British weather? I was accustomed to the Mediterranean sun on my mountain, not driving rain – most of the year at least.

I needed to go and check out off-gridding for myself, to take a tour of every kind of off-grid home, and meet every kind of person living that way: businessmen and aristocrats, gypsies and hippies, boat-owners and caravan-lovers; eco-campaigners, hermits, tree-people, students, bushwhackers, survivalists and skivers. Understandably, off-gridders tend to value their privacy – they stay out of trouble that way. Keeping off the radar of bureaucracy is one of the things that many find attractive. So setting off in search of the perfect off-grid life was not going to be a walk in the park.

I began by phoning companies that sold renewable energy and rainwater harvesting systems. On the whole, nobody was interested in the 'off-grid market'; they were focused on selling 'grid tied' systems to city dwellers who wanted to help save the planet. Later, I visited Dulas, one of the oldest renewable energy consultants, with solar, wind and hydro projects all over the world. One of the senior staff pulled out a folder 'we call the off-grid file. It's full of enquiries from people saying things like "I live on a remote farm" or "I'm building a place in the woods". We'd like to help, but we haven't got time to do anything about them.' I was reminded that I was skirting the edges of a booming industry which had its sights fixed on a very different place to my own. The more I met suppliers of renewable energy, the more I realised that the industry which is evangelising this brave new world is staffed by people who don't live that way themselves. They (and their customers) want to run a blender, a washing machine, a dishwasher, two TVs, stereos, phone chargers, lights, a toaster – the full checklist of modern domestic gadgetry. Still, perhaps they knew something I didn't about what was possible with a solar panel and wind turbine. Whatever it was, I planned to find out.

My round of calls to energy companies did yield a handful of names, and I could depend on word of mouth to slowly build an off-grid address list. I had started a website a year earlier as a clearing centre for information about the off-grid life (www.off-grid.net), and I received a regular trickle of emails from visitors who did not want to drop out of society, just to keep it at arm's length. The Internet allows widely-dispersed people to stay in touch as if they lived in a city centre. To encourage traffic I was always looking out for famous names who had joined the ranks of off-gridders, whether they bought a beach hut, like Stoner Keith Richards, spent the occasional night camping in Notting Hill, like Annie Lennox, or lived in a completely off-grid home, like Daryl Hannah in the Rocky Mountains, George Bush's ranch in Texas or Cameron Diaz in Beverly Hills. In doing so I was flirting with the celebrity culture I criticise. But people search the Internet by typing terms into Google, and terms like 'Cameron Diaz' are searched more often than 'composting loo'.

Even supposing I could find enough people willing to let a stranger come and write about their living conditions, I still had a problem. How would I travel? I was visiting places most people did not know existed. These outlandish destinations were usually far off the public transport network, and even when there was a train or bus connection, the schedules all too often ended at 6.30 p.m. The most ecological means was by bicycle or horse, both of which I ruled out, if only because I didn't want to travel light on this trip. My aim was a taste of real off-grid life, but I wanted to experience it as I would really live it if I were to commit to it part- or full-time, not as some kind of camping holiday. And the way I live is with a panoply of gadgets and comforts, so it would be unrealistic to leave behind such things as a computer, a stills camera, a film camera, battery chargers, a change of clothes, drinks, books, plenty of food, cooking equipment, bedding, cushions, table and chairs . . . Going off-grid was not about punishing myself or denying the benefits of the electronic age.

I would have to drive. But that left me with the horny issue of where to stay. I could hardly ask to plonk myself down on the sofa after I had invited myself into people's homes. I felt it was going to be touchy enough just parachuting into their lives during daytime. Yet for me, heading back to a hotel or a nice warm B&B afterwards was somehow not in keeping with the spirit of the project. Nor would I be able to afford it.

Essential camper van features

While I was still wondering how to find off-grid people, Fiona and I were invited to a wedding in a decrepit stately home in Somerset. Twenty-four of us were going to camp on the lawns and eat meals in the stone-flagged dining room. About half the party turned up in camper vans, and I realised that these friends who used to own nothing except a bicycle were growing up and having families; they'd found they could keep at least some of their freedom by bundling the kids into a camper. Someone had an upmarket vehicle called a Hymer, which was more like a bed-sit on wheels (later, I would discover that an above-average camper van can cost more than the average house). I was introduced to Strider, who had arrived in a converted LDV van which cost him in total about £250 plus parts. Strider lived most of the time in Wales, in the only valley which still had no electricity. He had renovated the tumbledown cottage himself, and lined it with second-hand books for insulation. His neighbours had a wind turbine on their land, but Strider had no time for that malarkey. 'Twenty-year payback period?' he scoffed. 'I want to be in California long before then, smoking spliff and soaking up the rays.'

A camper van was the answer. My choice would be both a sign that I had joined the off-grid army as well as a practical solution to the logistics of spending time with off-gridders. The statistics show that there are 150,000 camper vans in the UK, and even if half are mouldering on their owners' drives, the other half, 75,000 households, have the means to go off-grid tomorrow. I call this being 'off-grid ready'.

Leaving till later the task of persuading Fiona that this was a worthwhile use of our time, I began to question Strider about his set-up, and he told me what to look for in a camper. 'For a start, make sure you get one you can stand up in, otherwise you are gonna end up living like Gollum under the bridge.' That was pretty rich, I thought, coming from someone who looked and lived like a hobbit. But I knew he was right.

Next thing on Strider's list was ventilation. If you have a completely sealed interior then at night your own breath ends up condensing on the windows and walls and running down onto your bed. You wake up damp and shivering. Even at the risk of being cold, ventilation is essential. One of those little wind-vanes in the roof is all you need.

Don't bother with plumbing, he said. It might all seem very attractive in the camper-van showroom, when you realise you can flush a chain just like on a normal loo, and turn on the tap for water just like a normal kitchen. But you actually have to fill up those huge water tanks and, sorry to mention it, empty the toilet. You are better off with a few twelve-gallon plastic water tanks with little taps on them, and using the great outdoors as your toilet.

And the last crucial item, he advised me, is . . . curtains. Shut out the world when you want to. I agreed with him there, having experienced in my early days in Majorca waking up in a hire car to find the local populace staring at me curiously.

By the time Fiona arrived on the scene I had, of course, established enough of a routine to render this car-sleeping unnecessary – which is just as well because car-dwelling is not her style. I doubted that she would look on camper-van life any more favourably. Fiona is an artist with a studio in east London and a string of galleries in LA, New York and Berlin as well as the West End. I thought carefully about how to raise the idea with her.

'Fi?' I ventured as we lay in bed one rainy Wednesday morning. She had just told me for the nth time how the arrival of Caitlin had plunged us into an unprecedented and worrying routine from which we needed to break free. 'We have to try to do something different every day,' she'd said. I sensed my moment had arrived. 'Fi,' I cooed again, 'how about we just jump in a camper van and get away for a few months, go and check out the way people live, you know, away from the rat race?'

'Are you kidding?' she said, reaching for the cup of tea I bring her every morning, which takes about ninety seconds to make using our energy-burning 5kW designer kettle from Habitat.

'But we love it whenever we go to the country,' I persevered. 'You're always saying you want to spend more time out of town.'

She shook her head. 'I belong here in London. We'd go bonkers after about five days.'

She's right, I thought (I am so easily led).

'Well, can't we try it out for a while, at least?' I whined. 'We could go for quick trips, and see if they get longer.'

Silence. This was a good sign.

'We could use that Japanese Army camping cooker I bought you when we first met,' she said, eventually.

I was home free! Saved by the stainless steel, highly complex Muji camping stove that had loomed over us from the top shelf for the past four years. By the end of the trip it had yet to deliver a meal – the instructions were all in Japanese, and although we did run into a Japanese woman on a camp site, her English was not good enough – but it had served its purpose. From now, whatever absurd adventures I had on the way were pre-authorised. I'd get no comeback if I was arrested for overnighting on Glyndebourne or 'wild walking' through private shooting estates. I had the go-ahead to park the camper on Hampstead Heath. It was all part of an experiment Fiona had signed up to.

That discussion with Fiona was my turning point. We would go on the road for a week or two at a time to begin with, and then see whether we wanted to spend longer living this way. I also planned to travel alone when Fiona's commitments kept her in town. I began to plan a schedule in this theoretical vehicle, forgetting that I had no idea how to acquire one. Perhaps a visit to Devon and Wales for starters, both hippy redoubts since the 1960s. Then there were the remoter parts of Yorkshire, and Scotland, not to mention the possibility of finding the occasional yurt in the Home Counties. I could, I realised, live an off-grid life as I did my research – perhaps buy a wind turbine for the camper van, solar panels for the roof, and an array of mobile gadgets from the camping stores.

I did a double-take. Wasn't 'off-grid' at least partly about quitting the spendaholic's consumption habit? Yet there is a mini-industry in gadgets and systems for off-grid life: rainwater collection units, pole-mounted wind turbines, foldaway solar battery chargers, meditation retreats in organic country homes ... the list is endless. Did I have a moral dilemma here before I had even started? I decided I did not. If I invested wisely, the products would pay for themselves in reduced stress and consumption. That would be better for me and better for the planet. And it would be better for the businesses that adjust to this new reality. They would build longer-lasting, better-quality products, and give better value for money.

Some of the time we would travel *en famille*, because now, of course, we had Caitlin to consider. My mind turned to how we could adapt an off-grid life to make sure she was safe and healthy. Bottle sterilisation, laundry, hot water ... all the things that had not mattered before in my deliberations were now crowding in on me. And what would happen when she could talk and walk? How much fun could a three-year-old have on her own with us flitting from one isolated venue to another? We would have to find off-grid kids for her to play with, as well as off-grid schools and crèches.

I realised that only once we had the camper van would our education begin. Whether it's a solar sauna, a fifteen-minute meditation technique or a full-fledged four-bed house in the woods, visiting someone who has already done it and wants to share their experiences is the best way to learn. Seeing all these off-grid solutions would allow me to decide whether it could work for someone like me, someone who wanted to step off the treadmill without dropping out of the race.

As it happened, I was part of a trend. Campers, or RVs as they are known in the States (short for 'recreational vehicles'), were enjoying one of their periodic revivals. I was one of perhaps 10,000 who bought a van in the first six months of 2006. According to media reports they were in short supply because this was a World Cup summer: supporters were buying anything they could drive to Germany and sleep in. Prices had allegedly leapt by 35 per cent. The media reckoned the camper-van boom was a temporary fad, but they were wrong. Even without the World Cup there had been a sharp rise in sales. And it will continue, because there is a freedom in being able to just leave when you want, with no booking, and park in some tiny lane, or a friend's field, or a stranger's field if you think you can get away with it.

Previous camper and caravan sales booms had been led by older or retired people trying to see the country on a budget. They shelled out large amounts – typically £15,000 to £20,000 – for a purpose-built vehicle with hideously ugly seat coverings and a shrunken-down version of all the facilities they had at home. Then they drove around staying in camp sites. But younger people were leading the latest sales boom, according to reports. 'Camper vanning for the Big Chill generation' journalist Rhiannon Batten called it; 'in other words, those who are too old to rough it but too young to admit it'. And the UK boom is just part of an international trend. In Australia, North America, and across Europe, thirty-somethings are buying more mobile homes.

In search of the perfect van

With only a few weeks till the World Cup kicked off, I had to move fast. I began my off-grid odyssey one rainy Monday morning with a train journey, gliding past east London tenements on a visit to a camper-van showroom in Essex. When I arrived, Steve the salesman seemed quite grateful for some company. He was planning to spend the next few weeks in front of a telly with a forty-eight-pack of beer and a few mates, and it didn't look as if business would interrupt him. Despite what the media reports said, Steve's car-park had no customers, at least not while I was there. But his range of retirement vans were built for a life in camper parks, where couples rig up the satellite dish on the roof as soon as they arrive, make tea at 4 p.m., and start on the G&Ts at six. I couldn't quite envisage buyers of this kind of vehicle driving it across fields, or parking next to a yurt for the night. I concluded that I could stop searching for my vehicle in caravan dealerships.

A brief visit to one or two camp sites for a viewing of some modern camper vans confirmed my belief that the big-money camper vanner is a completely different animal. Technically, new things are happening in the world of campers, and the sector is becoming ever more sophisticated. The £685,000 Terra Wind mobile home, for instance, can hit 80mph on land and seven knots over lakes. Anyone willing to pay even £34,000 for a new Volkswagen Caravelle, for example, or £50,000 for a Fiat Ducato has to be fully on the grid, a totally paid-up member of consumer society. They want to leave home without leaving home.

I pushed aside this uncharitable thought and focused on my own search, for a cheap camper, preferably under £5,000, and no collector's item, just one of the hundreds of thousands that have been mass-produced since the 1950s. As soon as I had it I would hop in and drive. I would never stay on a camp site if I could avoid it.

But resolving to buy a van and set off in search of the off-grid world was the easy part. Actually getting hold of an appropriate vehicle threw me into a miasma of unreliable advertising claims and complex technical issues, not to mention the competing criteria my wife and I applied. My checklist, inspired by my conversation with Strider, comprised the following points: the van must be tall enough to stand up in, it should have ventilation to stop it becoming damp, and it should not have a vast water reservoir that would go stale and add extra weight to the van. But that did not rule enough out. And as I started looking, more criteria presented themselves. For instance, thanks to Daryl Hannah, who campaigned for years before it was fashionable to persuade people to convert to bio-diesel fuel, I was prepared to try various alternative fuels in my van. Used vegetable oil from fish and chip shops, or fresh veggie oil from any grocery, or proper bio-diesel from the few places that make it – all are cheaper than 'real' diesel. They are arguably better for the environment, too, and most importantly, using alternative fuels allows us in a very personal way to stick two fingers up at the oil companies. It is, to use that awful word, 'empowering'. So it had to be a diesel van. Then, instead of choosing between Shell and BP, I could choose between Shell, BP and the little Indian cash and carry at the end of Hackney Road.

I headed off in search of the famous London street where

hundreds of camper vans were allegedly bought and sold each week. I knew it existed because every time I mentioned my new mission to friends, they all told me about it. It was in Waterloo, or Kentish Town, or Richmond – on a Sunday, or perhaps a Thursday evening. Apparently Australians 'doing Europe' were the mainstay of the market and I had to go there with an expert or I'd be rooked.

While I waited for confirmation of the precise location and time, I went to visit my friend Julienne Dolphin Wilding in Broxbourne, Hertfordshire. Like me, she had a portfolio career. Part artist, part furniture designer, part web entrepreneur, she split her time between her studio in the UK and a flat in Barcelona. Her steely-hearted landlords had just thrown her out of her Hertfordshire home, so she bought a caravan for £200, decked it out in galvanised steel, and moved it into a farmer's barn while she decided what to do next. We spent a couple of days driving round the area to see where she could park the caravan, and discovered an off-grid community living in caravans and trailers in a piece of woodland near Hertford. The rain was pounding on the roof of her Volvo estate (needed to cart all her wood and tools around) as we sped down a tree-lined country road. We had just driven past a sign saying Buck's Alley when we saw a chimney smoking deep

Julienne in her aluminium-lined caravan.

in a bluebell wood on the other side of the road. We looked at each other. It was dusk, but there was no doubt we had to check it out.

My first off-grid community

We found the entrance to Bayford Wood – an open five-bar gate – drove in and crawled along a path that described a giant U-shape around the wood. We must have passed a dozen beautiful trailers, several with firelight glowing through the windows. But we were too embarrassed and scared to knock on any doors. I am six foot two and Julienne is almost as tall, a statuesque, mixed-race forty-year-old with giant dreadlocks. Nevertheless there was something ominous about the closed doors of the caravans, even with the friendly smoke puffing through the chimneys.

We were out of the car by now, standing next to dripping rhodo-dendrons, when the sound of dogs baying broke the silence. Julienne sprinted for the car, but I was rooted to the spot in terror. The dogs rounded the corner followed by their owner – two miniature Labradors at most a foot long (perhaps it was just a strange echo that had made them sound so fierce). They seemed terrified when they saw me. Their master, however, was not in the least abashed. 'How did you get in?' he demanded. He was about five feet tall and fifty years old with the wrin-kles of a confirmed smoker. He was wearing a leather jacket and had bouffant dyed hair, in the manner of a retired rock star, albeit one who had presumably fallen on hard times. He was soon joined by his 'lady', who was the same height. With her bottle-blonde hair and dirty grey tracksuit, there was an air of the grunged-up former rock chick about her.

I had calmed them down by the time Julienne crept back, and was explaining that my lady friend needed a place to park her caravan. 'Oh, you couldn't do that 'ere,' said the man. 'No, Bob's clearing all these out. There used to be so many people staying in vans 'ere but they were the wrong sort, always making trouble, so he's closing it all down now.'

Julienne and I exchanged glances. We had seen nothing to confirm this story, no empty patches where trailers had once stood nor any trailers that looked untended. No, this was a working caravan community all right, in the leafy heart of Herts. But I could understand why the rocker was telling us this. It's the sort of story I would use myself if some stranger came onto my land asking for a place to park.

The blonde glanced at Julienne, who used to be the drummer in an all-girl band, and softened. 'Well, she could ask Bob. No harm in that.'

In the end it was agreed that although Bob Orme was staying on the edge of Bayford Wood, and had owned it for about twenty years, it would be best not to bother him just now. We would write a letter, and await a response.

Months later, when I had forgotten all about it, the reply finally arrived. Bob called to confirm that the place was indeed a legal caravan park, founded in the 1960s when there was a short-lived relaxation of the rules. Unlike most other sites, where the caravans are lined up a few feet apart, this was a delightful spot – a Kool Karavan site – with each caravan in its own little clearing, out of sight of the others. It was at the very least an option for Julienne – but before too long she'd be making a life-changing decision of her own.

The hunt continues

Back home the next night there was still no news about the street market, so I started a search on eBay, which had hundreds of campers advertised, some at rock-bottom prices, as well as trucks and vans if I wanted to kit them out myself. The temptation was to find the first bargain and buy it, but I learned to look for the signs. No mention of the MOT means the vehicle does not have one. If the seller claims it's 100 per cent reliable, then you must look at their track record to judge their claim. Many of the ads had been placed by dealers, but the only way to tell this was to see how many previous trades they had done on eBay (careful records are kept on every member's transactions and what the other members thought of it). I was looking for someone who did not spend all their time online buying and selling, as their prices tend to be higher, and they attach greater value to things I consider unimportant, like the paint job. They also usually provide some sort of guarantee, which requires returning the vehicle to them, and that's too time-consuming unless they happen to be local.

Before long I found a beauty, a six-ton former local authority mobile library. The seller, Jake Cake, had painstakingly converted it into a split-level family home. It looked terrific in the ad, army green with central folding doors. It had a Bedford 330 turbo diesel engine with five-speed overdrive gearbox; according to the ad, 'she flys' (*sic*). It was set up for off-grid living rather than mere camping with 'diesel heater, double bed, 2 bunks, child's cot. Fitted stainless steel & wood kitchen; Full size 4-ring stainless steel gas cooker. Dining table with seat belted coach seats. Unique wood burning stove. Four bicycle rack . . . Any questions don't hesitate to call.'

I phoned Jake Cake immediately, and he seemed like a really nice guy. At this point I was not even aware that anything over three and a half tons was out of the question, as it needed a special licence and insurance. But anyway, as Jake rambled lyrically about the engine and gearbox I realised I was listening to a man who thought nothing of sliding underneath this behemoth of a vehicle. I, on the other hand, had no aptitude or skill for, and to be honest no interest in, maintaining a diesel engine the size of a double bed. I am not proud of that, but it's best to know one's limitations. Living the off-grid life would eventually give me the skills to be independent and self-sufficient – or at least that was the plan. I would have been jumping in at the deep end if I had taken on the library wagon. I had paid my dues to romance already, in Majorca, so I decided this romantic travelling library had to be passed over. When it went for £2,717 I felt a twinge of regret, but luckily it was too late to do anything about it.

I continued to scan the small ads online and in magazines. There were three main websites: eBay, Gumtree and Autotrader, the online version of the print magazine. Autotrader's website allows you to type in your postcode and price range, and returns all campers with the distance from your own home and the owner's phone number. The problem was that there were never any in my area, and all the advertisers I contacted had already sold their vans. The best site was Gumtree.com, which had only recently been bought by eBay and so was still run along simple, communitarian lines. Ads were free and divided geographically so I could restrict my search to London if I wanted to; the interface was simple, too, and prices were low. Gumtree had a smaller selection than eBay, but it felt more authentic, and when I was finally ready for my first actual visit to view a van, it was in response to a Gumtree advert.

I was ignoring anything Volkswagen. For some reason the VW

Camper still carries an enormous cachet. The best-designed VWs have been collectors' items for years, and by the time Jamie Oliver travelled to Italy in one (beautifully done up with a Cath Kidstone interior) for a TV series, prices were topping £10,000 for a twenty-year-old vehicle. The owners I know tell me they break down often (as indeed happened during Jamie's trip to Italy), they guzzle petrol, they are noisy and uncomfortable, and you cannot stand up in them. All in all they are a puzzling purchase, except that they look nice and retro.

The first likely candidate for me was an elderly Talbot. At £3,500, the price was right for a purpose-built camper with a double bed in a little protrusion that overhung the driver's cab. Simon, the seller, lived in deepest north London and was moving back to Newcastle. Being shown around the van by its owner proved unexpectedly to be an unnerving experience, rather like being shown around someone's home only more . . . intimate. The normal things you say to people when negotiating for a second-hand car sounded in the practice room of my mind like personal insults as I struggled for the right words. At last, I could see the point of estate agents. How do you tell someone that you find their (motor)home a mite depressing, that the oven is miserable, or that you can smell the musty odour of the curtains? When Simon showed me the heating system I was sure I could smell something else – gas. It may be OK to buy second-hand electrical goods, but a leaky gas cooker? I don't think so.

Simon wasn't going to let me go without a struggle. I weakly agreed to a test drive – my first in a camper van. Simon slid into the driver's seat to show me how it all worked; I would take over on the return journey. We shot out of the drive and onto a windy back road as he proudly demonstrated the vehicle's turn of speed. It was noisy and not ideal for long hours travelling across country. When it was time for me to assume the controls, I discovered another vital requirement – power steering. This 1987 baby didn't have it. Turning, parking, even rounding a corner needed concentrated effort, and since I was visiting obscure places on my trip, I realised that power steering would be as important as standing room. I thanked Simon and sank gratefully back onto my Honda 90.

I knew what my wife wanted, a large designer van, well pro-portioned, snug, solid, reliable and above all safe. With a child along on the trip, safety had to be the primary consideration. But a van that fulfilled those criteria would not come cheap – £10,000 at least, judging by the ads I had seen. Viewing Simon's Talbot was a useful trial run, though. It made me realise that the off-gridders I visited would judge me by the van I drove. Appearance is all, as Oscar Wilde said; 'what else is there to judge by?' I reckoned the only people I would put at their ease with the Talbot would be other Talbot owners.

There was a whole class of campers built out of converted vans, and I figured one of these would be the best bet. Overall, they were at the low end of the price range, which was a big plus. I returned to my hunt for the mythical London street market where dazed Antipodeans sold their mobile homes for the price of a final multi-stop trip round the world. It didn't exist. Months later a camper enthusiast explained that it had come to an end a few years before when the markets were over-run with sharks who shipped unsellable vehicles from around the country to palm off on the Aussies. A piece of carpet over a rusty hole in the floor; brakes that had no more than a few miles of life in them; that sort of thing. The police had decided to close the operation down. In earlier times the van sellers would have moved to another street, but simultaneously the Internet was becoming the market of choice for the Aussies, and just about everyone else. Why restrict yourself to a Sunday morning in the rain when you can do the whole thing from the comfort of your own keyboard before even arriving in the UK?

Pitfalls of on-line processing

Back on eBay, an ad for a Ford Transit caught my eye. It was unequiv-ocal about the quality of the engine, and since that was the subject in which I was least qualified, it gave me some peace of mind. 'Here's what you get' ran the ad:

N Reg Ford Transit 100 SWB Hi-Top Camper 2.5 Diesel 2 Berth
(+ 1 small child at a push) ❑ MOT ❑ Power Steering ❑ CD Player
(Speakers front and rear) ❑ TV (240V) ❑ DVD Player (240V Brand
new, still under guarantee) ❑ Gas Cooker (4 Burner Hob & Grill)
❑ Paloma Gas Water Heater ❑ Shower ❑ Portable gas heater

❏ Sink ❏ Fresh water tank (40l Aquaroll) with pump ❏ Portapotty Toilet ❏ 3 Way Fridge (240V, 12V, Gas, a bit temperamental, could probably do with a new one to be honest) ❏ Front swivel seats ❏ Leisure Battery ❏ 2 x 12V to 240V Inverters ❏ 25 Metre Mains Hook-up Cable ❏ 12V and 240V lighting ❏ Mul-T Lock ❏ New brake pads and timing belt.

A 'small child', it said. I had one of those.

The van had not yet reached its £2,000 reserve in the auction, and with a few hours to go I sent an email offering £2,500. The sellers were from Nottingham and they did not react at first, hoping for a better bid online, but naively I overlooked this. Another bell tolled when, after they had accepted my bid and I had sent my deposit of £250, there was a long silence. As I had bought outside the auction I had lost the right to comment publicly on the seller's performance, and thus any hold I might have had over them.

Before I could collect, I had to take out insurance. This proved to be a minefield of its own. Most mainstream insurance companies do not cover motorhomes unless they are professionally converted by a limited number of recognised businesses. After considerable research I found a broker that would take on the job, and they found an insurer that did not demur at my grimy east London postcode. For about £450 I was insured for a year, as long as I did not cover more than 5,000 miles.

The van vendors eventually got in touch and we arranged to meet at a convenient station, Wellingborough, chosen because it was about halfway on a direct line between Nottingham and London. Two hours after our meeting time I was still waiting at Wellingborough station. At that point I should have just taken the final train back to London and forgotten my £250, but I had already bought the insurance, and anyway, after two weeks of looking, this was my van of choice.

Martin from Nottingham arrived in the van just after the final train to London had departed. If I decided not to buy it, I reflected as he pulled up, he would be unlikely to offer me a lift home. He was trailed by his wife in an expensive-looking Subaru estate. They made a strange pair: Martin a gaunt, roll-up-smoking hippy, his wife the cheerful, chubby apologist. Martin was ready to spend all night going over the details of the van, but the bed was all I looked at carefully, and at about five feet eight inches long it was fine for Martin but too small for either me or Fiona to stretch out fully. It could be lengthened by spinning round the two front seats to add extra foot room, but that wasn't much comfort. But it was now nearly 11 p.m., and after a cursory examination of the main points I was ready to make the purchase. Martin had already knocked £150 off because he had forgotten to bring along the Portapotty. He had also installed a new exhaust, as the receipt he pulled out of his top pocket proved, because the old one had fallen off that morning. The inside of the van was dirty and badly made, but that didn't worry me as he knocked off a further £100.

I drove back to London relieved rather than delighted with my purchase. There were only two seats in front and therefore nowhere to put Caitlin. Never mind. My Internet research had turned up a removable Ford Galaxy chair with a built-in baby seat which would allow Caitlin to sit comfortably and safely in the back. At night the seat could be stowed outside, and the bed could be made. We would be a bit cramped when there were three of us, but when I was travelling alone and space was not an issue the low fuel consumption would come into its own. A yellow light with a picture of an oil lamp was blinking, but I paid no attention to that.

The following morning I took the Ford to a local mechanic who confirmed that the engine was in good condition, and had miraculously survived a long journey with almost no oil. He poured in twenty litres, and as far as I was concerned it was now time to head out on the road and live the off-grid life.

Then I showed the van to Fiona. She could not have been more disappointed. It was, as she immediately pointed out, too small. Small was beautiful, manoeuvrable, economical, I argued. The sort of people I was planning to visit might not be too impressed if we turned up in a glossy love-wagon. And some of the narrow dirt tracks I was anticipating would be impassable to larger vehicles. The killer criticisms I could not overcome were that the van had no space for the baby seat, and it had been converted by someone who was both visually illiterate and incompetent at DIY. The shower area, with its doorway made of surplus architrave from a building job on a gated community somewhere in the north-west, was perhaps the most pointless feature since there was nowhere for the water to run off. I dared not test the fridge and the cooker as I would have been too depressed had they failed to work. The ugly wall tiles, the pointless shower area and the dirty old fridge would have to go; Fiona also insisted on the replacement of the ceramic floor tiles (in a camper van?), which were cracked and therefore dangerous for Caitlin. Never mind the time it would take to do the work, I thought, the cost could well be on the way to another thousand pounds. And whatever improvements we made would never be enough. When arriving to stay with friends, or at a small, select literary festival we were planning to attend over the summer, I could sense Fiona's rising fear that she would be judged by my bad taste.

Months later I was vindicated when a lifelong van dweller called Adrian, who had spent twenty years studying the question, 'including measuring vans in the street', concluded that the Ford Transit and its short wheelbase is the best vehicle for long-distance off-gridding. But after just a few days of domestic negotiation it became clear I had made a serious error and had better put the van back on the market immediately. I returned the Ford Galaxy seat to the breaker's yard where I had bought it a few days earlier for 'a ton', and accepted £75 back. Then I wearily turned on the computer, posted pictures of the Transit on Gumtree – making sure that I stressed the deficiencies to deter all but the most seriously interested – and went back to eBay's camper-van section, a website I had thought I would not need to look at again for at least a year.

This time we got lucky. Within a few minutes we had found a van we both liked – a Renault Master converted hospital bus that had just been refitted by James, a carpenter whose hobby was ... refitting camper vans. It looked great, and it had three seats in front, so Caitlin would be up there with us in the cab. The bidding had ended at £3,500, but that was not enough to secure the van because James had set the reserve at £4,000. I had to have it. I just could not stand another weekend in London, nor the thought of another week looking at tiny photos of camper vans taken from careful angles. A quick phone call to James and an offer of his full asking price was enough to seal the deal. Because I was still within the fourteen-day cooling-off period, the insurance I'd bought for the Ford Transit was transferred to the new vehicle at no extra cost, so it remained only to make the trip to Clacton-on-Sea and hand over the cash. Again I was buying outside the auction system with little or no recourse if things went wrong.

A few days later, with the scent of sea air and fish and chips in my nostrils, I was shown around my new motorhome. This time there was no doubt in my mind. It was the Ikea of campers, with tasteful cork-tile flooring, cream curtains sewn by James's mum, and hessian-style cushion coverings. It was noisy, but I had now seen enough vans to know that in the trade-off between price and desirability, I had done well for the money. Most importantly, Fiona would love it. The sink and cooker were stainless steel and brand new, and the fridge was free of others' smears and stains. It was twice as long as the Transit – so long that I scraped its gleaming white panel against the side of a Ford Escort as I turned a corner the very next day. It also consumed double the fuel of the Transit, but at least it was diesel, so I could try to run it on vegetable oil. Numerous websites assured me this was possible. It had a diesel-powered heater that would keep us warm as toast and two big ventilation panels in the roof. The stereo had four speakers wired in under the roof insulation. The small water tank meant we would be carrying little excess weight and the water would not go stale and brackish in the summer heat. Sure enough, Fiona approved, and she soon got to work, adding silver foil camping blankets as backing to the curtains, to insulate us against the cold night air, and see-through black blinds against the daytime sun. She also began a search on eBay for a camper-van awning. There was no shower or loo, so we would depend on pubs, garages and the countryside for our toiletary needs, and rivers, the sea, municipal showers or the people we visited for a proper wash every few days.

The engine was good and the van was running perfectly, but I still took it round to my local garage for a service. Mistake. Inner-city garages don't really get diesel camper vans, as they freely admitted after I had paid the bill. And although they charged me a fortune, it was several days before I was back on the road. From then on I always took it to little roadside garages well away from towns, and had faults dealt with when I could fit them in.

Tooling up

I put the word out in the PR community for gadgets and gizmos to take on the road with me. The freebies flooded in: a wind-up torch and a wind-up digital radio from Freeplay; a mini vacuum cleaner from Electrolux; a rucksack with built-in solar panel from Selfridges; rechargeable batteries and a charger from Energiser, along with an LED torch you wear on your head; a press card and guidebook from the Camping and Caravanning Club, entitling me to preferential treatment in their network of camping sites; a watch with built-in digital compass and GPS satellite tracking from Suunto; phones from Nokia and Sony Ericsson; a cool box and electric fan from Halfords, both running off the cigar lighter, and perhaps the best gadget of all: a little lead you could plug into the cigar lighter that turned it into two cigar lighters.

I was far more excited by the double lighter socket than by the Blackberry, a mobile email gadget supposedly so addictive the media have renamed it the Crackberry, much to the delight of the marketing department at Blackberry. I did not take to the Crackberry, with its tiny keyboard. If you are downloading emails, you might as well have a proper-sized screen on which to read them and a proper keyboard with which to reply to them. And if you are sitting at dinner and trying to work at the same time, then, unless you are a news editor, it seems to me that firstly you should give yourself a break, and secondly you could just send text messages on your mobile. Business execs tell me that such is the speed at which they are now expected to operate that they have to stay in the loop on the hundreds of emails a day sent within teams they are leading or else the group might spin off on some hare-brained sidetrack. But even then the Blackberry is the wrong device. A Japanese phone called SPV allows you to do all the things a Blackberry offers and in addition to download and read full-size Word and spreadsheet attachments.

I also received a total of six GPS navigation systems (dozens of companies were entering this new market at the time), but however hard I tried I literally could not understand how any of them worked. Every time I made contact with an off-gridder – and after weeks of emails and phone calls I had assembled a reasonable list of them – I had asked for their postcode and made a mark on a large map of England

Double socket blew my fuse.

I kept pinned to the grey carpeting material that insulated the ceiling of the van. The dots made a nice pattern and gave me an overview of the off-grid hotspots across the UK. I had visions of simply tapping in the postcode for my next visit, then sitting back and enjoying the metallic voice as it told me which of countless little side roads and dirt tracks to follow. But it was not to be. Having failed the basic IQ test that is the lot of all those who won't read manuals, I would have to rely on my limited wits to find these places. It was some consolation to hear stories of drivers who had followed their navigation-system instructions straight into rivers or marshland. Anyway, the gadgets were all extremely energy hungry, and by the end of each journey their batteries would need recharging. Some had cigar lighter attachments, but that power source was already needed to feed the phones, the computer and the cool box.

I was worried about our power supply, and the first time the fuse blew on the cigar lighter I turned to Bert Hagley, who had contacted me through the off-grid website. He ran a large engineering company on the edge of Birmingham – the heartland of British manufacturing industry, which once ruled the world. Bert's company made die casts – bits of machinery for other manufacturing companies, chunks of metal that could then be assembled into production lines both in the UK and round the world. The way Bert told it, the company was a success story, but it had seen better days and he had decided to sell out and switch his talents to the renewable energy industry. He was very untypical of the kind of people who were going off-grid, with his golfer's haircut and brand-new powder-blue Jaguar with personalised number plates, but why would he lie?

A couple of the people I was to meet on my journey asked me to change their name or omit their surname, to protect them from legal reprisals, and I have always made it clear in the text when that happened. But there is only one name I decided to conceal. 'Bert Hagley', then, was a classic Brummie, and I felt humbled when he first contacted me by phone. Here was a true fan, an avid visitor to my website, who told me at our first face-to-face meeting that he had been inspired to change his life because of what he'd seen there. At first he came across as a simpleton, with his thick Birmingham accent, moon-like face and torturing of the English language. Perhaps this was the secret of his business success. First impressions of Bert must have fooled many over the years. He had a way of hanging his mouth open between phrases, and he spoke in simple sentences with a language all his own. Wind turbines were 'wind terblinds' in Bert-speak, solar panels were 'sowlar flannels'.

Bert made a special trip down to London to meet me, and after just a few hours talking to him I felt here was a man I could trust, and a good engineer to boot. He offered to fit some solar panels and extra batteries to my van, made in China and costing a fraction of the going rate in the UK. He would come back some time soon to do the work.

While I was waiting for Bert to give me a date, I decided it was time to hit the road anyway. I had a powerful diesel engine, a lorry battery with a cigar lighter power adapter, and a Vodafone 3G card that could find an Internet signal in the middle of nowhere. I was ready to roll.

4

Meet the People

Residents moaned,
Complained by phone,
All in an angry tirade.
I suffered abuse;
They said my tree hoose
Spoiled their views o'er the glade.

'The Tree Hoose Song' by Barnie McCormack (2001)

O^{N A RAINY MORNING} in June, Fiona and I loaded the van with anoraks and duvets, food and cooking equipment, cameras, laptop computer, mobile phones and chargers, clothes, shoes and books. Anything left in the house by the time we finished packing could probably have been given to charity with no effect on our lives. Caitlin, almost a year old, sat between us in the front of the van with her own baby steering wheel (and associated sound effects). She alternately babbled and slept on our road trips together. Splayed out on the floor in the back was the final member of our party, our dog Olive, a piebald cross between a pointer and a spaniel. She had been badly mistreated by the pet shop from which we'd rescued her two years earlier, and seems to think of herself as a cross between a human and a small marsupial. At twelve months she was so timid we took her to a pet psychiatrist who told us that it was not Olive who had the problem, but Fiona and I, and suggested that a year's joint therapy – yes, all three of us – should resolve things. We never went back.

It stayed wet through most of our first sortie – a real test of the systems in the van. Anyone can be off-grid in the summer sun; a spot of cold and rain sorts out the men from the boys, I reflected as we sped through deserted London streets, windscreen wipers on full speed, our departure carefully timed to coincide with an England World Cup match. I thought of all the millions of people in front of their TVs, nipping into the kitchen at half-time to put the kettle on, going to bed that night with their red standby lights glowing reassuringly in the dark. I was leaving all that behind. Would I ever want to go back?

The artist and the woodsman

We were heading off to meet Sarah Harvey and Marcus Tribe, both of whom are now semi-public figures after Marcus's five-year legal wrangle with Mid-Devon Council over the right to live in his six-acre wood. The battle was almost won by the time we arrived near the village of Nomansland on the edge of Dartmoor. We rolled up at what was probably Marcus's domain, but to my untrained eye it looked no different from other woods. A statue of an owl carved into a tree stump by the entrance was a clue, although it had not featured in Sarah's directions. I left Fiona and Caitlin in the van and wandered along a narrow path. There were little fairy garlands of flowers in the vegetable patch, and some distance away I could see a yurt of green canvas, half-hidden among the trees. Unless the whole area had gone yurt-crazy, we were indeed in the right place.

I found Marcus sitting at a table outside this yurt, which the locals had described as an eyesore during the first few months after Marcus built it. The council was tipped off and an eviction notice sent. The woods had always been privately owned, but the locals saw the place as rightfully theirs. The fight over planning regulations went all the way to a public inquiry (see chapter 7). Marcus was wearing a thick padded lumberjack shirt, his greying hair cropped close to his head. His life as a charcoal burner and forest warden has left him looking older than his forty-eight years. His girlfriend, thirty-six-year-old Sarah Harvey, was sitting on the ground beside him, painting a big flower pot in lurid colours. She jumped up to congratulate me on finding the place without the several phone calls they usually get from first-time visitors. She had long dark hair and shining eyes, and was wearing a long skirt with a hand-knitted multi-coloured top. Sarah works part-time teaching art and poetry to alcoholics and ex-prisoners at a residential centre in the local town, paints gypsy caravans for a bit of extra income, and is a published poet. She finds her artistic inspiration in a little woodshed-on-stilts Marcus built for her.

Five minutes into saying my hellos I remembered that Caitlin and Fiona were still in the van, and returned to fetch them. Fiona was making coffee and feeding Caitlin pre-packed organic baby food. I briefly wondered how best to relate to these strangers whose houses I was visiting. Would they respond with more enthusiasm to a professional writer or to a person like themselves with a family and a child? They had been through years of media interviews about their planning battles, I reasoned as I carried Caitlin over to the yurt and introduced Fiona to Sarah, so they would prefer to meet another human, not an interviewer. I resolved to do my best not to ask the same questions everyone else must have asked.

If she was a bird, Sarah would be a swallow, darting around her domain. I guess Marcus would be a woodpecker. He has worked for the Forestry Commission all his life, on contracts that have taken him everywhere in the country. You walk into his yurt and it's instant feng shui, but the way he found the enchanted spot was anything but instant. He searched for twenty years before being offered his six acres near Nomansland seven years ago. He had watched prices rise inexorably over that time, always staying just out of reach of his tiny income. Now at last this fifth-generation woodsman who has not lived in a conventional house for eighteen years has his own wood, bought for cash with literally his life savings. 'I didn't find the land – it found me' was Marcus's mantra, delivered in a soft yet gruff West Country accent. Its most important feature, he told us as we sat together cross-legged that evening, was that it was flat. And it had a well.

The couple had prepared dinner on a tiny gas stove in a little kitchen extension to the warm, cosy yurt, as they did every night. Music came from a solar-powered car stereo. They had become quite used to entertaining visiting writers, journalists and TV crews over the years since the planning battle started. They had not sought the notoriety that comes with appearing on local TV and having their lives raked over in national newspapers, but Sarah at least was enjoying it. She read us some of her poetry and talked about her work with ex-prisoners. She is a voluble counterbalance to Marcus's rather laid-back presence. He seemed uncomfortable in his role of host, but who could blame him? He had signed up to manage a wood, not a PR campaign. And anyway, he had Sarah to handle all that for him.

They make a lovely couple, Marcus dour and hard-working, Sarah flitting poetically between the trees. Hard and soft; practical and imaginative. All they need to make their life perfect is a bigger yurt.

If they had to do it all over again, they would make one change to their strategy: wait until the battle with the council was over before Marcus built his workshed. Now that he is fully legal, he has a crippling rates bill on what is no more than a well-made shelter for his wood and himself. Had he known he would be charged rates he would have made

Marcus and Sarah, the swallow and the woodpecker.

the building much smaller, or constructed it as a wood store, not a workshop.

It had been dark for a couple of hours by the time we strolled back to our bedroom on wheels. Caitlin was asleep on my shoulder. The moon and stars were obscured by the canopy, but white stones placed along the path by Sarah showed us the way. To me the spot felt tranquil and inviting, but Fiona did not think she could live in a place like this. It was too dark, too damp and, for her at least, a little bit frightening. She also had a practical objection: it was too near the road, which ran along one side of the wood. Although it was barely a two-lane highway, it had become a cut-through for commuters in the years since Marcus moved in. 'What's the point of giving up all the comforts if you can still hear cars as you lie in bed?' she asked.

At daybreak we went for a walk around the woods with Marcus. He showed us his woodshed stacked with different lengths and types of saplings, used for building yurts and teaching people to build them. We passed several more carved owls, some of them finished, one still half-carved. He was not sure he would complete any more though, especially not near the road, because after pub closing time someone was in the habit of slicing the owls off their perch. After breakfast we had to move on, and with Sarah's reluctant permission, and a promise to return soon, we loaded up the van and went on our way.

Back on the road after those first tranquil twenty-four hours, everything seemed easy. We already felt at home in the Renault Master, but we couldn't keep calling it 'the van'. As it was an old hospital care bus, we decided to name it after its primary characteristic: 'the Bus'.

Traditional farm living

I heard about Lizzie Purchase from Clive Menhenett, a legendary solar power specialist who can usually be found at any festival where solar energy is being used to run the stage or the cybercafé. Clive's company, Magrec, was one of the renewable energy providers I phoned during my first round of research, and although he lives firmly on the grid in Okehampton, Devon, he spends a large part of the year off-grid, either recording dolphin song during long sea voyages or at festivals where he sells solar panels and has a nice sideline in CDs of dolphin song. He had installed Lizzie's solar panels and batteries, and a sophisticated control panel to monitor the system, switch on the generator if the battery ran low, and convert the power from 12 volts to 240. 'This probably won't interest you,' he told me as soon as I explained my interest, 'but it's a ridiculous situation.'

Liz is a youthful, energetic and very spiritual woman in her forties whose care for the environment, as with many conservationist farmers, stems from her devout Christianity. She sees herself as a steward of the land she inherited, preserving it for her children and keeping it the way God made it. Liz lives next door to her sister. Each lives in her respective half of a Devon long cottage inherited from their father. But the contrast between Liz and her sister could not be greater. While Liz has decided to live exactly the same way their father did, her sister has been equally determined to modernise and improve. The result is that Liz is off-grid with PV (photovoltaic) power and a generator, while in the other half of the building her sister has PVC windows and mains electricity.

Their father was a classic self-reliant farmer who recycled everything down to the sawdust from the log cutting, and mended everything from the fifty-year-old tractor (still working perfectly in Liz's barn) to an equally ancient Lister engine that drove the generator, which he had finally scrapped shortly before he died, four years earlier. 'He would not be dependent on power from the outside,' Liz recalled as we sat in her kitchen looking at photos of the farm in the 1970s when she was a teenager.

The oldest of three sisters, Liz was brought up to be the son. Her father bequeathed each sister a third of the land on his 120-acre farm, the house was split in two for Liz and her middle sister, and the out-houses and farm equipment went to Liz. Before Liz had renewable energy installed, both families shared the £7,000 generator that had been Pa's last big purchase before he passed on. 'We were having arguments about the generator,' Liz sighed, tilting her head towards the other half of the building. 'They used it all the time and it's noisy.' While Liz tried her best to conserve energy, her sister gobbled it up. 'It's all right for her, she doesn't have two children,' said Anne when I met her briefly. The voice was gentle but you could hear the resentment. This was not just about the relative merits of renewable energy versus mains. On some level this was personal.

Alone, Liz tends the fields, herds the animals, and fills in the end-less forms with which the Department for Rural Affairs (DEFRA) tortures the modern smallholder. Before her father died, Liz was living in an ex-council house with a field at the back where she grew her veg-etables. 'I was living on a shoestring. I had a goat in the yard . . . people would give me pigeon, deer, pheasant . . . they knew I was struggling. It was very much a barter system.' Four years after her father's death, Liz is still running the farm the way he would have done it: taking the tractor up to the top field and using its engine to drive the circular saw and cut the logs, and laying down animal manure as fertiliser instead of buying chemicals. The main innovation since she moved in was the £8,000 invested with Clive Menhenett in solar panels and batteries (supplemented by the generator).

I could not quite tell whether Liz was farming in this way to pre-serve the memory of her father or for its own sake. I guess she managed to make a living out of it, but perhaps the justification will only become fully apparent if or when energy prices shoot up and food becomes scarce, as James Lovelock is predicting. 'I'd like to think whatever happened to the world outside, there's always this little bit of land,' Liz remarked, looking round at the farm. 'It will be here for my grand-children to experiment with.' In the meantime, one thing is crystal clear: everything works on this farm, and everything is where it is supposed to be. The fields are all producing crops or supporting cattle and sheep. The tractor works. The hay loft is full of hay. The farmhouse is warm, comfortable and welcoming. It was a standard by which to judge other places as I continued my travels – the Lizzie Purchase test.

We woke up the next day knowing we would be coming back some time. Liz had made us feel welcome, and it was hard to leave this beautiful spot, miles from the main roads. I reversed onto the track and promptly dropped one wheel of the Bus into the ditch. My heart sank, but I needn't have worried. I was on a farm, part of the community; people simply deal with minor problems like this. Ten minutes later a local labourer was revving up the tractor while his mate tied a steel cord round the front axle. Two minutes later and we were heading down the road to Moretonhampstead.

The eco-commune

On the edge of Moretonhampstead, at the north-east corner of Dartmoor, teetering on a fearsomely steep piece of land that none of the locals would have dreamt of buying, is the Steward Wood commune (www.stewardwood.org), launched six years ago. There are now ten adults and five children living there, most of the families in semi-permanent dwellings they built themselves, but the commune has not yet managed to integrate with the locals. The neighbours are given to complaining about guest parking (they have even set up a website at www.stewardwood.co.uk), and the commune's temporary planning permission is up for renewal in 2007, so I had strict instructions on where to park the Bus to avoid breaching any of the planning conditions.

I had found Steward Wood on the Internet while searching through the Eco-Village website (www.evnuk.org.uk). I tried the phone number and it was answered by Merlin Howse, who spoke in low, serious BBC English. When we arrived, Merlin was waiting at the bottom of the track – from there it is another half-mile up a footpath to the main part of the site – but not just yet: his girlfriend's mother lives locally and she was due to drop off the weekly washing in her 4×4. Who was I to frown at this, seeing as I had turned up in an eighteen-foot-long, three-ton bus? I waited in it until the family meeting was over, then we trudged up the hill, Merlin carrying a huge rucksack full of washing on his back. He was six feet four inches tall, with long red-blond dreadlocks, a scraggly beard and a faraway look in his eye.

Merlin, Steward Wood's tech supremo.

The path began as a wide bridleway and ended up twisting through trees and around rocks. About halfway up we passed the commune's market garden. It was a long way from the kitchen. There was a smaller herb and veg garden, and it was on the only large flat area of land on the holding. Once up at the kitchen, you could see part of the commune. There was a shared building, used for eating and as a library. Next to it was the fire pit, covered against the elements with a large piece of canvas. The commune is built on a series of terraces to compensate for the steepness of the hill, so a narrow footpath snakes up the hill past other buildings that house either people or equipment. Some are made of wood, others of a mix of wood and canvas.

Steward Wood seemed well organised. Although it had only been in lawful existence for about four years, it was beginning to come together. They even had a micro hydro power system, its water being one of the reasons the residents bought the land in the first place. It was summer and the water level was too low to run it, but the level rises in the autumn, and as the days shorten the need for power increases, so it works out fine.

It did not meet the gold standard set down by Lizzie Purchase, but on the other hand the Steward Wood commune does not have big money behind it. I could see that the place was well kept, neat and tidy. And the people were friendly. Fiona, Caitlin and I were invited to stay for a meal, and made to feel welcome.

The Steward Wood biofuel store.

We wandered around as our hosts raced to meet their work commitments. I briefly met some of the other residents, including Merlin's partner Beccy, who was very sweet and shy, and his son Rowan, one of the least shy children I have ever met. He seemed intent on hijacking the role of guide from his father and telling his audience everything he knew about the commune, including some things I'm sure his elders would rather he hadn't mentioned. His descriptions of the composting toilet were particularly colourful.

Merlin's home is a green canvas bender. It is a timber frame construction with an apex roof, and it has double-glazed south-facing windows (reclaimed locally). Because it is on a steep hillside, it is built on stilts made from larch trunks supporting a platform made from beams (also from the woodland) and sterling board reclaimed from stages at the 2000 Glastonbury Festival. The main room is about sixteen by twelve feet and contains a wood-burning stove, a sofa, a mini kitchen, wardrobe space, lots of toy storage and a low second storey for the bedroom. There is a second smaller room that contains an office and storage space.

Another key member of the commune is Radiant Light, otherwise known as Dan. Formerly one of the leaders of the anti-McDonald's campaign in the UK, Dan has short hair and a scraggly beard. He wore a permanent slight smile that reminded me of Archbishop Rowan Williams, as though he had learned the secret of the universe and it was jolly good news. Dan is in charge of planting and gardening, which is run according to the principles of permaculture. He is almost always busy during the days at Steward Wood because there is so much to do.

Permaculture is a method of horticulture that follows nature and encourages the cultivation of a wide range of plants and vegetables that interact with and support one another. Sarah Harvey told me she had planted marigolds next to her cabbages because it made them 'happier', and that in a nutshell is the essence of permaculture: its aim is a mutually supporting combination of diverse crops that feed off different ground nutrients and also provide one another with nutrients. As far as possible all waste is recycled back into the planted areas. These areas become the commune's food store, and the aim is to live off them without the need for shopping and packaging, so that nothing ends up in landfill sites.

And permaculture is not just about growing things. It can be a whole life design that includes how we deal with waste water and human waste, and what we eat at different times of the year. The most widely known example of permaculture is probably Prickly Nut Wood in Surrey, which was twice featured on the Channel 4 series *Grand Designs*. It's a ten-acre woodland near Haslemere managed by woodsman Ben Law, one of the founding figures of the off-grid movement in the UK. He uses a 'whole system' permaculture approach, and the TV series focused on his house which was built almost entirely using products from the woodland.

Steward Wood has close relationships with other eco-communes around the country, including my next destination, which was also run along permaculture lines.

Battle of the benders

I contacted the Land Matters commune in Allaleigh, Devon, via an activist group that helps off-gridders and others win planning permission for their living spaces. I spoke to Charlotte, one of the main organisers, who had been living there off and on for three years. There are many eco-communes across Britain, some of them relatively long-standing, like Brith Dir Mawr, Tinker's Bubble and Kingshill, but Allaleigh is the newest, and possibly destined to be the shortest-lived, for it ran into local opposition almost from the outset. Still, despite some planning permission problems, over the phone it all sounded well organised and competent, and all appeared to be going well with their project to turn the mixed woodland and meadows into a sustainable eco-commune. Charlotte promptly invited us to come down and visit.

We found Allaleigh quite easily, but Land Matters was harder. Allaleigh is more of a hamlet than a village, with no pub or shop and perhaps a dozen houses. We stopped at the largest to ask the way. A tall, patrician lady came to the gate having first let loose two large dogs by her side. Somehow I knew it would be a mistake to ask for Land Matters so I named a neighbouring farm I had spotted on the Ordnance Survey map. 'Oh, it's up there.' She pointed disdainfully at the narrowest lane I had ever seen. I thanked her and climbed back into the Bus. We squeezed down the hill, leaving her still watching suspiciously in our wake. Maybe our choice of vehicle had been a bit misguided after all. And having the off-grid web address displayed in foot-high black vinyl letters across the bonnet, which had seemed perfectly innocuous in London, was perhaps rather unsubtle.

A few hundred yards down the steep, winding lane, at the bottom of the hill by a stream, was a gate bearing a hand-painted sign that said 'Land Matters'. I executed a ten-point turn onto the land and parked alongside a car and another van. From there it was half a mile up another hill into the heart of classic Devon countryside, as beautiful a piece of England as you could ever find. It was a hot day and the birds were trilling madly, together with a few crows. The hills rolled away into the distance, each a collection of small fields, and we could hear echoes from farm machinery across the steep valley – which presumably meant they could hear us too. Other than the nameplate on the gate, the only indication of human habitation was a black Darth Vader-shaped letterbox mounted incongruously on the fence leading into the second field.

We continued up the hill, through a gap in a hedge, and there was something quite startling and eye-catching about what I saw next. At the top of the hill, ten benders stood in a loose oval formation around a large field. Benders have been used for centuries by the rural poor. The 1880 Census recorded 11,000 in use, and there were probably just as many that went unrecorded. They were made popular again during the road protests of the 1990s. They are constructed out of anything available,

A bender at Land Matters: note the useful step up to the door.

but mostly have a canvas covering pegged down over a structure of interlaced willow or ash branches. These benders had recycled domestic windows built into them, and wooden duckboard flooring to raise them above ground level that was covered with carpets. The field was surrounded by high bushes and a few trees which lent some shelter to the benders, which were ten to twelve feet high. Some had fences around them to give the impression of a front garden – a little personal space within the wider commune, perhaps, or a way of creating a sense of smallness and domesticity on this exposed hilltop. Directly opposite the gate, up against the hedgerow on the other side of the field, was the largest of the structures, a kitchen tent with a fire circle to the left of it. A couple of people were cooking over the smoking fire. Solar panels abounded, leaned up against the bender walls or on frames standing in the field, tied down to the ground against the wind. But for these few touches of modernity, it was a timeless scene, almost Hardyesque. It was certainly about as far from the madding crowd as you could ever get in southern England.

As I sat in the fire circle that night, with Fiona wheezing in the Bus and even Caitlin suffering from the damp, I too felt the flu coming on. Thankfully there was a kettle boiling on a fire-stand made of three horseshoes welded together on thin metal legs, and I accepted a cup of herb tea offered by a voice out of the darkness. I was grateful because

I could sense the group was wary of me, an emissary from the straight world. I'd arrived just after they were denounced by the local Tory MP, and they felt like they were being watched. Their move to the land had been a bid for obscurity; now they were locked in the grid of planning permission bureaucracy.

'The locals think we are getting one over on them as they sit in their million-pound houses,' said a voice in the darkness.

'I think they want us to pay council tax,' said Charlotte with a throaty chuckle.

'Well, we're not paying council tax,' said another.

Charlotte, a veteran of the hippy movement, an attractive forty-something with greying blonde hair, gave me the background. She had a serious, almost monotonous way of speaking, and ended each sentence with a pouting movement of her lips as if challenging me to refute or interrupt her. Charlotte had worked as a copy editor in London for a while, and then moved to Totnes, the nearest town, where she had 'various admin jobs'. She still shares a flat there with other members of the co-op. They bedded down there during the early days of the commune when there was little or nothing in the way of facilities, and they sometimes still do in the winter.

Three years on, there did not seem to be as much progress as I would have expected. There was a small vegetable plot near the kitchen

Charlotte with her morning cuppa.

tent, and another half an acre of vegetables in the neighbouring field, but little evidence of cultivation anywhere else, so I am not sure it passes the Lizzie Purchase test, even though it is neat and tidy.

There was a maypole in the middle of the field, left over from a spring festival held a few days earlier. I was sorry to miss it as I imagined the place had been thronging with merry local villagers dancing in lockstep with their bender-dwelling hosts. But contrary to my speculation, the party had been attended mainly by visitors from other eco-communities and friends of the settlers, from Totnes, London and elsewhere.

I needed to use the toilet, and was directed through some bushes and across to the other side of the next field. I smelled the composting loo before I saw it. I took a deep breath and opened the door, then changed my mind and decided to wait for another opportunity.

By the time I returned to the fire, it was smoking badly. I was dodging and closing my eyes against the stinging smoke whipped towards each of us in turn by a changing wind. They had been there three years, but they were burning green logs. I felt a sudden concern at the hardship they were enduring. Notwithstanding the smoky fire, it was all pleasant enough in the height of summer, but what did they do when the weather turned really cold, other than huddle in their benders, only some of which were fully finished with inviting wood-stoves, or decamp to Totnes?

The most impractical element of Land Matters' set-up was the water supply, which was hand-carried from a stream at the bottom of the hill half a mile away. The local MP had denounced a grant of £4,000 from the Big Lottery Fund for the purpose of drilling a bore-hole. 'These are a group of nomads,' he fulminated, 'they should not be allowed to set up their camp.' As they discussed the possibility of using a donkey to turn a hand pump, once the borehole was eventually drilled, I wondered why they had not just used a couple of water pumps and a reservoir halfway up the hill to bring up water from the stream at the bottom. In a conversation with me, one local pointed out where the commune had really gone wrong: 'They put their living spaces up on the top of the hill where it's bitter in winter, instead of on a sheltered slope. And they planted their vegetable patch next to the houses on the worst soil. They should have it down near the stream where the best soil is.'

Even the purchase of the land itself had been a sort of accident. Christian Taylor had the original idea after he won a sealed-bid auction he had entered more to understand the market and to practise bidding than with any expectation of actually buying anything. He came away owning forty-two acres of prime Devon countryside for £60,000 or so. He contacted his mates, and they all paid £3,000 each into a

Housing Co-operative, the legal entity that owns the land. Everyone who joined committed to living there and devoting their time to making Land Matters a fully functioning, sustainable settlement. Christian made the first down payment, but when the contract was signed and the rest of the money paid over, it was in the name of Land Matters. This was the first inkling the local villagers could have had that things might not be as they seemed. Now the villagers were furious that Land Matters had been less than honest about their plans, and I was thinking that what I would learn from Land Matters was how *not* to live off-grid. The combination of lackadaisical planning and a lack of community relations made me pessimistic about their chances of making a go of it. Still, in a way I had to admire the impracticality of it all. These are, after all, some of the most idealistic people in Britain, who have transmuted their anger with the road system into a sincere attempt to live out their ideals. Despite the shortcomings that had struck me, they were certainly making a better go of it than I could, if I ever dared to try.

Other figures joined us around the fire: Josh, a musician responsible for the market garden; Ollie, the group's technical wizard; and Robin, who I later discovered had been named Prince of Wales organic gardener of the year in 2002. He was the most thoughtful member of the group, with a highly developed philosophy of the natural world. He spent hours practising his bushcraft skills in the woods below. Young, focused and clean cut, he was the perfect spokesman for Land Matters.

I persisted in trying to draw out their story. For the first year the co-op did little beyond visiting and watching what happened on the land through the changing seasons and thinking about how to organise their commune. They were aware that the villagers might object if they knew what the co-op was planning, so they didn't tell them. When the Land Matters crew finally moved in they built their benders at night, and swiftly; when the villagers finally found out, because someone was searching for a lost sheep, they felt they had been misled. That meant the village immediately formed an opposition to the incomers. It was a bad start.

The Land Matters planning application was quickly rejected by the council, and a planning inspector held a public inquiry in July 2007.

Planning inspectors are there to provide a dispassionate decision, applying national standards free of the prejudices or favouritism of local council politics. They are, however, a priesthood, with their own set of criteria that they apply in reaching their decisions. Journalists are not permitted to interview them, but I searched for a way into their secret world. They are appointed by the National Planning Inspectorate, which comes under the Department for Communities and Local Government. Both bodies refused to offer any help or advice in my attempts to contact an inspector, but eventually I succeeded (see chapter 7).

The locals in Allaleigh expected that the benders would be allowed to stay, for a few years at least, with the same kind of temporary permission as had been granted to Steward Wood. I was not so sure. I thought that the combination of the powerful elite lined up against them and the lack of significant progress in cultivating the land, plus the tiny narrow lanes that barely supported the existing car population, would all count against them at the public inquiry. And the fact that some in the group had identified themselves on their planning application as lacking agricultural skills meant they might have trouble arguing that they were actively working the land. Now that the local Tory had found he could win easy brownie points in the community by speaking out against them, they were on the defensive. They weren't even sure they should be talking to me. They had a figurative as well as a literal mountain to climb.

With all three of us wheezing and snuffling, we decided to head back towards London the following day. But I knew I would return to Allaleigh for two reasons. Firstly, Robin had invited me back to learn more about foraging. He said he would show me dozens of edible and medicinal herbs and flowers and teach me how to 'walk like a fox' – a bushcraft technique for treading lightly on the land. I also needed to meet Land Matters' opponents. Planning permission was clearly one of the key elements in the struggle to live off-grid (see chapter 7). I wanted to understand the mentality behind the widespread resistance to what I saw as a completely harmless and forward-looking idea, even when it was executed rather chaotically, as seemed to be the case at Land Matters.

Not in my back yard (Nimby)

A few weeks later I was back in Devon. There had been at least one national newspaper article on the planning battle by this time, and the residents of Allaleigh (population twenty-four) now found themselves, or saw themselves, in the spotlight. A little work with the local phone book gave me the number of the house where I had stopped to ask the way on my first visit. It was owned by celebrated restaurateur and food writer Tom Jaine.

If Tom was surprised by my phone call he certainly didn't show it. Here was a man who stood accused of pettifogging narrow-mindedness, of failing to understand or to welcome the strangers in his midst, but who responded to my phone call with an instant invitation to visit. 'You're writing about the hippies!' he roared down the phone. 'Well, yes, come over, come over. Of course.'

Would his wife remember me? I wondered as I beetled over in the Bus.

On closer inspection, the ancient hamlet was as immaculate as it had seemed at first. The outstanding feature was a complete absence of parking spaces. The narrow lanes in and out were bounded by walls, and even where the roads met there was only just room for two cars to pass. As the roads entered the hamlet, high hedgerows gave way to high dry-stone walls and fine detached houses. Tom had the most prominent, a double-fronted white mansionette with a lovingly tended front garden and views across the valley to a wood of hundred-year-old oaks.

I stopped outside and rang the bell. If Mrs Jaine recognised me, she showed no sign of it as she greeted me in the front garden, this time without the dogs. She introduced herself as Sally; her husband would join us shortly. I had squeezed the Bus as tightly as I could next to the garden wall but this was not enough for Tom, who appeared at the front gate apparently beside himself with excitement, although I soon learned that his strange jigging was a default behaviour. 'Good heavens, what's this? Is it really as close as you can? Will the neighbours pass?' I had to confess that they might not. 'Another few feet in, I think.' I leapt back into the driver's seat and manoeuvred even closer to the wall, trying to position the Bus so that it would intrude only minimally into the crossroads. Once this implicit admonishment had been dealt with, I was ushered in.

Tom, King of the Kitchen.

Tom was tall, thin as a rake, with a high balding dome of a head. He blared rather than talked, and in his buttonless designer shirt he bobbed and swayed about continuously, punctuating his sentences with guffaws and snorts. He had spent the hour between my phone call and my arrival checking me out on Google, I learned as he showed me through the well-stocked kitchen and simultaneously introduced himself. Now in their late fifties, the couple had bought Allaleigh House in 1983 and for twenty-one years had lived in one of the quietest corners of England. Cars rarely passed, except for the neighbours. The occasional cyclist or walker was the only stranger they ever expected to see. And now this.

It was seven o'clock, and I had feared being drawn into pre-dinner cocktails. To my relief I was not offered so much as a glass of water, but led straight into a formal sitting room with each cushion and magazine arranged at precise intervals and parallel with the surface it was on. The couple placed themselves in two white armchairs facing each other but slightly turned towards me. I sat on the matching sofa. The conversation that followed was largely between Tom and Sally. I was allowed to ask questions, but otherwise I was more like a spectator to their dialogue.

As soon as his bum touched the seat, Tom got on to the subject of my visit. 'Of course possession is nine tenths of the law,' was his opening remark. 'Once you're in situ you can adopt the moral high ground. Anybody who disagrees with you is making eighteen people homeless and thrusting them onto the rates.' He harrumphed at Sally, who pursed her lips as if she was about to disagree. But before she could say anything he was off again.

The essence of his argument emerged slowly between tumultuous but good-humoured shouts of rage and frustration. If it had been one or two households then he would have had no problem, he said. Sally agreed. 'We thought they might camp there for a week or two a year,' she said, but nine households, none of whom had any background of working on the land, was in Tom's opinion clear evidence of a scam being perpetrated on the local council. 'There are so many you feel it might double again,' Sally chipped in. Tom was more specific. 'We couldn't object to the present numbers,' he told his wife. 'They don't impinge on us, but in five years, if they all have 2.4 children there will be twenty-five people up there. How will ambulances or the fire brigade get up and down these narrow lanes? What happens when they get *E. coli* and start asking for water to be piped in?' He had now worked himself up into a real state. 'It's bonkers, just unacceptable.' I certainly would not tell Tom and Sally what I had just learned on my visit to Land Matters – that three of the women were pregnant, and within nine months there would be four children living on the hill. The population explosion had already started.

The conspiracy theorists in the village, said Tom, expected the initial temporary planning permission to be followed by a further application for temporary permission for upgraded homes. Further upgrades would follow over the years, 'and then they'll all bugger off with a million quid'. Over the years, Tom had opposed every single barn conversion in the area, and together with other residents had managed to buy up land to prevent the expansion of a nearby golf course. He had seen two farms go in the previous two decades, one to the golf course and another to become 'some sort of activity centre for kids'. 'Golf courses, hippies – it's all the same thing. Shoot the lot of them!' he roared in tones that no doubt went down a storm at the local village fête. But he had also done his research: he quoted Paul Waddington's book *The 21st-Century Smallholder* as evidence that you need a largish group if you are trying to cultivate a piece of land without chemicals.

Despite the colourful way of putting his argument, I felt Tom could not be dismissed as a knee-jerk scaremonger. He admitted himself that his opposition to developers was partly nimbyism, but nimbyism, he maintained, was one of the finest and most British of feelings. To some extent Tom blamed the small farmers for failing to manage their land properly and ending up in a situation where they were forced to sell. But he also cited the farmers as examples of why local resentment against the 'hippies' at Land Matters had run so high. His neighbour, a hard-working farmer, had recently applied for planning permission for an agricultural cottage, but he was turned down. 'A real farmer with a real son who wanted to build him a house on land that he owned,' Tom shouted at his wife, 'and he lost.'

I suggested that perhaps places like Land Matters could be treated in the same way as agricultural cottages, which received planning permission only for so long as its residents had some form of employment on the land. 'No,' Tom countered. There were two agricultural cottages nearby, one inhabited by a motor mechanic and the other by 'an emphysemic trustafarian who is selling, for £220,000, because he cannot get up the stairs any longer'. They are not working the land, said Tom, any more than the hippies are working the land – 'there's nothing going on up there'. He rocked back and forth like a rabbi at prayer. Tom had seen the planning application, and I hadn't, so I could hardly contradict him when he told Sally, 'They are all from W4 or Totnes or Brighton.'

It was now about 8 p.m., and time to go. As I drove down the hill I realised I was heading back directly towards the Land Matters co-op. I was sure, for no good reason, that my departing vehicle was being watched from Tom's top window, and much as I wanted to stop I decided to go straight past 'the hippies'. As part of their campaign to win planning permission, they had to be careful not to be seen to be generating traffic, and my ungainly bus squeezing down the narrow lane would not help their cause. So I passed the Land Matters gate and stopped at the next pull-in I found, a solitary barn, in use but deserted now until at least 6 a.m. I would be awake by then as I wanted to reach Somerset by breakfast time.

It was my first experience of wild camping – stopping somewhere I was not invited. Technically I was on private land, but I was parked outside the gates of the barn on what I presumed was a quiet country lane. A few more cars passed that night, one loaded with lads who stopped and shouted at one another rather than me. I locked the doors. But then all was quiet. Next day I was up before dawn. I did not need to meet any crusty old tractor drivers demanding I move on. It was a delightful morning and I enjoyed a long coffee listening to the birdsong before setting off. It seemed like wild camping could work.

A caravan on a farm

Off the main road a sign points to the farm shop. From there it's another mile straight into the country, then a couple of sharp turns bring you to a cluster of small farm buildings and two fields with a dozen piglets darting in and out of the chicken coops and a few sheep and cows. Behind the polytunnels, well out of sight, is a blue gypsy caravan built by Paul Score to house his wife and three-year-old daughter. The adjective most usually associated with gypsy wagons is 'minute', or 'doll-sized'; Paul and Susie's van is super-sized like an inflated version of the traditional design.

Paul first lived in a caravan when he was about twenty, in his second year of university. He tired of shared housing, dirty kitchens and arguments about bills, so he bought the cheapest caravan he could find, figuring he would make the money back on rent saved, and persuaded a nice farmer to let him park it in a field. Pretty soon he was told to leave – not by the farmer, but by the council on planning permission grounds – but he found another farmer, another field, and relied on friends with cars to tow him to a new site, which happened every few months. Eventually, after he left uni, he was able to afford his own car.

His years of being moved on taught him that 'if you live in something that looks a bit quaint you are less likely to be moved on'. If it was drawn by a horse instead of a car Paul discovered that a caravan would be welcome on any village green in the country for at least a night. He

had a solar panel for basic electrics and became adept at finding discreet hedges for his toiletary needs, but described that phase of his life as 'pretty grim really. It's much better if you are somewhere you can build a composting toilet.' Now they are settled on the farm, Paul and Susie's toilet follows the instructions in *The Humanure Handbook*, the leading US reference work on the subject. 'I was pretty sceptical at first,' Paul recalled, 'but it works really well. There's no smell.' The Humanure website has instructions on 'how to build a $25

Paul in the kitchen section of his gypsy caravan.

toilet' which are well worth following if you are in need of temporary facilities (visit www.jenkinspublishing.com/sawdustoilet.html).

At one time Paul was a road protester. He didn't want to give me his surname at first – a hangover from the days on the Convoy, where anyone from the straight media is the enemy. But he has to some extent joined the straight world now. He is, for instance, a skilled roofer, working on high-paying high-wire jobs four days a week, and spending the other three with his family. He is also a natural marketer, salesman even. Paul left university with a degree but then travelled and joined up with a group of other travellers, all of them educated, clever, clean and technically skilled. They were older now, and wanted to settle down. That meant finding land and working out a way of being allowed to live on it. Paul was planning a highly engineered, legally watertight off-grid eco-housing development on a piece of land in Somerset for which he was still negotiating. That meant they had to consult the veritable oracle of all the ways in which to win planning permission, Simon Fairlie.

Planning permission campaigner

Turn off the A303 at South Petherton, go down the first side road you find and along a winding lane to a sign saying Flaxdrayton Farm, and in the former potato store you will find Simon Fairlie, probably working in his book-lined office, crammed with carefully filed old alternative magazines and dusty planning applications, writing an angry tract about the land, or rather 'The Land', and simultaneously helping some random smallholder in his tangle with the planning authorities.

Simon is the éminence grise of the off-grid movement. His father was 'a dissolute journalist', and as he grew up the family moved around to stay one step ahead of the bailiffs. With a mound of dark black hair, an old shirt open to the waist, a week's stubble and a droopy moustache, Simon reminded me of a vagabond from a children's story, with a red and white spotted handkerchief on a stick, sitting by the side of the road smoking roll-ups. A gentleman of the road.

Beneath that unassuming exterior is one of the finest legal minds in Britain. He has given evidence to parliamentary inquiries into the future of planning in the countryside, and has launched a magazine, *The Land*, to campaign for the rights of smallholders to a fair hearing. Simon lived in France in the 1980s in a self-built wooden shack on a smallholding. When he returned to England he found it was illegal to live this way. After a period in a van he became co-owner of a bare landholding in Somerset and together with his fellow purchasers moved into tents on their land. That was in 1994, and 'Tinker's Bubble' gave Simon his first education in planning battles. Two years later Simon had fought his way through every part of the planning appeal process and won temporary planning permission (since renewed). The Bubble has been going for over a decade now.

Simon's passion is land politics, specifically the issue of why so many people want to live in the country but so few can. He has been campaigning for sustainable rural development since the mid 1990s and the Bubble was one of the first sustainable settlements to take on the planners and win. In the end, however, this particular version of the commune life was not for him. He left the Bubble because it was not communal enough, and not big enough for the sort of farmers' co-operative he had hoped it would become. 'It was a number of people with different little projects meshing together, and I didn't think it was efficient,' he said. So Simon now runs his multiple activities from a tiny office in the farm-turned-organic craft centre. He had to take the office after he accidentally started a scythe business. What began as the importing of a few Austrian scythes for friends is now what he relies on for his living, as his other activities do little more than cover his costs.

When I arrived, Simon was in conversation with a client, a posh local landowner with Raybans pushed up on his forehead. They were both bent over a huge scythe with a sweeping blade and long wooden handle with sidebars for each hand. I made for the toilet, which was shared by the other work units on the farm, and opened the door only to find a blonde woman in black underwear hastily adjusting her dress. 'The lock doesn't work!' she screamed at me. 'You're supposed to knock before you come in!' I hastily retreated. There's no point in telling a woman in her underwear that you don't believe her.

'The lock was working this morning,' Simon scoffed as he made me a cup of tea. The phone rang; Simon receives about 'five hundred calls a year' from people asking for his help and advice in their attempts to live part-time or full-time on agricultural or forest land. He helps them

Simon – relaxing for once.

if he does not feel they are simply trying to buy a second home on the cheap. 'The Old Store, the Old Post Office, the Old Barn,' he growled as we sat in the sunny yard outside his office. 'They're ripping the heart out of the countryside.' In his experience, the same people who are turning the pubs and shops and vicarages into suburban des res are the most likely to be vocal in their opposition to off-grid developments. To sum up Simon's essential attitude to the incomers: they are not country folk. They don't know about live-and-let-live in the country. They bought the view out of the window and they are buggered if they will let anyone else change it. If these arriviste middle classes have their way, they will squeeze the final few breaths of life out of a country community that has already been squeezed to near oblivion.

It would have been churlish to point out that Simon was a middle class writer and campaigner. The guy had paid his dues, living in agro-communes, squatting farms to prevent them being sold to city folk, and going out scything himself when he was not selling scythes. He was simply adapting what he did to the local circumstances.

After a while he went back to his many deadlines, and as I had no appointments until that afternoon, I stayed where I was to make some phone calls and write notes. As I opened the laptop, I made a useful discovery. The local businesses had a broadband connection to the Internet that was not password protected. With the wireless card in my computer, I could log on to their network and do all my high-speed computing. This was great. I was able to download three days' worth of emails – hundreds of items that would have taken hours at dial-up speed. Normally I piggyback on other people's bandwidth by driving round town with the computer on the passenger seat, scanning for a connection. It is known as war-surfing, and it works most of the time. Although technically it's stealing, war-surfing is a truly victimless crime. The bandwidth required to download some emails will not noticeably affect the quality of service for the actual paying customer, even if they are online at the same moment. Chances are they just left the computer on. Things would be different if you sat outside their window downloading videos or music, but I like to think a few emails is an acceptable piece of opportunism.

I had a lunch of strawberries and cream from the organic vegetable box business run by none other than the woman in black underwear, who had calmed down by now, then it was back to the Bus and on to meet Dylan Evans.

Utopia Experiment

As I crawled through the Bristol traffic, I reflected on Simon Fairlie's theory about the strange relationship between the car and the planning rules. We had allowed the car unrestricted access to almost every part of the countryside and simultaneously halted house-building. In so doing we had both shattered the tranquillity of the countryside and forced property prices up. We had looked to the car to make us happy and set us free. For Simon, at least, it had done neither.

Dylan Evans felt much the same about robots. A former philosophy lecturer, he had joined a multi-disciplinary team developing the next generation of worker robots. He had once believed that robots could make us happier, and fulfil the early-twentieth century dream of freeing man from his enslavement to drudgery and repetitive work. Now he had performed an intellectual U-turn, and was about to leave his job and explore a life off-grid as perhaps the only way to free us all from enslavement.

He showed me into his workplace, a cavernous room, perhaps 500 feet square, with sixty-foot ceilings, housing dozens of separate robot

Dylan on the land at Utopia.

experiments. In one corner was the Arena, an electrified floor where scores of robot drones are released simultaneously to perform simple rule-driven tasks that replicate the behaviour of termites. On the other side of the building was an experiment in robots powered by eating flies.

Dylan is in his mid-thirties, with small, delicate features and mousy hair. Behind rimless glasses, his eyes, I have to admit, were glinting madly, and with his deep, almost expressionless voice and self-effacing mannerisms, he fitted the stereotype of a scientist who believes that humanity must be saved from itself, whatever the cost. He explained the latest thinking in robots.

Terminator-style robots which cost millions and only need a small part to go wrong in order to break down are so last century. The fashion is for group intelligence – up to a hundred cheap, disposable robots 'modelled on ants, for example, which have no leader, nobody in charge. This makes them robust against individual failure. Each individual is relatively stupid, but if you have the right set of rules, what emerges is something that exhibits global properties hard to predict from the parts.'

Sitting on Dylan's desk was Eva, a startlingly lifelike head of a woman. Dylan was researching how a robot could both read emotion in others and display emotion itself. Eva could not feel emotion, or understand it, but through a USB camera in each eye she could be trained to detect patterns in the facial gestures of humans, and respond with ones of her own.

Over the years Dylan has come to think that science and technology add nothing to human happiness. Whatever benefits they bestow are outweighed by the feelings of powerlessness we all experience through no longer being in control of our lives on a physical level. A century and a half of industrialisation and specialisation means that many of us are unable to perform even the simplest tasks to maintain the complex machines we all depend upon for eating, communication, working and entertainment. We can't even perform simple tasks on relatively simple machines, like fixing a generator or changing a leaky tap. It was Dylan who introduced me to the work of Thomas Homer-Dixon on stresses in the global system, as quoted in chapter 2, with its warning that we may be heading towards some form of collapse as a result of 'synchronous failure'. 'If it all crashes then people will be unhappy, but perhaps not as unhappy if it crashes sooner than if it crashes later,' Dylan commented as we sat in a sparse, utilitarian canteen overlooking a car-park. 'There are countless examples in history of the overuse of a key resource such as trees leading to eco-disaster.'

Dylan was leaving to embark on the biggest experiment of his career, a Utopia in western Scotland on a thirty-acre off-grid patch of land. One hundred and seventy people volunteered after he announced his plans for a Utopia Experiment to the media, and the following month he would start to prepare living quarters for the fifteen or so who would be initially selected to take part. 'It even sounds crazy to me,' he admitted, 'but I have to follow this thought wherever it leads me.' As with his robotics experiments, Dylan believed that key to the project's success was the right set of rules. But he was not so arrogant as to believe he could come up with the perfect set first time, or enforce them on his volunteers. The rules they all set together would be the first outcome of the Utopia Experiment.

With the world's media on at him to let them film, it was flattering that I found myself the first outsider invited up to his Scottish Utopia. And after my conversation with Simon Fairlie, I wanted to reflect more on the right rules for off-grid communities. For now, though, it was time I returned to London. Fiona had headed home with Caitlin a few days earlier, and I wanted to see them both.

City Park houseboats

Back in London, I made a surprising discovery. I live in Hoxton, which until recently was a run-down, forgotten area just east of the City of London where artists starved in garrets waiting for Charlie Saatchi to turn up and discover them. Pete Doherty, before he met up with the rest of The Libertines, played music, recited poetry and took his drugs in The Foundry a few streets away. My grandparents, East European Jewish immigrants, struggled for decades to move out of the area. Now they would struggle to move in. The long upward march of property prices finally reached Hoxton a few years ago, bringing with it bars and restaurants and clothes shops, just like everywhere else.

A couple of miles north of here lie Hackney Marshes, which have become my favourite place to take Caitlin for walks when Fiona is working in her studio. The same weirdly dressed Orthodox Jews I remember from my youth, with pallid faces and huge black fur hats, walk their children to and from the synagogue past the dowdy frontage of the Egg Stores, a delicatessen that has become a bit rough around the edges since I waited there as a boy while Granny bought the weekly Hungarian salami and half-pickled cucumbers. Middle-class goyim are just beginning to move in, along with the new influx of Poles. Races and religions mix in Springfield Park, a lovingly tended collection of landscaped trees and smooth lawns sweeping down to the Regents Canal, and across the river Lea to the marshes beyond. It's still a landscape of industrial decay, though. You can see the last of the scrapyards from up on the hill next to a café housed in the restored Georgian park-keeper's cottage. Soon the skyline will be dotted with cranes as the transformation begins for the 2012 Olympics.

Down the hill, boaters and canoers mix with dog walkers on the canal towpath. There are dozens of houseboats, too, mostly clustered together for safety in a marina on the other side of the canal, but a few narrowboats are moored on towpaths on both sides of the canal. And that is where I made my discovery. Pushing Caitlin along in her pram one day past a mottled purple houseboat with flower pots lined up along the roof, I realised that here, in the middle of a near-Dickensian London scene, are a number of off-grid homes. The boats in the marina are all hooked up to the mains, but the ones on the towpath are self-powered and their inhabitants fetch their water from a tap. It was a weekend, and as I considered how to introduce myself, I saw a passer-by doing the same thing.

'Hi,' he said to a woman sunning herself on deck. 'Do you live there?'

She gave him a bored, 'Yeah.'

He didn't notice he was getting a brush-off. 'That's amazing. Any chance I could look around?'

She pulled herself up on her elbow. 'What would you think if I turned up at your front door and asked if I could look around your flat?' she growled before sinking back down to her book.

I decided to come back on a weekday to investigate canal life more carefully. As a result of the exchange I had just witnessed on the tow-path, I knew I would be viewed with suspicion if I just turned up, so I consulted my friend Dan Langton, an artist who lives on a boat near King's Cross station. The canal network is particularly diverse around there, and Dan lives just a few minutes' walk from the new Eurostar terminal, through a door in a brick wall and down a flight of steps to a towpath with just four other boats. They share a mains power connection and run hosepipes from a standpipe on the shore to their boats. Dan's vessel, the *Onion Bargee*, is like a student flat that has just been trashed after an all-night party – and that's after he has tidied it up.

Sure enough, Dan did know people who knew people who lived in Springfield Park, and a few phone calls later I was heading back to

Renee parked just near the Olympic Village.

the park to meet Renee Vaughan Sutherland, who lives on one of about 3,000 off-grid boats in the UK. Renee is tall, with short dark hair and a couple of facial piercings; she wears flowing gypsy skirts and mohair tops. In Australia, where she comes from, 'all my family have two houses each'. She arrived in the UK for a few months and has stayed nine years. Now aged thirty, she works for Sutton Council a couple of days a week doing 'change management consulting' but prefers to spend the rest of the time, when she could be earning more money, studying art at Middlesex University and making non-narrative films, which she shows in a makeshift outdoor cinema stored in the back of a friend's car.

Her boat is over fifty feet long with a deck at each end and a bicycle chained to the roof in between, next to the rusty smokestack chimney from her wood-burner. You enter at one end down some stairs and in via the bedroom containing just some shelves and a high double bed, designed so that Renee can look out of the window when she wakes up in the morning. Through the doorway is a small galley with everything you would expect to find in a tiny urban kitchenette. Beyond that is a sitting room, long by comparison with the tiny bedroom and galley. It contains an elegant 1950s sofa almost as long as the cabin, capable of housing two overnight guests sleeping end to end. Next to the stove with its flue poking out through the roof of the boat there is another door leading out on to the small deck. Plywood-lined ceilings have oblong, silver-framed twelve-volt lights embedded in them. The shelves and kitchen surfaces are rosewood. Cooking and water heating are from gas bottles and there are four marine batteries to run her lights, stereo and computer.

Renee made us excellent black coffee while Caitlin played with her collection of pens. I watched in terror in case she left baby drawings on the furniture. Why had Renee chosen to live on a boat? was the first question I asked. 'I'm in love with water,' she said, sipping her coffee out of a Wonderwoman mug. 'I grew up near the coast in Brisbane.' But there was another, more practical reason: 'I didn't want to fall into the mortgage trap. And I got tired of shared flats.' She had spent the last four years on the boat, which she bought as just a hull for £10,000 and fitted out for another £6,000. 'I made the mistake of moving on before I finished the work, which slowed everything down,' she recalled as the boat rocked gently under the impact of the wake from a passing canoe. Caitlin staggered into the galley and started emptying Renee's groceries, which were stored in a box under the sink.

Her water supply is kept in a large tank under the front deck. At the moment she can fill it up by driving thirty feet to the other side of the canal and using the tap shared with the other boaters. 'When you have a full tank of water you feel really good because you know you can have a shower,' she said, pulling back a curtain to show me the shower unit. Hot water comes from the kitchen mini-boiler, and a small pump propels the waste water into the canal. Supply boats come past at regular intervals selling diesel, wood, coal and gas bottles.

Some of the boat dwellers are quite hardcore anti-capitalists, like Olivia, a herbalist who shares her boat with her dog, a 'Doberwoman' called Vigera. Olivia has been living like this for over a decade. Her boat has the same kitchen, bathroom and wood-stove set-up as Renee's, but also a workbench where she mixes her herbal remedies. She collects the raw materials from the fields where she sometimes moors at night. Olivia has spent most of her time moored in Oxford, Bath and London. In Oxford the places to go for are the canal, the Thames and Duke's Cut; in London she favours Hackney – Springfield Park, Victoria Park, Bow Locks and a mooring east of the Islington Tunnel where 'they lock the gates at night so it is quite secure. Years ago there were a lot of places you could stop as a travelling boat person in London. Nowadays there are not as many places to stop. They still exist, but the amount of people who live on boats has increased, so it's harder to find a spot.' But there are benefits to the increasing boat population. She would never have dared moor in Hackney's Victoria Park ten years ago 'because the kids used to cause riots. Now there is a solid group who stopped there and weathered it.'

Renee does not always live in east London. At times she chugs along the canal to Ladbroke Grove in the west, but she has been there less since a girl in the next door boat woke to find a peeping Tom staring through her window. And frequent stories of muggings, torchings and opportunistic theft reminded me of the vulnerability of boats on towpaths that are deserted at night. Occasionally Renee treks out of London for a bit of fresh air, but she is basically a city girl with a packed agenda of films, plays, parties and art performances. She says she would never survive in the country.

Neighbour problems

After a day spent equipping the van for the next trip, and taking delivery of fifty litres of vegetable oil from Ocado, we headed towards Wales, an area I hardly knew but which has a well-recognised open policy towards off-grid living.

On the way I wanted to stop off in Hay on Wye. Thanks to the literary festival that is held there I have been to the area several times before, and on one visit I stumbled across Ross Kennard-Davis after my Range Rover broke down on an isolated road in the Golden Valley. Needing rescue, I rang for a cab, and as we passed the end of Ross's lane the driver mentioned casually that he had been called there a couple of times. 'They have these raves, see,' he confided as we bumped and jolted along. 'They couldn't even drive their car, the people who phoned. And it was nine o'clock in the morning. *And they were naked.*'

These were people I had to meet. But I did not feel I could just drive up to the house. Supposing they were on some drug-fuelled bender and came charging at me with machetes – or, worse still, came charging at me naked? A couple of days later the problem was solved. Driving by in the newly and expensively repaired 4×4, I saw a chap standing at the very gate the cabbie had pointed out. He was wearing jodhpurs and a hard hat which he took off just as I skidded to a halt, to reveal a near-shaven head, owlish glasses and what looked like a duelling scar across one cheek that added a rakish and mysterious quality to his persona. He smiled coyly when I asked him as my opening gambit whether he was 'the guy who had the great parties I had heard about'. In fact it tickled his sense of himself, and although we could not talk then as he was about to drive down to town, he happily handed me his details.

Months later, we were finally about to meet. Driving down the long bumpy track to his house, which passes over Ross's neighbour's land before reaching his own, was a post-apocalyptic experience. There were old cars on either side, buses, junk – seemingly the detritus of a group of New Age travellers. Some of the vans and buses were semi-inhabited. It would never pass the Lizzie Purchase test, but it didn't need to. Planning permission was the least of Ross's concerns.

At first, Ross seemed almost disappointingly sober and well organised. He had, he revealed, inherited the small quarry with no power and its own water supply, and had decided to leave the urban jungle behind and make a new life on his land (this story was to change several times as I got to know him better). Ross himself is Afrikaner-British, from Cape Town. He is in his early thirties, fit from years of manual work since he moved here. I was visiting him at the same time as the annual literary

Ross at the only place where he can get a signal.

festival, and the two ladies I took with me to meet this off-gridder said he had the animal aura of a character from a Wilbur Smith novel.

When he first moved to London, Ross worked as a data analyst for Reuters. It was well paid by his standards and after three years he could afford to give up the job and escape here. For the first five years he lived in a caravan on his forty acres of land, but his fully off-grid house is now nearing completion. The roof had gone on a few months earlier. 'I didn't really understand what I was doing leaving the city and leaving modern conveniences like hot water,' he told me. 'I just wanted to give it a go, and get stuck into a nice big project that would take me fifteen to twenty years.'

This sounded just like my attitude, so I was interested to hear more.

His first priority was the energy supply. 'I costed out getting connected and it came to £15,000 to £20,000, and I worked out I could get a fantastic renewable energy set-up with grants available at the time.' Ross feels at home with technology and is not scared to give things a try and make a few mistakes. Before his solar power was installed he relied on a generator to power a few batteries, a large Lister which ran on bio-diesel, 'old chip oil which I get from local pubs and restaurants. I did the rounds and went and asked a few, and they are happy to let me collect it once a fortnight. I have the space and the time to filter it and add methanol, but it means you have to change the filters on the generator.' Water comes from a spring and is pumped into a tank in the barn. At the moment it's piped to the caravan where Ross washes, but eventually it will go all the way to the house. The batteries power lights, a computer and a stereo – as it turned out, the stereo that was rather central to Ross's story.

As I mentioned, when we first met, Ross gave me the carefully edited version of how he came by the land. The final story was rather different. After I had stayed overnight and we had spent many hours talking and walking around the land together, he began to explain. 'I bought the farm from my aunt, after my uncle died,' he said. Where others had just seen an isolated farm building on low-quality land, his uncle realised the potential of the disused quarry, which yielded good-quality sandstone tiles. Such is the demand from listed buildings for the type of stone in the quarry that Ross was making a clear £250 a day whenever he wanted to work.

At first, Ross was elliptical in his criticism of the locals. 'People over here are more conservative, less willing to try new things, different things, things which might not work,' he said. I thought he was talking about local opposition to his weekend-long parties with the nakedness and drugs. But it was more complex than that.

Slowly, the story came out. Ross's uncle had put everything into the farm, but one day he had to shut down because to everyone's surprise the right of way across his neighbour's fields from the road to the farm house was under dispute; the lease did not contain a residential or agricultural right of way. Whether it was jealousy, greed or simple conservatism, the neighbours wanted Ross's uncle to pay them for the right to drive down a path. After a ten-year legal battle, Ross's uncle won his case. But it was too late. Broken by the stress of the court case, he died, leaving a wife and child. He was only forty-three. Ross's aunt did not want to stay there after that: the place had too many mournful associations, and she was not cut out for off-grid living with just her child for company. So she put it on the market, and Ross bought it.

Every so often Ross plays loud trance music at his parties, on huge speakers, and invites hundreds of hipsters and travellers from the area and all around. The way he tells it, he just wants others to enjoy his land, and he likes the company. But I have a different explanation: whether consciously or unconsciously, I believe Ross is punishing the neighbours for what happened to his uncle. I worry what might happen to him on a dark winter night while he walks his dogs in the nearby fields. It may be perfectly reasonable for a farmer to shoot a dog off-lead in a field of lambs, but neighbour disputes have a nasty way of escalating.

Beauty and the beast of bureaucracy

Ross told us of a clever spot where we could stay in the middle of Hay, a tiny car-park by the river in the middle of town. It was beautiful, peaceful, and best of all free. Two minutes away was a café with free broadband, and I sat there for a few hours, plugged into their power supply, sending emails.

Over breakfast I chatted to a local who advised me to visit Nigel Dodman and his wife Sandy Boulanger just north of Hay. Nigel is a horse vet who lives and works in an isolated house in the middle of Forestry Commission land. Compared to Ross or the Allaleigh settlers he and his wife are the epitome of middle-class country dwellers. They are managing to turn into reality that idealised vision of country life so many others aspire to, both farming the land and running a separate business.

As we arrived, half a dozen week-old puppies spilled out of the pantry in a picture of cuteness, and two cats padded around proprietorially, until Caitlin chased them away. Although Nigel's job gives him a clear connection to the land, he seemed more like a writer or an artist, with rumpled, smiling features and a smock-like shirt. Sandy was like all the Hampstead housewives I had ever known, relaxed, self-confident, and at home with ideas as much as with things. And the kitchen was also a cross between farmhouse and Hampstead chic – messy, book-lined, with pretty blue-painted cupboards. And where you would expect to find pictures of the family there are photos of animals: two happy pigs on their hind legs, their trotters perched on a low door; horses; dogs with tongues lolling at the camera.

The following morning was a Saturday and we joined our hosts for breakfast at about 10 a.m. Nigel, his face still rumpled by sleep, and Sandy, equally bleary-eyed, bustled around as they recalled their house hunting. 'We weren't looking for anything off-grid,' said Nigel, 'just wanted a little bit of land, somewhere where we could ride. This whole area is open riding. Sandy had lived with a generator before so it wasn't a problem.'

Sandy and Nigel with their dog Mega.

Sandy had been married to an editor who had reluctantly become a farmer when she wanted to go back to her own farming roots. Once their children had grown up, he returned to London and she was left to follow her dream alone. Both Nigel and Sandy, in fact, had left relationships to live together, and were left short of money as a result. That's why they bought their little house in the woods, along a wide track a mile or so off the main road. It took them five years to find the place. 'We wanted somewhere with a little bit of land,' Sandy recalled. They got more than they bargained for, a giant forty acres in fact, and they decided to farm it themselves.

It would be a step too far to say they made it seem easy, but they did make it seem fun, and not too much like hard work. The biggest difficulty, they told me, is dealing with all the form filling.

Only industrial-scale farmers can afford to have a full-time clerk pushing the paper to Whitehall and applying for a dizzying array of grants from London and Brussels (grants necessitated by outdated farming techniques or world competition or hard-nosed supermarket buyers, depending on who you believe). Sandy filled me in on this secret world of farming. Anyone with less than a couple of hundred acres is left to scrape a living and use their day off to inform the pinstriped civil servants every time a calf is born or when they are about to take in the harvest. Fail to submit the forms on time and you risk being ordered to have the calf slaughtered with no compensation, or even losing the annual grant – part of the taxpayers' subsidy to farmers.

Nigel and Sandy were told it would cost £30,000 to bring in electricity from half a mile away, so they decided to spend half that on a power system of their own. The payback was immediate – power instead of no power – as well as long term, in savings compared to paying utility bills. And they were lucky because the grants that usually paid 50 per cent of the cost had been supplemented by an additional EU subsidy, taking the total to 75 per cent. So a £40,000 system cost £10,000. Their wind turbine is on a hill 500 yards from the house, and the solar panels are on a frame that faces south-west but could move around if it is important to maximise energy input by tracking the sun. In effect they have their own power station, capable of supplying more than their house needs, though there are no others around. Another shed contains the many boxes with dials and flashing lights. Next to that is yet another shed housing the generator, which comes on automatically if it senses that the battery power is low (i.e. less than 60 per cent).

Nigel and Sandy's kitchen was dominated by a huge 1930s coffee grinder with a big white glowing sign that read 'coffee'. 'This is why we had to get the electricity,' Sandy joked, 'so we could have fresh coffee every morning.' They buy green beans and roast them in a frying pan. Once ground, they are transferred to a Gaggia to produce as fine a cup of coffee as I have tasted. Their Rayburn is used for all cooking and heating as well as hot water, though they burn ecologically unsound coal at a cost of £10 to £12 per week.

Nigel and Sandy do not have much money, but they don't need much. 'This is one of the poorest areas in Britain, and my fees have to reflect that,' explained Nigel as we sat on a low bench under a porch outside the house, watching the rain and the chickens running around on the lawn. 'I don't get paid the same rate as a vet in Oxfordshire. I work in a thirty-mile radius, and I keep my name out of the phone book. We chose how we wanted to live, and part of that is a very low income, but it's a very low expenditure.'

That night they took me to a neighbour's for an event that qualified as my first off-grid party. We parked at the house, a large seventeenth-century cottage, and walked to the party 500 yards away in the cleft of a tiny valley. There were two marquees, a whole sheep cooking over a fire, and loud music that could not be heard from the house, or else-where, because the sound was enclosed by the contours of the land.

I liked Nigel and Sandy for a simple reason: they were not dogmatic. They are living a 'green' life, and they hold strong beliefs about how the planet is threatened by man's behaviour, but they don't try to judge others by their standards. Sandy has a Welsh word for it, *harateg*, meaning 'fair play'. 'If you treat others as equals, and if you contribute to the community' then any eccentricity or lifestyle will be accommodated. 'They'll help you if you help them.'

Generator-only generation

My conversations with Nigel and Sandy were punctuated by phone calls and the occasional visit from horse-owning customers. One of them lived off-grid. Her name was Annette Potter, and she bred horses in the mountains twenty miles away, on a high moorland near Knighton.

You drive out of a nearby village, under an old aqueduct and into a farm, then up a steep hill via a bridleway, and finally onto open moorland, and you are almost there. I only got as far as the steep hill before mini-disaster struck. I had stopped to find my bearings, and allowed the Bus to roll back down the hill a few yards. In doing so I had let one of the back wheels roll up a steep bank, and now the other wheel, on the driver's side, was several feet in the air. As it was the front wheels that powered the Bus, I was completely stuck. I stepped carefully out of the cab to assess the situation, and the wheel lifted another foot into the air. Fiona passed Caitlin out to me, and then sat in the driver's seat herself in order to weigh down that corner.

Some distance away was a house, but as I approached it I realised it was shuttered and closed up – one of those wretched weekend cottages, which destroy communities and confuse travellers in distress! Further on was a possible farmhouse, though. I walked over and knocked on the door. A dog barked, but other than that there was no answer.

I walked back to the Bus and sat down to assess our position. I had passed some old boys a mile down the hill, but even if they were still there, what could they do to lift a three-ton bus off a bank of earth and grass? A gust of wind made the vehicle tremble, and I realised there was just a chance the whole thing would tip over on its side. Plus all the weight was on the front tyre, which could blow, leaving us up the mountain with nothing but my AA card to protect us. I checked the signal on my Vodafone and was reassured to see it was strong. By now Fiona was standing on the running board outside the driver's door, leaning back to maximise her weight.

Then I heard a quad bike coming from the direction of the farmhouse. Perhaps he had been asleep after a hard day's farming. The farmer, a fresh-faced blond man of about thirty, took one look at the Bus and with the words 'Tractor'll do it' spun the quad round and raced off the way he had come. Two minutes later he was coupling a steel cable to the Bus. 'Put her in neutral!' he shouted above the roar of the tractor, but I could not even manage that, and the Bus shuddered violently as the tractor pulled it forward, still in second gear. 'All right?'

said the farmer when he was finished, but before I could answer, or thank him, he was gone, racing the tractor back to the house. I expected the Bus would feel wobbly after its ordeal, but the near-disaster had no effect at all.

When I finally arrived at the Potters' gate, it did not look like the entrance to a farm, more like a gate into a field. We drove on and down a fiendishly steep track. By the time I realised I had gone too far it was too late to turn round. The Bus would never make it back up the hill. My only option was to drive to the bottom of the valley, then ten miles round the mountain and start again. Who knows what the GPS navigation devices would have made of the situation. On this isolated moorland, I doubt if they would have done any better. Luckily, it was high summer; in winter the terrain would not have been so forgiving of my multiple driving errors. The Renault Master was the wrong vehicle for wild camping in winter, I realised. Mind you, perhaps wild camping in winter was a bad idea anyway, unless you happened to have a massively insulated stretch 4×4.

When we finally arrived, Annette was waiting at the gate, wearing tight jodhpurs and with her jet-black hair swept back over her head. As we walked down to the house she told me about the small thorough-bred breeding stable she ran, and the drawbacks of siting it on this sparse piece of moorland. 'I like the peace and quiet,' she told me. 'Not

Annette doing the early-morning feed.

that we are unsociable, we just like to get away from everything.' She was twenty-five when she moved there. 'It was a great place to bring up kids, the serenity of it. Away from the hustle and bustle. But winter can be harsh. It's a long winter up here. All the necessary feeding to do, we pick up logs, make sure the animals are OK, and that we have enough stores left if we are snowed in. We are lacking in various trace elements up here, which the horses get out of a bucket rather than the land.'

As well as twenty or more horses, there were four of them living up on the moor: Annette, her daughter, her mother, and Dennis, her father. They were going through hard times. At one point they had owned the farmhouse next door as well, a very large building. They had always lived in strange, out-of-the-way places. Prior to that it had been a seventeenth-century mansion near Bath which Dennis had found the same way he found this place, by driving for miles down windy back lanes, looking for tumbledown dwellings, then asking around until he found someone to sell it to him. That was how he had bought Upper Heath, and now the whole family's future was staked on the horses Annette was breeding and the possibility that one of them in a few years might become a champion. A horse breeder is on a percentage from their winning horses for life. Annette had a string of horses descended from Irish champions that she sold for quite large sums, but only enough to keep the business going. Now they were waiting until her one-year-olds became three-year-olds, and ran in major races. Meanwhile, they had been forced to sell the bigger property, Annette told me without any hint of regret. Over coffee in their tiny kitchen, Dennis described how he had originally found the place, and bought it for a song.

Spring water comes into the house by pump up to a header tank located higher than the house, and is then gravity-fed back down, travelling about 250 yards in all. But unlike almost everyone else I met, the Potters have no wind or solar power. Annette and her family survive entirely on one petrol generator. No batteries, just one generator, which they turn on when they want light, or to run machinery, or to watch TV, or when Annette's daughter needs the computer for schoolwork. Annette admitted 'a storage battery would be preferable'.

The generator is kept in an outhouse across from the property; it runs the stable and yard light as well. Dennis took me in to see it.

I found it sitting next to three or four broken-down generators amid shelves full of spare parts from long-dead equipment. The old boys who used to travel around fixing these vintage pieces of equipment have all retired or died. There is only one person left in the area who can do the job, and he is rushed off his sixty-seven-year-old feet. 'It's noisy, I'm afraid,' Dennis said, 'so that's a good reason for getting wind or alternative power, especially on a summer's evening.' But the family can barely afford the cost, and even if they could, the palaver of filling in forms for the grants, and even choosing the right system, is too much for them.

CATs and caravans

From Annette's we made our way to Machynlleth, near the North Wales coast, a hotbed of renewable energy since the early 1970s when a few far-sighted hippies launched the Centre for Alternative Technology (CAT) just outside the town as a base to campaign for wind and solar power, and at the same time to demonstrate a sustainable life in practice. At first the locals were openly resentful of the takeover by these English hippies, but over the years that has softened to something more like uninterest. It has nothing to do with an English–Welsh divide; I expect the same thing would have happened in a small town in Dorset or Gloucestershire. It's just that the cultural gap is wider here.

Slowly, more and more off-grid idealogues have moved into the Machynlleth area. Some of them are interns at CAT, others have been attracted by the community and the free-thinking Welsh environment, which tolerates alien points of view without endorsing them. Wales in general has become the centre of the UK off-grid movement over the past few years. Partly thanks to devolution, and partly to successive waves of hippy migration in the 1960s and 1970s, the Welsh authorities have grown accustomed to eco-development. This is not to say that they welcome it and foster it, but that they have in a rather surly way been persuaded to put fewer obstacles in the paths of those who want to live a greener, cleaner or just more independent life.

At a more local level, however, it became apparent to Fiona and me that there is still a curious disconnect in Machynlleth between the CAT people and the locals. The ideas pioneered at CAT have not exactly taken off among Welsh speakers. The free thinking extends to tolerating the outsiders, although you would have thought that as some of the incomers have been living there over twenty years they are hardly outsiders any more. But on the whole the Welsh have not adopted or adapted to their green philosophy. CAT's own need for green sources of power recently led them to support a community-owned wind turbine (by forward-buying its power). The initiative came from English settlers, but by bringing in the indigenous locals as share-holders, opposition was muted, if not non-existent. That strategy is being copied elsewhere in Britain. Thanks to EU grants and the revenues to be derived from wind farms, the indigenous Welsh renewable energy movement is now beginning to take off. But it remains the case that most off-gridders I met in Wales are English.

It was a sweltering day, so after a look around the CAT eco-living displays and a visit to Dulas, the renewable energy company, we drove to the nearest beach for a couple of days' R&R. It was a fantastic spot, but before relaxing I felt I had to check the Bus, which was still acting up after being serviced at our London garage. As I pointlessly prodded around under the bonnet, my mobile phone slid out of my pocket and into the engine. We were near an activity centre manned by young, suspicious locals who lent me an adjustable spanner and stood over me to ensure I did not make off with it, but this was not enough to remove the various engine covers needed to dislodge the phone. I would like to say that I was able to shrug my shoulders and leave the phone to look after itself, but that would be a lie. I was completely hooked on it – as bad a case of dependency as you will ever find. I decided to drive to the nearest garage where the mechanic let me onto the ramp and I was able to get into the engine from the well underneath and remove the phone. I then went straight to the nearest pound shop to buy a toolkit, one of the few items we had not thought to include until now.

Returning to the beach covered in grease, I lined the Bus up along-side another dozen camper vans right down on the sand. It was legal to park there and the wardens in yellow T-shirts and blue shorts came round to collect the daily £1 fee. It was illegal to stay the whole night on the beach but we decided to do so anyway. As the wardens began locking the activity centre and the last remaining camper van made a U-turn in the wet sand and headed off the beach, we followed suit, drove to a mini-market, and returned half an hour later to what was now our own private beach. Was there a catch? we wondered. We searched around for notices about high tides, built a fire, barbecued some chicken and polished off a bottle of rosé to the sound of the waves lapping harmlessly a hundred yards away.

Around 9.30 p.m., as Caitlin lay sleeping and we were thinking of turning in, we heard the roar of cars sliding across the beach towards us. I stuck my head round the corner of the Bus and saw several pimped-up Cortinas performing balletic figures of eight in the damp sand. They lined up facing the sea and a posse of local youth scrambled out and began chugging beers in the last of the sunset. Had they been having sex or taking drugs I wouldn't have minded, but why did they have to choose this beautiful spot to rev their engines? Fiona and I looked at each other feeling vulnerable and square, and retreated into our Bus with the curtains drawn. The drivers disappeared once the last of the light had faded away, and we had the beach to ourselves again.

I woke to the sound of seagulls and skylarks. Fiona looked angelic, asleep with the soft morning sunlight playing on her face, and I let her sleep on while I took Caitlin down to the water's edge for a bit of skinny-dipping. By the time Fiona joined us, Caitlin and I had prepared a huge breakfast. We watched the sun's reflections on the water as we ate and played in the sand, until it was time to inspect the next off-grid location.

An unmarked turning off the main road near CAT leads up a wide forestry track, similar to the one at Nigel and Sandy's house. The Bus lurched up the breathtakingly beautiful mountain road, and plateaued out at about 750 feet above sea level. Despite the altitude there was no view; we were in a sheltered plain surrounded by higher peaks. It reminded me of photos I had seen of the Andes.

We pulled up in a large clearing with a stream running alongside, fed from the top of the hill and providing both power and water to the residents of a house called Dynyn, a very special farm. Over the past two decades scores of CAT staffers have passed through; some have spent years there, others no more than a few months. Many babies have been brought up there, and Charlotte Cosserat, one of the current residents, was about to give birth to the next generation. It was

Charlotte who showed us around the legendary hydro reservoir, built decades earlier by one of the founders of CAT, and still fully functioning. The water rushes in from the top of the surrounding hills (which must look like distant mountains when you are down on the ground, but felt more like hillocks from where we were standing). Much of the year the flowing water could power the generator on its own. But at the height of summer, the reservoir is both a power source and a swimming pool, with red kites diving and swooping over the bathers. 'The reservoir is our battery,' said Charlotte's partner, Aragon. The 250-metre pipe from the reservoir to the turbine drops twenty-three metres on its journey, which is enough to give the house 1.5kW in summer and 2kW in winter, allowing seven people to run lights, an immersion heater, underfloor heating (in winter), TVs, DVDs and stereos, and even a blender, but not kettles or toasters. 'There have never been any arguments about overusage' between the residents, Aragon informed me, though 'sometimes we have to turn some lights off if two people want to watch different TVs in the evening'.

When I phoned months later, Charlotte and Aragon were parents. Little Leila had been born right there in the house, with two midwives

Charlotte showing us round her hydro power.

from the local hospital who had encouraged the couple to have a home birth when they were undecided. It was a long birth, but problem-free, Aragon told me.

We stayed the night on that sheltered high-altitude plateau. It was an enchanted spot, with air like crystal, but it does not make it onto my list of the top places to stay in the UK for one small reason: midges, the worst I've encountered outside Scotland. At dusk that day and the following dawn they forced us into the Bus where we battened it down into a sealed capsule.

Normally no more than six people live at Dynyn, in the main house and in an outbuilding, but in the winter that number sometimes increases to seven. Iona Sawtell was brought up near Slough, and went to a 'posh girls' school'. Now aged thirty-five, she summers in an old mud-coloured Sprite Alpine on a very quiet back road a few miles outside Machynlleth. It's a 'standard little touring caravan', fourteen feet long, with a bed at one end, a home-welded wood-burner, a table and a gas cooker in the middle, and cupboards and a sofa at the other end. She scavenges fuel for the wood-burner from the field behind the caravan. Iona has one light, run off a solar panel, and takes a twenty-litre water bottle to the house to fill it up. Her only other gadgetry is a wind-up chargeable Freeplay radio. When she can, Iona walks or cycles everywhere – not for ideological reasons, she just likes to stay fit. In the winter she has to make the hour-long walk up and down the road to Dynyn because the conditions are too rough for cycling.

She studied engineering at Warwick University and arrived in Machynlleth as an engineering volunteer at CAT. 'This is my sixth summer in the van,' she explained as she stood outside it on a floor of brown leaves next to a big bramble patch at the bottom of a friend's garden. The metal chimney from her wood-burner rose out of the van's roof, and dotted around the outside was a collection of blue, green and white buckets, each touching the van, to catch rainwater. Two mini-benders, one a toilet tent, the other a washing tent where she keeps a two-foot-high water barrel, stood a few yards away. Outside the caravan's kitchen window was a large blue Calor gas container for her cooker. Iona is very contented there, and apart from the vague possibility that the owner will return one day, she is as happy as anyone I met on my journey.

Her only difficulty was the damp. 'When it's cold and wet what I most need is space,' she told me, 'for hanging clothes and drying things. If it rains for several days the clothes in the drawers are all damp.' The other thing she lacked in this tranquil space was complete privacy. 'It's a narrow stretch of land – there's the road on one side and a farmer's field on the other.' But the road could hardly be quieter. It led to just two other houses. Off to the other side was some young forest land screening the farmer's field. 'It's important to me that I am in a clearing,' she continued. 'I would not want to be in the woods. And it's south-facing, which is important – there's lots of sun. And the field behind is gorgeous – rocky, with trees, and sheep and cattle. You quickly reach a spot where you can see for a long way around. And the farmer's great, friendly and open, which makes a big difference.'

Like Sandy and Nigel, Iona doesn't want to impose her views on anyone else; she just feels lucky that she can live a free, independent life. She is absolutely a part of society, with a regular job and many friends living on the grid in the area, but she is doing it her way. 'I do like the idea of having minimal impact,' she explained. 'I feel guilty if I use resources when it's not necessary. I like to think, "Is that what I really want or what I really need?" and if it is then I can justify anything. I went on holiday to America, and that was fine, but if I feel like I haven't really thought about it, then that's selfish – and that's my theory about the amount of energy that gets used generally by everybody.'

Iona's landlord was away when I visited: he had gone to his dentist in Bristol 'to have all his teeth out'. But he was not the ultimate owner of the property, which he rented from an ornithologist who visited the place once every two years. The absentee landlord had wanted a spot he could turn into a bird sanctuary. He had also bought a small adjoining wood from the local farmer. It was full of high beech trees, and as the canopy kept out most of the light, the floor of the wood was free of brambles and carpeted in soft decomposing leaves. The ornithologist's absence means Iona has an idyllic nature reserve as her home, and the road means it is conveniently situated for all local amenities. I could live like Iona with no difficulty, especially as my 3G card picked up a clear signal when I sat in the Bus that night.

And Iona has plenty of company in her friend's garden. There is another caravan, currently inhabited by a woman called Kestrel who

Iona and Luca brave the Welsh weather with dog Tazo.

recently split up with her husband. And at the back of the garden is a large yurt used as a workshop by an Italian carpenter called Luca. He arrived in the rain the next morning with a sopping wet Irish wolfhound at his side and a big bag of yellow mushrooms he had picked on the way.

Luca arrived in London from the Dolomites on the Austro-Italian border at the age of twenty and was quickly 'discovered' by a talent scout while selling copies of the *Big Issue*. He became a high-earning male model, and featured in Calvin Klein underwear ads. But he soon tired of the fast lifestyle, the sexual exploitation and the superficiality of the fashion world. He still had the body of a model when I met him, though it was now hidden under a drab one-piece overall. At twenty-five he decided he wanted to work with his hands and to live a more spiritual life. He was due to be enlisted for military service in Italy 'but I couldn't stand the idea of it'. He could have done voluntary service instead, 'helping old people . . . but it's not fair that the state wants a year of my life just because I am a man. What's that all about? I was planning to be a conscientious objector, but that would have meant military prison for six months, so I wanted to find another way.' By working abroad until he was twenty-seven he knew he could avoid the compulsory year. 'Then I fell in love with Wales. I like the freedom you have in this country, the fact that you take civil liberties very seriously. In Italy there may be better food and so on, but the politics here is better.'

Luca lived in a truck and then in a caravan before moving into the yurt for three years, but his girlfriend shared both Iona and Fiona's dislike of damp dark woods as a residential setting. (It seems that men like woods and women don't.) So Luca and his girlfriend moved to a static trailer in a field a few miles away, and the yurt became his workshop. Apart from a smidgen of maintenance, the space cost Luca nothing, and that allowed him to pursue his career as a self-taught furniture maker on a very low income. He told me that if he had to pay any rent or rates it would tip his enterprise into bare subsistence. As it was he made very little – just enough to run a car and feed himself.

Luca summed up for me much that was valuable about living off-grid. He felt free. He was living a happy, gentle, uncompetitive life, following his dream. His compulsion to make things out of wood reminded me of the way Fiona felt about her art. I do not know if he pays tax, but he sometimes buys some wood, and he sometimes sells a few plates and chairs at the market, so he is contributing to the local economy. The key to his existence is his free working space. He just could not pay rent and still make a living.

We could have headed back to London that night, but I wanted to see more of the area. It was so dramatic, and I was still excited by my discovery of Wales, this new land I had been ignoring all my life. I also hoped to discover at least some evidence of the impact of CAT on the locals. We drove to another village, Corris, which had a pub the CAT people recommended. We passed a lad mending a car by the side of the road. I stopped and asked him where would be a good place to park for the night and still be in walking distance of the pub. He pointed to a spot on the other side of the tiny valley, and described how to drive there. It was high up with a view across the village, and though the whole village could see us, nobody minded. (The photo I took of our parking spot near Corris is the cover of this book.)

We walked down to the pub together as soon as we'd parked the van and set up for the night. Fiona is a real ale connoisseur, and I wanted to find out what the regulars thought of the environmentalists. The Slater's Arms was the heart of the community. Kids kept running in to buy crisps and chocolate. With Caitlin in my arms it was easy to meet people, and soon we were leaning on the bar with the local vicar, John Martin. Over a few pints of Best, he gave us the low-down. Essentially Corris is still a coal-based community, he told us; 'a pall of smoke hangs over the village on November evenings'. Incomes are low, so the price of fuel is important. The vicar has solar water heating on his roof, as do several other houses around the area. So my impression that the locals ignored the environment was wide of the mark.

After a couple more pints, we walked through the village, past rows of terraced cottages and up the hill carrying a two-litre water bottle filled with beer. With Olive and the Renault Master waiting loyally for us up in the woods, it felt like we were arriving home just like any of the pub's customers. The Bus had a good heart, a solid, reliable engine, and it was surprisingly comfortable as we sprawled out over dinner that night. We cooked fresh mackerel on the grill and new potatoes on the gas ring. The twelve-volt internal lights made it all quite jolly as the three of us lay around, reading and listening to the radio.

The next day we went for a long walk in the woods above the village. Two fighter jets screamed low overhead, at once awesome and terrifying, negating a year's carbon savings from living off-grid in one pass. We walked for miles through the sturdy, craggy landscape past long-closed mines. I was shocked at the condition of the trees themselves, evergreens with a serious case of defoliation. I don't know what

caused the leaves to go missing – age or insects or acid rain. It may need decades, and heavy reclamation work, before that wood can yield good timber again. But who will do it? The locals seem to ignore the problem altogether, and wood is not valuable enough for outside investors to take any interest. Perhaps that is why the off-grid community is to some extent tolerated here. They try to make their lifestyle work on a piece of land others spurn.

You can take Caitlin anywhere.

Green legend

In June 2006, Wales' claim to be the off-grid HQ of the British Isles received a boost from Pembrokeshire Regional Council, which issued a new set of priorities for planning permission designed to encourage people to live on forest or agricultural land if they are not using mains power or water or sewage. The new policy appeared to be a major breakthrough for anyone who wants to live off-grid, and the first few applications went in while I was doing my research for this book. It is fitting that the policy is being piloted in Pembrokeshire because some of the first pioneers of eco-communes set themselves up in this small county in the south-west corner of Wales.

The very first application under the new rules was from Tony Wrench, who lives in the eco-commune at Brith Dir Mawr. Brith has mythical status in the green movement. It exemplifies the key values of self-sufficiency and standing up for one's beliefs in the face of interfering officialdom. It was founded by Emma and Julian Orbach, who bought the fifty or so acres in the 1980s. For his job Julian classified listed buildings all over Wales, so he knew every nook and cranny of the countryside, what was possible when dealing with planners, what kind of land came up for sale, and how often. Brith Dir, as its friends and neighbours call it, is a spectacular piece of land with fields, woods, lanes and, most importantly, a classic Welsh farmhouse. It's more of a hamlet, with a large house and two terraces of small labourers' cottages plus barns and outhouses.

The next door neighbours once included John Seymour, author of the first guides to self-sufficiency back in the 1970s. The area had pedigree, then, but that was not enough to prevent the commune imploding a few years ago. Julian and Emma split up, and Tony, with his long-time partner Jane, decided that he did not want to live in a commune any more, with its rules about weekly meetings, consensus decision-making, group meals and numerous other restrictions on his freedom of operation. Julian went to live in a nearby town. Tony, Jane and Emma left the built part of the commune and each split off some of the land into his or her own holding. Each then transferred that holding into a trust, in Emma's case because she preferred 'sharing and co-operation' to ownership.

I wish my house was like Tony and Jane's.

Tony and Jane built a roundhouse on their plot, a turf-roofed circular building with windows on all sides, similar to a large yurt but made of wood rather than canvas. Tony wanted to live in his own version of low-impact housing, by which he means housing you cannot see until you come right up to it. And it works: the roundhouse can be spotted from the air because of the glinting of its solar panels, but it is totally unobtrusive. Its low impact was not enough to convince the planners, however, who slapped an enforcement notice on the building as soon as they saw photos from a spotter plane. Tony is still fighting it. He is hoping that the new rules will finally win his battle for him, and, of course, he has just put in a new planning application.

Tony's struggles (see www.thatroundhouse.info) have been inspirational to many. He has used guile, enthusiasm and carefully selected media coverage to counter opposition from the local council and National Park authorities. It helped that he had himself been a council employee for many years. Not only had he learned their rules from the inside; it was there, while watching the slow progression of his superiors up the career ladder, that he framed the reason for his own departure to the off-grid life. 'I saw that what they all wanted was to end up living somewhere quiet and rural and private, and I thought, "Why wait until I'm fifty when I can have it now?"' That is a desire I wholly identify with. Who was it who said 'Life is what happens while you are making other plans'?

Emma is even more hardcore than Tony. While he wanted to get away from the tyranny of 'The Group', Emma turned her back on technology altogether. (Though there is one exception to this retreat from electrical and mechanical implements: she keeps a phone in a box in a hedge near her section of the land 'to remain available to people like you. It's my concession to those who can't reach me via telepathy.') She greeted me wearing two feathers poking out of her hair, like homemade deelyboppers. Masses of beautiful curly hair framed her strong face, and like a witch of the woods, two magnificent growths – warts, I guessed, though I did not dare ask – adorned her chin. She sat me down and launched into a tirade against electricity, and in particular electric lights. She would like to buy candles made only from vegetable products, she told me apologetically, 'but they are not cheap so I still have paraffin candles'. 'We have become scared of the darkness,' she added, with some justification. 'We need to dream.'

Emma's world of dark skies filled with nothing but stars and moon is the opposite of my own image-saturated city existence, where no space can be left empty and it is almost impossible ever to experience total darkness. In my part of London 44 per cent of businesses keep

Emma – the most off-grid of us all.

their lights on all night, according to a recent survey. Emma also felt there was too much noise in our society as well as light. 'Silence is really important,' she said, 'because we have to be able to tune in and listen to all the other beings that share this planet with us.' In her field of dreams she certainly has plenty of silence.

Emma has built a few sheds around her piece of woodland, but in the summer months at least she spends most evenings outside. Like Tony, she has applied for planning permission for an eco-community on her new piece of land, but with low or no technology. Her application does not specify where her buildings are to be placed; at the moment she has 'three little residential roundhouses and one which is officially a wood-shed'. She is expecting a deal where she is given permission for a certain number of buildings, and is trusted to decide on their precise location. She is also expecting a band of volunteers to emerge serendipitously to help fulfil her vision of this next phase of Brith Dir Mawr.

Reuben's retreat

After a morning spent talking to Emma, Tony and some of the commune people living in the stone-walled houses, I was ready to move on to meet Reuben the wood-carver, who lives about an hour away. But back in the van I discovered I'd left the ignition on since the early morning, when I sat having coffee looking up at the black hill opposite. Zoned out on the beauty, I forgot to keep an eye on my energy consumption. The solar battery already had a warning light built into the regulator which flashed orange when it ran low, but there was no way of monitoring the main battery. Now I was stuck, though hardly stranded, and not for the first time I wished I could just stay in this field for a few days, or weeks, or months. The people were lovely, the place was lovely. I could live here, I thought.

I had to force myself to walk back to the house and round up a car to give me a jump-start. I managed to recruit Pete, whom I had met at dinner the previous night. An hour later we located the jump-leads in the bicycle shed, and drove back to the field where the Bus was parked. Pete suddenly remembered that there was a fee for overnight camping of £5. I was only too pleased to pay, especially as dinner had been fantastic. The meal had started with one minute of holding hands around the table. To my surprise I'd found it touching rather than toe-curling. There was no ceremony, just a silent holding of hands, allowing me to feel that I had been let into this commune and given their trust, rather than just their food. I nervously tried it at my next dinner party, and sure enough my smart London friends gagged at the idea.

One jump-start later, I was finally on the road and heading off to visit Reuben. As I pulled out of a turning, a small brown car shot up alongside, perilously close, and the driver waved me down. 'You nearly killed us!' he cried in a strong Welsh accent. Judging by his haircut and tracksuit, he was some kind of retired boxer. A woman in the passenger seat identified herself as the owner of the car. 'I have a heart condition, see, and you may have brought it on, like,' she said, pulling out a pack of cigarettes with trembling hands. I resisted the temptation to advise her of the relationship between heart disease and smoking. I had not heard the slightest bump or felt any kind of impact. Were these two honest-seeming, God-fearing people having me on? Once she had taken my insurance details she told me not to move and phoned the police, but not before she had ordered a third person out of the car, a young girl carrying a baby, and stationed them in front of my wheels to prevent me from moving. I sighed and settled back into my seat. I could have just ignored her instructions and gone on my way, but in this close-knit community on a small road that went in only one direction, I was bound to be pursued and stopped. My best hope was to stay put.

After half an hour the local bobbie arrived. He agreed with me that the dent the smoker pointed to on the wheel arch of her brand-new chocolate-brown VW Dobler did not correspond with any dent to my vehicle. Nor had the paint on her vehicle transferred itself to mine, despite the driver's claim that 'the two cars had locked together'. I was breathalysed, with a reading of zero, ordered to produce my driving documents, and sent on my way. I suppose I was lucky not to have many of these outlandish incidents. I wondered yet again whether a smaller camper van wasn't the answer.

By the time I found the bottom of Reuben's path it was late afternoon. I parked the Bus off the road and began to walk up a track along which a boy was pushing a bicycle. Fortunately he was a friend of Reuben's oldest son, because without him I would never have believed I was in the right place. Off to the left and right were old ruined cottages more conveniently situated than the one I was heading for. Had the boy not been marching beside me I would have given up two or three times in the belief that no residential track could be so long, steep and impassable to any car other than a four-wheel-drive. The trees grew so densely over the path that it was almost dark despite being broad daylight. The boy seemed to think it was perfectly normal to march up a one-in-four gradient to visit a friend. There should be no obesity problem in this part of Wales, I thought, as the mist began to close in.

I had puffed my way to the house and met Reuben Irvine and his wife Laura when it started to rain. We were still not on the top of the hill, but on a ledge part of the way up. The boy continued to climb the road past the house as it snaked further up into the mountain, towards a caravan where stood a lad I assumed was Reuben's son. I made some comment about it being a pity to be up so high but not to be able to see the view. 'Oh, it's almost always like this,' said Reuben, 'so you haven't really missed anything.'

Their turf-roofed building had been a ruin, but now it looked like some sort of eco-chapel from the outside because of the fantastically tall windows, salvaged from a skip while Reuben was restoring the cottage, alone, with no experience of DIY or self-building and only Laura to help. The building was like a skewed Gaudí interpretation of a conventional house, with wavy lines where you would expect straight ones, and an ornate chimney, again salvaged because it was in the skip that day. They had been sitting tenants in a farmhouse until they moved here with a small pay-off that allowed them to buy this land. 'Most of the materials were already on site,' I was told, namely the stones and wood and turf.

They had put everything into this house on this inhospitable hilltop, but they were in danger of losing the lot for lack of proper planning consent. Both Reuben and Laura were intelligent people, but they had

Reuben & Co. – and the house he built.

never thought about planning permission, never challenged the various letters from the council. They had only just seen a lawyer a few days before we met, years after first hearing from the council planning department. Instead they had taken advice from friends at nearby Tipi Valley, a collection of tipis (or tepees), vans and caravans that had managed to beat the council for the past fifteen years until the planning department gave up because they were spending too much on legal bills. Swampy the notorious road protester moved there recently.

Reuben and Laura's was the first 'normal' family I had visited on my travels, with a husband, a wife and children all from the same parents. I had spoken to other off-grid nuclear families on the phone, but they were among the most reluctant to be involved. It made sense. These were people who had turned their back on the mainstream world and would feel naturally protective of their children's privacy as well as their own. So it was a bit of a thrill to realise that Reuben, who is in his late thirties, had three normal healthy kids, even if the oldest one was skulking in his caravan with his pal who had walked me up the hill.

I left Reuben's threatened house wishing him good luck in evading the enforcement notice, or at least in getting the chance to challenge it in court one day. I passed through the famous Tipi Valley on my way west. Everything was still shrouded in mist. It seemed unwelcoming, but if I was an illegal asylum seeker trying to avoid detention, it might be the perfect refuge. The few people I spoke to as they loomed out of the thickening gloom were spookily uncouth, suspicious to the point of aggression, but I guess this was just fear of strangers. As the mist became fog, I found a spot where I could see no other vehicles, parked, and went to sleep in my invisible, anonymous space.

The next morning brought no lift of the murky weather, so, resolving to return one day, I set off for a place where I could at least be sure of a friendly welcome from someone who lived off-grid but who had been a regular visitor to my website for many months.

21st-century hermit of the woods

Judy lives on the edge of a tiny village with a population of maybe twenty and a large cemetery containing a total of 175 tombstones – which neatly symbolises the emptying of the countryside around here. Some agricultural jobs are being replaced with tourism and leisure pursuits, but not in these parts, it seemed to me. The point has been made before: the townies buying the land and houses as the farmers retire or die tend to become the most vociferous opponents of any further development. That is why places like the one I was about to visit are so hard to find.

I followed Judy's directions until I reached the dirt track that led up to her land and pulled the Bus off the road a short way up the track. I left it parked there because Judy told me her neighbours would be away and I doubted whether anyone else would be coming up or down. Something about the area made me think the residents of this particular village might include a few boy-racer types on trail bikes who were not well disposed towards camper vans. A hundred yards or so further on was a cattle grid. It was a narrow track, with forest on the left and verges bursting with life on the right; berries of all sorts and tall pink flowers (known locally as fire flowers, I later discovered) topped the hedgerows like purple-haired pensioners. Robins flitted from tree to tree, and buzzards circled overhead.

I walked on enchanted, and eventually spotted the blueish tinge of photovoltaic panels among the trees up ahead. The path veered slightly to the left. I made towards the spot. Even when I was a few feet away, it was hard to discern the house. In fact there were three buildings close to one another, but each was buried in trees and bushes, the surrounding vegetation carefully cut to allow light through windows without being too visible. Even in the middle of her 22.5 acres, Judy does not wish to attract attention.

She has been there for eleven years now and her arms and wrists show the muscles of someone who is used to physical labour, yet at five foot six and of slight build, she is no Amazon. Amazingly, Judy built her three cabins entirely alone, cutting logs and moving them into place. She paid for a digger to cleave a mile-long gravel track from the road into her woodland, but other than that, the water system, the buildings, the composting loo, everything is her own work, made from materials painstakingly accumulated from scrap yards or cut from her own trees. Just the water butts dragged into place were testament enough to her extraordinary determination.

Some weeks she didn't see another human being, and she liked it that way. But she was always pleased to have a visitor, and under the stern gaze of two ancestral portraits that adorned her tiny sitting room-cum-office, like a satire of a country-house interior, we talked late into the night about weird neighbours, hydro power and defending the woodland from local hunters.

The next morning I made coffee in the van, still tucked away discreetly at the bottom of Judy's track, then walked in blazing sunshine over to the local cemetery, picked some early blackberries and sat on a bench feeling the weight of centuries of sadness emanating from the gravestones. I thought of my own mother and father, cremated for reasons of atheism. I have nowhere to remember them but in my heart and in any place where they come back to me. This valley cleaving through low hills away to the horizon was somehow an appropriate place for such wistful reverie. Oaks and pines and high hedgerows decorated the fields, like the best, most intimate Devon land.

As I finished my coffee, a sudden heavy shower produced a rainbow so close I could see where it ended in the valley below.

I walked back to the van and then into the deepest part of the wood with my spade. Reflections and ablutions taken care of, the rest of the day was spent touring the land with Judy and learning how she had managed on her own all these years.

Having just celebrated her fiftieth birthday, Judy has spent the last twenty-five years in a steady march towards total hermitage. Until 1993 she lived in a conventional if isolated cottage a few miles into the countryside. It was peaceful, she said, and her only neighbours were a couple in their seventies. None of them had cars, and the old people occasionally walked into the local town. Judy hitched rides when she wanted a change of scene. She would probably never have found the woodland she now lives in had it not been for a chance meeting with a writer who stopped one day to give her a lift. He wanted somewhere isolated to stay for a few months, and he told her that he liked to look after people's houses where it was quiet. Judy was returning to her native Canada for a month. She had a few cats, so she invited the writer to house-sit. Like many writers, this one spent time nosing around the area when he should have been at his desk. It was he who discovered the wood for sale just a mile or so from her cottage.

Judy had thought of becoming a forest ranger, but never of buying woodland. On her return from Canada she visited the wood, sat in the centre of it for an entire day, sent away to the Forestry Commission for the particulars, and made an offer that was accepted just before Christmas. She immediately sold her house to a friend and moved into a trailer in the garden while she waited to complete her purchase. There were numerous technical hitches, but she managed to sign the contract the day before a Forestry Commission deadline for putting it back on the market. The Forestry Commission are a good source of woodland (see chapter 6). Although they sell only a few hundred acres per year, they do not inflate the price, and they do not ask too many questions about what you are planning to do with it. Later, back in London, still under the spell of Judy's infectious enthusiasm, I phoned a Forestry Commission representative to explore living off-grid in a wood, and she seemed rather supportive of the idea.

I left Judy working on her other major project – an organiser system that makes use of A7 notepaper and combines it all into a wearable diary, like a Filofax that has been turned into a jacket. It was her hope that this system would turn into a business one day. I was off to visit someone who had made millions from his business and was now diverting some of that cash into his off-grid home.

Project of a lifetime

Simon Marr-Johnson is a very precise man. The directions to his Welsh farmhouse were extremely detailed, and I felt like I knew every gatepost before I had even turned out of the village of Crickhowell onto the narrow winding lane that led to his drive. What I did not know, and wanted to find out, was why someone who could have whatever he wanted would choose to live full-time off-grid.

Past two cattle grids, a barn and a road sign, and through a gate, I found Simon's front drive. It was steep. The Bus skidded up the first incline and stuck on the corner. After twenty little backwards and forwards movements, I just about achieved a parking position. I jumped out next to an elegant one-room building that was too small to be the main Marr-Johnson residence. As I stretched and attempted to orientate myself, the words 'Well done, Nick' emanated from the other side of the vehicle in languid aristocratic tones. This was followed by the owner of the voice, Simon Marr-Johnson himself. His head was as bald and

Simon, Katherine, grass roof and turbine pole.

smooth as a billiard ball. Although the weather was warm, he was wearing a triple layer of clothes: brown jersey on top of olive collared shirt
on top of white T-shirt. As he strode ahead of me up to the house, past
a huge wind turbine and a startlingly lifelike bronze sculpture of a girl
staring across the Brecon Beacons, I imagined Simon as a James Bond
villain, playing the innocent landowner but all the while secretly
developing the ultimate force-field machine deep underground. In fact,
the only underground section of the house was a walk-in larder, stuffed
with enough supplies to last for two weeks in the event of being
snowed in. Next to the jars of home-made jams and pickles, Simon
tapped on a large metal filing cabinet. Had he said 'Step inside, Mr
Bond' I would not have been surprised. In fact, what he said was, 'That's
where we keep the supplies the mice like.'

A former chartered surveyor who still advises a handful of clients
in Belgravia, Simon, with his artist wife Katherine, has devoted himself
to the house since he sold his London home. They bought when
property prices were low and they had very little money. Katherine's
mother had lived nearby. They had since lavished hundreds of
thousands on it, adding a sitting-room extension to the south end of the

building, and a conservatory as a shield from the wind that buffeted the north wall all winter. I considered it as finished and perfect as any house could be. From the dark oak floors to the architect-designed skylights to the art covering the walls, the place cried out to be immortalised in *House and Garden*. But Simon still had plans: he was close to completing a sauna with an earthen roof. His next project was the 'loobrary', a combined composting toilet and library.

I didn't ask Simon how much time he had spent in total on remodelling the cottage, but I did catch myself wondering whether it was worth all the trouble. It seemed to contradict the pared-down nature of the off-grid life to do a place up quite so thoroughly. And I realised that my own outlook – how determined I had been to preserve all my comforts – had changed since I set off. Perhaps my recent visit to Judy had taught me how little one actually needs to be comfortable. Simon clearly had other priorities.

And were there not other more accessible, more beautiful, more worthwhile spaces? I was reckoning without the deep attachment to the land that steals up on us all if we stay in a place long enough. 'It's just the most dramatic site in the country,' Simon told me. When I asked what drove him to make his constant improvements, he replied simply, 'It's fun, and it saves the earth a little.' I couldn't argue with that.

As we descended the steep drive I paused for a last look at the valley dropping away in front of me, then rising up again to a high flat ridge, silhouetted by the setting sun. All it needed to be a scene from a classic Western was a man riding a horse along the ridge.

On the way back to London I wanted to make a final detour via the edge of Birmingham, to meet Bert Hagley again. I will always have a soft spot for this loyal visitor to my website – my first fan.

Renewable energy bandwagon

We had been staying in touch by phone, and Bert had been playing cat and mouse with me over when he was going to install the rooftop solar panel on the Bus. Now he had asked to meet in a BP service station just off Spaghetti Junction. It was a ridiculous venue, and Fiona fumed at this absurd detour. Bert was late, too, and there was nowhere to wait but in the Bus, which was in need of a good clean – rather like the three of us. When he finally arrived in his sporty Jaguar, we made rather a contrast: Bert in expensive leather trainers and brand-name clothing, us in rumpled shirts with a few marks where Caitlin had daubed food. He began his usual talk about wind terblinds and sowlar flannels at a fraction of the normal price. He certainly seemed full of energy. He had, he said, just become sole North European distributor for Whisper, an American wind turbine manufacturer (though I later learnt from Whisper that at no point has this ever been true). He also told us that he had bought a piece of land in the centre of Birmingham, and a two-storey log cabin kit-house, and was about to take on the council and build an off-grid home. Why I believed this nonsense I have no idea. Perhaps I just didn't want to be proved wrong for having trusted him in the first place.

Bert then announced that he was starting a company called Green Solar to sell and install renewable energy kits. Fiona sighed and rolled her eyes as he went into detail about the renewable energy packages he was planning. He said that if I displayed his new logo on the Bus somewhere, he would fit my panel for free. Then he showed me the logo. I blinked for a moment, then looked up at the BP sign. On Bert's logo, the BP yellow sun had turned green, and BP's green surround had become a yellow surround; otherwise the two were almost identical. 'Wow, who's your designer?' was the best response I could muster. Yet again Bert offered to visit me in London and fit a solar panel on the Bus. I suggested I ought to come to him since he was the one doing me the favour, but he would hear none of it.

The appointed day came and went, and somehow I wasn't surprised that Bert was a no-show. That was when I realised that the off-grid boom was going to be just like the Internet boom of a decade earlier – full of cowboys. Renewable energy had eerie parallels – the same sort of venture capitalists looking to invest, the same sales growth, the same feeling of being on the verge of a bubble. Every so often a new player would stumble onto the field, and quickly look for friends.

Some days later Bert sent me an email saying he was 'in the Far East' and his phone had been stolen at the airport. But he would drive down to install the system the following week.

I never saw him again.

Off-grid ready

While I was arranging my next trip, I came across another off-grid businessman, but this time he was the real thing.

Tony Marmont briefly featured in the *Sunday Times* Rich List after selling a soft drinks company he'd built up over twenty years. Since then he had devoted himself to spending his money as fast as possible to further the cause of renewable energy through top-quality academic research. He has never detailed exactly how much he spent, but when he appeared in the rich list his fortune was estimated at £45 million. He is not on the list any more.

Although he never received a university education, the seventy-six-year-old is now an honorary professor at several science departments, and he spends his time working with a range of academics both to improve his own home energy system and to develop new ways of extracting power from hydrogen, solar panels and waste vegetable materials. Tony receives hundreds of letters asking for a tour of his home and grounds. I was invited to be part of a group of environmentalists from the local area to join the official tour of his house and garden. This sort of tour is something he does three or four times a month to maximise the efficiency with which he handles the requests for a visit.

His home and research establishment, West Beacon Farm, is near Loughborough, just off the M1 within a network of fast roads in what must be some of the UK's most unromantic countryside. I set off early from London to make the 10.30 a.m. start, turned off the motorway, went past some drab fields and cottages, and into a leafy lane. Tony's drive is protected by a gate that can be opened with the right password.

Tony – the Charles Saatchi of renewables.

He was standing in the entrance when I arrived, long grey hair covering his ears, wearing the boffin's obligatory stripy short-sleeved shirt, with two pens peeking out of the breast pocket. The house was large but otherwise unpretentious, with comfortable, practical, unshowy furniture. It stood amid big lawns, a duck pond, woods and streams. He and his wife bought the former farm in 1969. It was a bare piece of land back then, fifty acres of bleak, windswept fields. Their first move was to plant a series of windbreaks totalling at least 25,000 trees, mainly fast-growing pine and larch. These are now being replaced by oak and other deciduous trees which provide food, fuel, shelter and breeding sites for wildlife.

It was the mid-1980s when Tony first started taking environmental problems seriously. 'As a pilot I was flying over the Alps and I could literally see the ice caps were getting smaller,' he told me. Tony collects renewable energy like other millionaires collect art, and has dedicated himself to pushing the boundaries in this respect, living as he does in the certain knowledge that the era of global warming is here and is about to destroy civilisation. He has been predicting it for years and has never entertained the slightest doubt that it would arrive. Now he is ready – off-grid ready.

Water comes from a natural spring fifty metres below ground, and from rainwater, which is collected from the rooftop in conventional guttering and then passed through a filter to remove any coarse dirt before being stored in a 6,000-litre underground storage tank. It is then filtered a further three times before being stored in a second underground tank, at which stage it is suitable for all household use though not for drinking. Water for drinking must pass through an ultra-violet filter and then a reverse-osmosis membrane purifier before being piped to separate taps in the house. On-site sewage treatment uses septic tanks. The naturally treated nutrients that are produced are used on the farmland.

Wind power? He has two huge wind turbines by the duck pond, and a smaller one near the hydrogen storage area. Solar power? He has an array of two dozen solar panels, some of them twenty years old and 'still working perfectly'. Water power? Two micro hydro generators can be found at the bottom of his land, where the stream runs fastest, and a few hundred feet away, carefully screened with wire mesh to allow the trout to leap upriver, a third mini water turbine powers the garden lights. He also has a ground source heat pump which transfers the warmth from the ground to your living room, and an electric car, a Solectra imported from America a decade ago, with a range of 120 miles and a top speed of 75mph. It runs off a new Chinese nickel metal hydride battery, and Tony plans to build a small fuel cell into the vehicle, to increase its performance, range and fuel economy. He has paid for the development of a new non-polluting aviation fuel made from vegetable matter which has passed all the safety tests but which the airline safety authorities refuse to adopt. 'They are very conservative,' he replied when I asked why all the effort put into developing the fuel had so far failed to pay off. 'But we are talking to Virgin,' he added, whose founder Richard Branson recently announced that he is planning to invest £300 million in eco-businesses. The local environmentalists have never heard anything like it. They look on Tony as though he is a god.

Part of the way through the tour he told a story about a recent meeting with a senior official from the Ministry of Defence. Tony was there promoting his new aviation fuel, and receiving zero interest. Apparently the official suddenly remarked that 'if the anti-gravity experiments come to anything', Tony's new fuel would soon be obsolete. 'What anti-gravity experiments?' Tony asked. The man from the ministry would say no more about it, but Tony is sure the government is working on something. He sees history in cycles. 'Think about it: fifty years of reciprocating engines ... fifty years of gas turbines ... now the next fifty-year change is due.'

At the end of the tour, Tony showed us the stand-out star of his collection – a bank of fuel cells that produces electricity by extracting the hydrogen from water. It cost about £250,000 to install plus another £250,000 for the blastproof building needed to produce the hydrogen safely. A team of PhD students from Loughborough University are on hand to develop the system, and Tony expects he will soon be producing hydrogen on a commercial scale. For now the fuel cells are connected, and feed back stored hydrogen as electricity when there is not enough being produced by his wind turbines, solar panels and hydro turbine. Next to the hydrogen plant, in the wine cellar, were a series of submarine batteries used to store power from the turbines and panels and deliver the energy to the house via a 240-volt inverter. Bright yellow, and each standing four feet tall, they were the most heavy duty of all the power storage units I would come across on my travels.

Tony is 'off-grid ready', meaning he is not actually off the grid. He has installed enough renewable energy so that he could switch over to being off-grid at any time, but he uses the grid as a battery or back-up. We could all be following Tony's example, in a smaller way. Instead of monitoring and replacing these heavyweight and over-sensitive lumps of lead and acid you can simply export your power to the grid when you have a surplus (and be paid for it) and take it from the grid on windless cloudy days. At least that's the theory. Tony stopped selling his power back to the grid a few years ago when one of the government subsidies was cut and the payment sank to 1.25 pence per kilowatt hour. But being 'off-grid ready' is still the most practical step most of us can take towards an off-grid future.

Despite his conviction that we are heading for an ecological collapse brought on by global warming, the favourite toy in Tony's box of energy tricks is a full-sized gas-guzzling helicopter, kept in a hangar on one side of the grounds. Now that he is getting on in years, he has designed a helipad that rolls smoothly out of the hangar and into the landing space at the press of a button. He finished by demonstrating this piece of kit, then beckoned me to join him for lunch in a nearby farmhouse. As I waited for him to say goodbye to the other guests I noticed a topiary by his front door that had been neatly clipped into the shape of . . . a helicopter.

'There is a 90 per cent chance' of a major ecological disaster 'in the next ten years' said Tony the moment he closed the door and started his other car, a Prius, to drive us to lunch. He believes this will be flooding- or weather-related, and quoted David Thomas's book *Frozen Oceans*, which warns that global warming could increase sea levels by 262 feet, forcing half the world's population to become climate change migrants. 'Nearly all major cities and oil refineries would be affected' by this rise in sea levels, Tony continued. He likened our unwillingness to prepare for this eventuality to the state of denial that existed around the dangers of smoking twenty years ago. 'There were rumours that it was bad for you, but smoking was still socially acceptable. Now it is slowly being marginalised.'

On our way to the farmhouse restaurant, the four giant cooling towers of Radcliffe on Soar power station loomed up on the other side of the valley. It was a coal-fired station, Tony informed me – he seemed authoritative on such matters – and it had deposited caesium across the country, and as far away as Holland and Scandinavia, 'with a half-life of two thousand years . . . The radiation losses from this power station are greater than Windscale. All coal is mildly radioactive. When you burn it you concentrate the radioactivity in the ash, some of which is carried out through the chimney. We are all getting radiation the whole time via the sun, but it's the hard radiation from these isotopes close to our bodies that is not good. I am sure it wouldn't have been permitted if it was known. You'd never get planning permission these days.'

For Tony, this was the enemy, the reason he spent his own personal energy and millions of pounds of his own money creating and popularising renewable power. It seemed ironic that the power station loomed so large in his field of vision. I was to see more of those towers later in the journey.

Building a social enterprise community

I headed north to meet Nigel Lowthrop, owner and founder of Hill Holt Wood. The directions were unpromising: make a U-turn on the A46 dual carriageway at the sign to Norton Disney, then take the first entrance on your left at the sign for Northamptonshire.

Nigel was waiting near the car-parking area when I arrived. It was rush hour and you could hear the traffic sweeping past, but along the track, past signs pointing to the visitor centre, amid the tranquillity of the woodland, a different mood took over. Logs were stacked in an orderly pile. There was a network of wide, well-marked paths. The bushes were clipped and tended. Alongside the car-park, a walled permaculture garden contained rows of orderly raised beds, and two long polytunnels stuffed with beans and tomato plants. Sheds, barns and huts concealed the tools and equipment a place of this size needs to function. Everything was neat and well organised. There was no pile of bric-a-brac lying around, as was common at other off-grid places I visited, indeed at most farms of any sort. The place looked more like a visitor attraction than a working wood, but in a good way.

(Right to left) Nigel, Karen and their son, Harry.

Nigel was an interesting combination. A tall, imposing, bullet-headed fifty-year-old, he started his career in the RAF before moving into forestry management. He has been a park ranger and a woodland manager, and once ran and sold a fencing business, but he is by RAF training and inclination a biologist. Just the person, in other words, you would want with you if you were thinking of taking over a damaged piece of woodland and turning it into a profitable business. Perhaps it was this background that gave him the confidence to set out on his plans to create a major 'social enterprise' at Hill Holt.

The details of Nigel's life emerged slowly over the hours I spent with him, but rarely in answer to a question. He had a tour planned in his own mind, and he was going to give it to me (which was OK by me). I was hardly out of the Bus before he had started on a madcap exposition of the wood, the houses he had built, the renewable energy, the water arrangements. An hour went by, and still I had not been able to fetch my notebook.

He'd bought Hill Holt ten years earlier for £32,000 and moved in with his family. This was no bijou wood flanked by anxious home-owners. It was a wood nobody cared to defend, a ravaged wood, all its best trees chopped down by a timber company. His first priority was to try to eradicate the rhododendron that had taken over. Since then, things had moved at a terrific pace. As soon as he could, Nigel opened the wood to the public and made sure everyone knew this was now a space they could visit with their families or dogs. The idea of opening at all meant opening hours had to be set, and therefore the wood was closed at nights. This resonated with the public, and it means that locals support the project (unlike Allaleigh residents and Land Matters, for example). It also gives Nigel a way of controlling the place at night. As a result he is not plagued by local kids or gypsies, or bothered by neighbouring farmers. Now Nigel has a large organisation, and disadvantaged children are brought in almost weekly for courses to try to calm them down, give them some social and life skills – in other words, make them employable. A combination of full-time staff and volunteers work in the wood and see to administrative duties.

Nigel built two houses overlooking a small man-made lake he created in an old quarry in a private section of the wood. We reached the brow of a small hill and the two beautiful log cabins came into view. Nigel and family had moved into the larger one just a few months earlier. It had been built from a kit and was not quite what Nigel had intended, but Karen, his partner, had put her foot down. After years living in an American trailer, she told him she would be out of there if they did not have a home, like, now.

My tour began on a man-made incline above the smooth water of the lake. We looked across to the small self-built cabin on the opposite side fifty yards away, where his teenage daughter now lives, and the much larger house on the left shore, made from the £31,000 kit (price not including VAT and delivery). We were standing next to the power plant, a pair of huts with solar panels on the roof containing batteries from China and a back-up generator from the UK. To power the two houses, Nigel bought the Chinese-made wind turbines next to the hut, and batteries from a local supplier. There were teething problems. The turbines were wonky, and the supplier had to refit them. The box full of gear to manage the power output had broken several times, too, but at £12,000 for the lot Nigel was saving about £10,000 on the normal retail price and resigned himself to having them re-engineered by the local firm. This was the kind of hands-on experience I could learn from.

It had all started to take off a few years after he was granted planning permission, when he contacted the then Minister for the Environment Elliot Morley and invited him to visit Hill Holt. Three times Nigel wrote to the minister, and three times he replied saying he was too busy, 'even though his constituency is nearby'. Finally the minister agreed to send 'a senior representative from the Forestry Commission'. The great day arrived, and 'the Forestry Commission's regional director came, who I now get on with very well, and the policy adviser to the minister, and a senior manager from Forest Enterprise [the commercial arm of the Forestry Commission] in Bristol, and the local man. They turned up here one morning at nine a.m., and being a woodsman I can move around fairly quietly so I overheard them. They were saying, "I don't know why we're here"; "We've seen it all before". They looked pretty uncomfortable when I appeared right behind them. I know what they were picturing: this eco-warrior who was smelly and dirty and lived in the woods They were getting ready to say, "You're a nice loony, but you are a loony nevertheless; this isn't mainstream." But by the time they had walked round the land once, you could see them thinking, "This isn't what we'd expected," and after they had a long talk with me they were really thinking hard. For lunch we had invited a load of representatives of local organisations who we had links with. They split up and just quizzed all these people, didn't want to talk to me. They just asked questions. "What's your involvement in Hill Holt?" "Do you think it works?" And after lunch Judy Collins, the policy adviser, said "Right, how do we make this happen elsewhere?"' Nigel sounded triumphant by this point. 'It was a complete change of attitude. They realised they had found something unique, although nothing we do is new, it's all been done before. What's different is the mix. It's the way you do things, it's not what you do. The core principle is sustainability in its widest sense, meaning the social, economic, environmental balance which is at the core of sustainability. That's the message that should come out.'

What Nigel is doing suddenly became rather fashionable shortly after we first met. It is called 'social enterprise', businesses with primarily social objectives whose surpluses are reinvested in the business or in the community rather than being given to shareholders.

Everyone at Hill Holt has done well out of Nigel's success. He and Karen have a nice piece of land with a house, a lake and a garage. The community has a valuable resource, and a former piece of wasteland is now a popular destination. Nigel has built a fair-sized organisation, too, which means local employment for sixteen staff alongside innumerable volunteers. The place enjoys regular, diehard local visitors, highly placed local supporters and a turnover of around £400,000, and it is run using renewable energy with a generator as back-up. However big his social enterprise grows, Nigel is determined it will not go back on the mains, at least not in his residential part of the land.

A couple of years ago they handed ownership of over half the thirty-four acres plus the numerous non-domestic buildings to a local management committee for a payment of £150,000. The committee paid more than the £120,000 Nigel proposed because the members felt they were being offered the land for less than market value. That's how good Nigel's relations were with his local community. So, ten years after he first moved onto the land, Nigel has a wood, a home, a lake, a barn and a garage for the very tidy sum of absolutely nothing (plus years of hard work), and the satisfaction of knowing that he has created an amazing organisation. The wood has helped to reduce crime in the area, given hope to some dead-end kids and brought a community together that was in danger of falling apart. Nigel has done all this with little or no money in grants. Hill Holt's revenues now include money from the council for training. This is paid work, not grant aid. The team are also paid a bonus for each boy who holds down a job after passing through Hill Holt, and they pick up regular bonus payments.

I spent the rest of the day with Nigel and then wandered round on my own for the evening talking to the staff and volunteers – mainly idealistic twenty-somethings. Each one admitted they secretly wanted to do what Nigel had done, in their own wood. It's a great thought: Hill Holt Wood spawning dozens of imitators, all inspired by the amazing energy of Nigel and Karen.

The next morning I was planning to drift around and take a few notes. By the time I was dressed and out, there were half a dozen expensive Range Rovers parked nearby. I learned that the meeting of the East Midlands section of the Country Landowners Association (CLA) was taking place on site that day. I walked past one of the buildings to see some earnest-looking men, mostly in tweed jackets or suits, sitting around a table. A huge pile of sandwiches led me to conclude that these were the honoured guests.

The CLA is an interesting ally for Hill Holt Wood. The members between them own 60 per cent of the rural land in Britain. They could all be running environmental schemes on their land, or encouraging off-grid development. They were more interested in the social aspects of the scheme rather than the environmental impact, I later learned, and they were meeting in this small room in what was little more than a shed rather than the baronial setting they were no doubt accustomed to because they were excited by the multiple revenue streams that had been created at Hill Holt.

The newbies

My next appointment was out on the Pennines near Bolton Abbey in Yorkshire. I arrived at the beauty spot on a white-hot morning in July. Even the smallest back lanes had scrolly signs outside the farms advertising cream teas. But no random passers-by would ever run across the place I was visiting. The entrance to the estate was via a road so narrow that turning into the gate required expert manoeuvring. Even in the summer it was a rough and jolting journey, for two miles, crossing numerous cattle grids. I began to wonder if I was in the right place – which is remarkable considering I had been there before. As I climbed higher and higher onto the bare moorland, the view across the abbey opened up to the hills beyond. It was a film-set of a panorama, and indeed several films and TV series had been made there over the years.

As I said, I had been to Broadshaw House before, with a Radio 4 *Today* programme crew, to visit the previous inhabitant, David Allender, a retired IBM consultant who rented it for £40 a week from the Duke of Devonshire's estate. For his money he had a large three-bed with two receptions, a massive kitchen, numerous outhouses and a stone barn. There were twenty-four heavy-duty batteries in one outhouse, rescued from a defunct telephone exchange, and two inverters, for transforming twelve-volt battery power into the 240 volts needed to run most household appliances. David had also installed all the renewable energy you could need: a wind turbine, solar panels and a micro hydro. His watch-phrase was 'multiple back-up'. If one or even two power sources failed there would be a third and a fourth.

The old systems were held together literally with string and will-power by the man who had rigged them up. When he decided to move to Spain, the property was put up for rent by the Bolton Abbey Estate. The estate did not particularly mind whether or not the place stayed off-grid, other than the financial implications if they had to install mains, but David did not want to see twenty years of effort wiped out by the new tenants, so he advertised for a family that would keep to his set-up. 'You have to have the know-how to manage the technology, and a love of peace, tranquillity and animals,' Allender had told me in his slow Yorkshire burr. With a few weeks to go, *Today* ran the story about David's search for a tenant who would keep the place off-grid, and that is how Louis della Porta and Annette Robinson heard of the house. Once the young couple had struck a deal with the estate, they became second-generation off-gridders, inheriting the systems but not the skills. I was interested to see how they would cope.

An early indication had come when I visited their house on a prim estate in Warwickshire on my way back from Hay. They

were preparing for the move but were still living in a perfectly conventional two-bedroom house with no apparent concessions to an ecological lifestyle. Most of their belongings were already boxed up when I arrived, but there were no solar panels, recycling bins or rainwater-gathering devices there. I wondered if they knew what they were letting themselves in for. Louis had already spent twelve frustrating

Easier days – Louis and Annette before the move off-grid.

weeks trying to negotiate a landline for Broadshaw House from BT. The lowest price they quoted was £123,000.

'We've both got rid of our cars,' he suddenly revealed as we sat in the small kitchen. I was impressed by this apparent display of green ethical correctness. I had put the couple down as a pair of serial property developers, moving to the country so they could maximise their equity. After all, there was that drive up a dirt track two miles from the nearest road, which in any case had no public transport. 'Yeah, I got rid of my Audi and got a Subaru four-wheel-drive, and Annette swapped her car for a small Golf,' Louis proudly announced. Hmm. It seemed as if these guys were not motivated by ecological considerations, so why had they decided to take the plunge?

I arrived three weeks after they had moved in, and there were problems everywhere. The phone line had not been installed and Louis badly needed broadband for his product design consultancy. At the time he was making the five-mile drive to the nearest cybercafé at least once a day, and his battles with BT were taking up hours every week. He hoped he had found a solution, he told me, which bypassed BT and meant he would pay only £18 per month for all his Internet and phone calls. It was a satellite broadband service, and as long as the company did not go bust it allowed Louis to catch the signal supplied to the nearest village on a hilltop a few miles away and make all his phone calls via the high-quality internet connection for the cost of a receiver station on a small pylon in his back garden.

When I caught up with him six months later, however, I found he was still testing equipment for reliability and remained without a dependable, always-on, Internet connection. The biggest struggle had been getting reliable power to the mast, he told me. 'It takes an hour to take batteries up to the mast each few days. We ran a wind turbine to recharge the batteries, but it blew away in the recent winds. I am trying to get my money back from the manufacturers, who are claiming it was never suitable for high winds (which makes it a rather pointless product, like selling a boat which dissolves in water). As soon as we have a reliable system I can then apply for planning permission to have the mast permanently sited.'

But that was in the future. Right now, the entire battery bank had to be replaced – David had warned them about this – but not within a few weeks of arriving, surely? Maintaining batteries is a special skill (see chapter 8), and I would learn from all my experiences how to do it and how not to do it. Also, one of the wind turbines had come down in a storm, and a local farmer popped in while I was there to agree on the spot where the new pole could be mounted.

Louis was reasonably practical. His product design work meant building prototypes after all. I watched him in his workshop as he dismantled the micro hydro generator. It was a simple little motor, essential to their electricity supply the following winter. He needed to check the brushes and clean the parts. He laboured over taking it apart, sweat dripping from his nose into the machine, and he was still at work when I decided to park for the night on the Pennine Moors a few hundred yards from the house. There was a nice flat spot there, one of few available along the length of the track, with the view I had enjoyed earlier across Bolton Abbey to the horizon thirty miles away, and a good mobile phone signal, even though there was none at the house. Louis and Annette walked out to the spot before dinner. 'Ah, you've parked on our office,' they exclaimed in unison. Louis had already spent many hours sitting there on a large flat stone in client conference calls.

Was it going to work? I wondered. Imagine having to relate to a client, perhaps some obsessive brand manager whose annual bonus depends on increasing sales 0.1 per cent thanks to Louis's design. Would Louis be able to get into the right head-space while staring at nature like this? I could imagine it working on a part-time basis, half a week in town and the rest of the time in this isolated retreat. I still didn't think I could do what Louis was trying to do, but despite my misgivings they appeared to be managing well. They still had a totally positive attitude in the face of the numerous breakdowns and disappointments. If anything, it was me who saw each of their setbacks as part of a wider pattern. Louis simply recounted each story as a separate obstacle to be overcome.

Maybe the Bolton Abbey Estate was working its magic on them.

Back in the van, I slid the Vodafone 3G card into the computer and downloaded 350 emails, most of them spam. Then I typed up some notes. I went to sleep as the very last of the light slipped away to the west.

The regretters

In the morning I was on the road at 7 a.m., on my way to Northumberland. This under-populated county, one of the poorest in England, was dealt a bad hand when it came to mains power. During the great electrification, thousands of houses were overlooked, left off the grid; many thousands more were off the water grid and had to make do with their own springs and wells. As a result there is now a stock of relatively cheap housing in Northumberland available to anyone who wants to live off-grid. The couple I was about to visit were living successfully in the way Louis and Annette were attempting, working from an off-grid home without farming or having to live off the land. The difference was they wished they were on-grid.

David and Anne Boon bought their bungalow near the beauty spot of Otterburn in 1985. It had just one bedroom, a big kitchen and a little conservatory. Although he was not in any way an environmentalist, David was excited at the prospect of living an authentic self-sufficient life. 'We'd seen *The Good Life* on telly, mortgage rates were 15 per cent, and we thought, "Sod this."' Over two decades later the dream had turned a little sour.

David looks and sounds like an English Joe Pesci, the actor who plays loveable but vicious villains usually opposite Robert De Niro. Small, fast-talking and hoarse-voiced, he spends his days working the phone and the Internet, breaking off to wander round his four acres, up a long track on the edge of the National Park. He is a vehicle broker, or, to put it bluntly, a car salesman. When he first moved to the house, David was commuting to a car showroom forty miles away, but now he works for himself, providing cars at a slightly better price than companies with greater overheads. 'I'm always here,' he explained in the little conservatory that became his office. 'I'm never on training, or flexidays. If I'm sick I can still drag myself into the office. It's about continuity. If anyone calls me I'll always call them back within an hour.'

His approach could be adopted by anyone in the service industry who wants to work from home somewhere affordable. David does have a landline, but the Boons' power, water and sewage are all off-grid, meaning outgoings are low. They have four large solar panels, a wind turbine and a Lister diesel generator, a large inverter from the US company Trace, and various other little boxes and gadgets which control the energy coming into their battery bank, and the voltage going out. But twenty years on this energy set-up is still not all that reliable, and living in an isolated corner of England, the Boons receive little or no support from the people who supplied them with the gear. David gets a fair number of calls from friends of friends asking for his advice on the right settings for the inverter, or who to go to when things go wrong, and he does his best to help them over the phone, so he is no technical illiterate. 'I'm one of those people who reads the manual really carefully, and if something goes wrong I try to figure it out.' When his own system fails, David tries to mend it, but if it's something he cannot fix himself he waits for the supplier to send a replacement part, or has to pay a princely sum for a mechanic or technician to come out to see him. Over the years he has changed suppliers a few times, but it is always the same story.

The day we met, David had rung to request I delay my arrival as he was having his generator repaired. I wondered whether this was going to be like some kind of royal visit. Was he having his generator serviced on my account? No, it turned out he did not want me to start my visit watching him haggle with the mechanic, who came from sixty miles away and charged £30 per hour just for travelling time. That was an extra £90 on every £150 bill. 'The people who supply it, none of them live it,' David complained as we sat with his wife in the garden during his lunch break. 'They might have it on show, but not at home. They know it's very limited. It was going to cost us £10,000 to get connected in 1985, and we didn't have the money. So we bought a generator and a bank of batteries instead. But if I had my time over again, I'd pay for the electricity connection.'

Since many choose to go off-grid to save money, I was not judging David's motives in this. I just wanted to know if it was possible to save money if you had David's level of expertise, which was several degrees above my own. The answer seemed to be in the negative. 'The solar panels I bought are only putting out half the power compared to when they were new. Now the people I bought it off don't want to know.' David later phoned me to admit that the wire from the solar panels to the battery was the wrong sort. He had decided to wire it up himself to save money, and had used a fairly thin flexible core wire.

David and Anne – more bad luck than anyone deserves.

Ever since he changed the wire for a thicker solid core, the panels had worked perfectly.

He also had problems with his 1kW wind turbine, which folds back on itself when the wind is too powerful, to protect itself from damage. The turbine was supposed to unfurl once the wind dropped, but after only a few months it stopped rectifying itself. The suppliers Winsund came to repair it, but only a few weeks later the same thing happened. 'It looked like a chicken with its neck broken,' David said. 'They admitted in so many words it was a design flaw they were aware of. Eventually they replaced it with exactly the same thing, which I never took out the box, I just sold it. The guy who sold it to me, Mike from Winsund in Muggleswick, is a lovely guy, a charming man, but if you think you are selling something that time and again doesn't perform, then wouldn't you question why you are selling it?' The turbine David had bought was a Whisper. When I remembered that Bert Hagley had told me he was planning to take over the North European distribution for Whisper, things seemed to make a bit more sense. David switched to a new brand, the Bornay, and had a series of problems with that as well. Nuts and bolts came loose and the cover came off, letting the rain in. He had to wait for fourteen months for a new cover, and six months later that one fell off.

I didn't know what to make of David's criticisms. He seemed sincere, and perhaps now I had found a reason why many of the renewable energy suppliers did not want to put me in touch with their off-grid customers. Eventually I contacted Winsund to ask them for their side of the story. Mike Seeley patiently explained to me that David was a rare exception. 'We know all our off-grid customers and their individual circumstances,' he wrote in an email. 'We try to respond and visit their remote sites (often unpaid) when they have a problem. In general, if customers opt for a DIY option then the attention we provide is bound to be limited. The manufacturer's warranty is a "return to base" – so he should be grateful that we went out to site at all.' So David, in his need to cut costs, had declined to budget for the suppliers to do the work he was now complaining about. 'David wanted to do most of the work himself,' Mike continued, 'but wanted assistance with the wind generator installation at the tower. It was an old tower and he did not want to upgrade it. He did his own wiring and then moaned that the Whisper H40 only gave two-thirds power. In the end it was exchanged under warranty, and we used it here for three years with no problem. We think that he may not have connected one of the three phases correctly to the controller – hence the two-thirds output.'

I filed away the information, and began to think that perhaps I had done the right thing in Majorca by sticking to the most minimal possible system. Even renewable energy is about owning more things, which then become more things that can go wrong. Perhaps the most obvious conclusion to take away from my meeting with David was that there are so many forgotten skills required for a successful off-grid life that you can only do it if you are either prepared to pay the full price or you have enough friends in the area to cover all the skills you will need for everything from energy supply through to plumbing and building, not to mention perhaps the most important thing of all – human companionship.

A few miles away at the bar of a pub in Longframlington I found the kind of friendliness and genuine interest in strangers that is rare in London. It demonstrated to me the real bedrock of rural community, and another approach to the off-grid ethos. I was chatting to the locals about the days before electricity in the area when I met

Patrick Scott, who had just finished two and a half years as a close protection officer in Iraq. Jack Straw was 'like a little hobbit', he told me. The pressure had taken its toll. After a couple of weeks back in the UK, Patrick was drinking and smoking like he was still in Iraq; it might be months before he settled back into the easy-going swing of things. But his close-knit group of friends and neighbours was folding itself around him, protecting him, helping him recover. He had a wife and a new baby, born while he was on leave, and someone had found him a job as head of security on a Northumberland aristocrat's estate. A large, commanding, jovial presence, he shot deer, rabbit, hare and pigeon. 'Anything that moves,' he said as he tried to press a huge fresh trout on me back at his father-in-law's farm that evening.

The farm had been off-grid until a few years earlier, when the local Electricity for Enterprise scheme swept through the valley handing out grants to switch the residents onto the grid. Until then the household had lived with a gennie and two car batteries. Their water was still from a local spring, like most of the valley. And Patrick was off-grid in another way: he hardly ever used supermarkets, except to buy Pampers and powdered milk for his new baby. His food came from the river or the local wood. His father-in-law ran the local gun shop, and in common with his customers, Patrick hunted. Like everyone else in the community he bartered what he had for what he needed – game for cheese and wine, for example; a bit of help on the neighbour's farm for milk and steak. The tax man would have a field day with him.

Managing isolation

Few places I visited felt more isolated than the Wilsons' farm. Gibshiel was only a couple of miles from the Boons as the crow flies, but seven miles by road. As I drove through the National Park I could not resist the tranquillity. I explored a few side roads and hopped out of the cab to sit on a log and tune in to the serenity of the land. I arrived gasping for a cup of tea, but I was to be disappointed. Before I was invited in, Roger wanted to give me the tour of the energy and water arrangements.

Roger left his job as a management consultant fifteen years ago and moved with his wife Jane to this lonely farmhouse five miles from the nearest made-up road, high up on the ridge of the Park. The track ends at a gate leading into the Kielder Forest. On the other side of the forest is the Scottish border. Roger's farm stands like a mute sentry to the comings and goings, of which there are few of the human kind. Two huge barns adjoin the house, dating back to the time when this was a 400-acre farm; Roger has just eighty of them, with eighty sheep and twenty goats. They are award-winning rare breeds, and one of the barns is festooned with rosettes; the other contains the renewable energy control units and a generator.

When we walked in a red light was flashing on the inverter control panel. The LED display informed Roger that the batteries were low, and the generator had failed to come on automatically, as it was supposed to do. He tried the generator manually, and it worked. He tried the back-up generator, and that worked. Therefore there was something wrong with the inverter. He stood there staring hopelessly at the grey box, for he did not have the expertise to diagnose the fault, and fix it. It would have to wait a few weeks until the next scheduled maintenance visit. Was there no neighbour who could come by and have a look? Roger answered only with a short, mirthless laugh.

As you would expect in a community of isolated homes, there are a range of organised activities, including a film club, a camera club, and even a leek club. They all get together once a month for a ceilidh, too. But there was no inverter club. In answer to my questioning, Roger said that the local pub (six miles away) was the core of the community. The last two owners had 'gone bust' so the locals do all they can to spend money there because they know their existence as a community depends on it.

At last we headed inside towards what I hoped would be a teapot. Mrs Wilson popped into the kitchen to say hello and give me an inquisitive stare. I thanked her sincerely for letting me visit, for I was reminded again how peculiar it is to enter a succession of strangers' houses, but despite my gratitude I could not help feeling that there was an air about the house that indicated a constant battle to keep the systems working, and an asceticism that may have been the result of years of hard work for little return.

My intuition was confirmed when Roger finally offered me tea. I accepted enthusiastically, but there was a problem. 'Do you really want tea?' he asked, emerging from the scullery after a short delay. 'I can't really put the electric kettle on because the power's low, and the gas . . .' He trailed off. I hastily assured him that I would in any case much prefer water, whose provision was just as dependent on modern technology. It came from a spring a hundred yards back up the track. It was first forced uphill by an electric pump to a Victorian-built brick reservoir that stood higher than the house, then gravity fed it to the water tank in the farmhouse attic.

This, it seemed to me, was the rough end of energy-saving. And despite all the claims that a modern off-grid system largely looks after itself, the truth is you have to get involved if you are going to run your own private power station. Just as most people tend their homes and gardens, and put a little of themselves into each square inch of the place, on some level you need to be equally involved in your own water or electricity supply. Being simply aware of it, monitoring the sun and the wind and the state of your batteries, is not enough. You need to adapt your behaviour to changes in the supply, and unless money is no object you need to be able to maintain it yourself. In the future, once domestic power generation is commonplace, there may be idiotproof systems and/or many with the skills to isolate the cause of a power outage and mend it. But at the moment, this is all customised equipment with special cables, special fuses and complex programmable electronics. If you are not the sort of person who can get stuck in and understand the set-up you will end up – excuse the pun – feeling powerless whenever some small but vital part needs repairing or replacing. Roger was not that sort of person, and when I started my relationship with the off-grid life, neither was I. But I realised as Roger handed me my glass of excellent spring water that I would have to change if I wanted to be able to relax and enjoy the feeling of independence from the grid. Freedom brings responsibility.

Independence does not necessarily imply isolation, but Gibshiel is by no means unique in being so lonely, and in winter so cut off from the rest of the area. The thirty-two-pence first-class stamp really pays off for the Wilsons: the nearest post office is ten miles away, so the postman comes all the way along the track to their door each day (when they have any post) and collects their outgoing mail at the same time as he delivers. I don't know whether Roger charged the same sort of fees as most management consultants, but the Wilsons were certainly living a low-cost life. They were clearly not hermits, but their location helped them resist consumerist impulses. At least it did until the Internet connection arrived. For the past two years, Roger has been able to order groceries from Tesco, and everywhere else, via the web. There was already a phone line when they bought the place, but it was not reliable for carrying Internet data. Then a technical breakthrough by BT meant that reliable broadband was available via the phone line up to ten miles from the nearest phone exchange, except when it rained. So Roger can work from his remote house almost as if he was in any city suburb, ordering books from Amazon and using the web as his global library.

Here is an ethical quandary of interest to all who live remotely, whether off-grid or not: it costs a few pounds in petrol (plus a couple of hours) for Roger to visit the shops, but the Tesco in Hexham, thirty miles away, will deliver all the way to the door for almost the same cost – £3.99 on Wednesdays and £4.99 the rest of the week. To that extent he is no longer off-grid. He has, as Professor Avner Offer had told me, swapped one grid for another. You could argue that his use of mail order is good for the local post office, but it is also bad for whichever bookshop or other local supplier he would have used if he did not sometimes have a Tesco delivery. In the long term that seems bad for the community. The danger to local small shopkeepers and farmers of diverting their revenue to Britain's biggest grocers is not compensated by the reduced emissions from the Tesco delivery van fitting Roger into its schedule. The miles clocked up bringing food from all over the world to the door of the delivery van also need to be balanced against the time and effort required for Roger to source as much of his weekly shop locally as is practical. Roger and his wife rear their own sheep, and eat them, but they are not growing their own vegetables any more than Roger is tending his energy system. 'Gardens and goats seem incompatible,' he explained to me.

After saying my goodbyes to Roger, I decided to contribute to the community and spend some cash in a local pub, the Holly Bush in Greenhaugh, and look for a place to spend the night as I drove there. It was wide open moorland most of the way, with a few impressive houses hidden away in copses here and there. I spotted a number of flat, sheltered spots as I descended to the pub on the edge of the village. Inside the Holly Bush local farm labourers were holding their pints standing next to glossy Chablis-drinking landowners. There was a warm heartiness that lifted my spirits and reminded me that for all its shortcomings – racism, narrow-mindedness, bad coffee – the British countryside is a joyful place.

Reassured by the locals that I could overnight anywhere in the National Park without hassle, I returned to the Park and a flat spot next to a wood with a fine view. From 9 p.m. that night to 8.30 next morning, a Saturday, not a single car disturbed me.

Off-grid kids

After breakfast I set off to meet Wigwam Steve. Apparently he lived in a wigwam and had nine children by five different women. According to the gossip I'd picked up along the road, at least two of these children were hugely talented, and worked for Spielberg.

I'd left a note at the end of what might or might not have been the track to Steve's place before going to see Roger Wilson, and sure enough Steve's wife had found it and phoned me to say they would be interested in meeting up. The first five miles back towards them were very slow, idyllically slow in fact. I sat back in my driving seat and enjoyed the scenery and the flock of sheep ambling in front of me. Then I realised I was driving in the wrong direction. I didn't mind, but it meant I would be late, and I had asked Steve to make the sacrifice of getting up early. At 10 a.m. I was still driving down tiny narrow lanes. I rang to say I'd be delayed an hour. A small child answered the phone and passed me over to Daddy.

'We'll make good use of it,' he said laconically.

When I finally arrived at the top of the hill, I could see a handful of the legendary kids in the distance, making a camp in the garden. The track was steep and slippery. I parked the Bus by the gate and walked a quarter of a mile down a sharp incline and up the other side, past a tiny roundhouse, built from recycled wood with a tin roof. There was nobody in. At the top of the hill I found the main cottage – a solid, confidence-inspiring, old stone building with walls half a metre thick. Steve was still in bed, but his missus made me a cup of tea in a farm-

Wigwam Steve – his life should be a movie.

house kitchen. The tables and chairs were all handmade and beautifully crafted. When Steve emerged it was easy to see why he had a Lothario reputation: tall, charming and handsome, here was someone who had lived his dream all his life.

Steve Hardman left Aston University after the first year of a PPE course and ended up in Northumberland with a few friends who wanted to do the seventies dropping-out thing. He'd bought the place for a thousand pounds, and until recently he had lived with a single battery and a generator. He had brought his kids up there, all of them, after his first wife walked out. It turned out Steve had more than nine children but fewer than five wives, which in a way was even more remarkable than the rumours had suggested. When Steve split with his first wife, he was left to look after five kids. Then along came his new missus, Pam, with six kids from her previous marriage. Steve and Pam had six children together, too, which made a grand total of seventeen, most of them boys. They had all been brought up in the three-bedroom house, and the little roundhouse I had seen on the way. At its peak population, Steve and Pam had to move into a big white wigwam, which became a local landmark, and gave Steve his name.

The first few years had been hard, man. Steve moved in fresh from college with little more than his idealism and a copy of *The Whole Earth Handbook* to guide his alternative lifestyle. He started with just firewood and lamps. It was a big moment when the first generator was installed. It allowed Steve and Pam to run a twin-tub washing machine. He shuddered as he remembered the Saturday morning wash before then. 'I got cured of Terry nappies,' he said. 'You know, we thought we were doing the right thing environmentally, but every Saturday morning there would be these buckets of steaming nappies. There was some sort of liquid we kept them in till they were washed and I can still taste that sour smell.' There were two candlelit births in the house, much to the disquiet of the local maternity unit, which had to put a helicopter on standby each time. After the second child popped out with no trouble, they persuaded Steve and Pam to take a private room in the Alnwick cottage hospital for the next ones. 'They said we could do what we wanted in there, but please, just come over and use the room,' Steve told me.

Steve must have been an oddity in this isolated community, but they had somehow accepted him. At times his brood comprised the majority of pupils in the local school, a distinctive gang of long-haired boys. In winter, the children were a vital part of the energy set-up. The coal delivery was dumped just inside the gate where I had parked the Bus, and 'the kids would get the coal from the top of the track in the wheelbarrow. Going down the hill was easy, but coming up the other side on snowy days, a posse of the smaller kids would pull a rope attached to the front of the wheelbarrow, and two older ones held the handles and steered.' Collecting firewood was also a group enterprise – each small child was expected to return with one log, the larger children with two – and in the summer, the kids played a vital role in the water system. 'Originally when we came here the water supply was the dew-pond that gravity feeds to the house,' Steve explained. 'In spring tadpoles would come out the tap, and in summer it was little white worms.' So the children would be sent up to another spring at the top of the hill with a container tailored to their size.

'Our clothes wouldn't be up with the fashions,' recalled one of the sons, Ruairi, when he met me in a Soho coffee bar. 'They started in charity shops and then got handed down from one brother to the next. We got our own private bus to school every day, paid for by the council – both ways. We were so far off the bus routes. It would drop us off at our different schools. We were very encapsulated in our little off-grid world. In a way that made us isolated. We weren't around other kids, apart from at school. When we got back we played together. We never went to school friends' houses, couldn't join in any TV conversations. We all always wanted to get a TV – it was a treat for us at Christmas when Dad would hire one in.' Then he admitted, on behalf of his brothers and sisters, 'Ultimately there is a feeling that he was imposing his view of the world on us.' But it does not seem to have done Ruairi any harm. He doesn't work for Spielberg after all (nor does the other film industry brother), but in a post-production house where he is learning the craft of film editing. And he is the first of the brood to plan a return to the area, in search of an off-grid home of his own.

There has been progress at Steve's since Ruairi was a lad: a pipe running from a stream in the nearby woods to provide the house with water; a new extension at the back of the house; and even solar and wind power, installed with the aid of local council grants. The wigwam has been taken down as the number of children has dwindled to manageable proportions and it is no longer needed. Steve, whose previous work had been of the less legitimate sort, has become a builder – an ex-directory builder, he quickly added, who only accepted work from word-of-mouth referrals. It is the customers who need references, not the builder, the way Steve sees it. Meeting the man, and looking around his property, it was easy to believe that Steve is the ideal builder – kind, clever, gentle, and highly intelligent. The white Ford van parked in the drive added a touch of verisimilitude.

We took a walk around the land, past the 400-foot-deep quarry, filled with rainwater, his own private swimming pool. A little further on we passed Steve's current bedroom, a small two-man tent. Our brief phone conversation must have taken place as he lay there a couple of hours earlier. 'I just prefer it,' he explained, though I hadn't needed to ask.

Community, not commune

I was now only a few miles from the Scottish border. The next leg of my journey would take me into a different legal system, especially when it came to land ownership, and a different off-grid mentality. In England and Wales I had met some resistance among those who lived off-grid to the idea of publicising their lives, but on the whole there was a feeling that it would help promote something worthwhile. The Scots were less taken with the idea of appearing in print. And those who did consent to be interviewed were in the main unwilling to be photographed. Even in the Highland township of Scoraig, on the west coast near Ullapool, which has had plenty of publicity over the years, including a BBC documentary, and where the idea of a visiting writer

Scoraig on the walk in – Alan's house is on the left.

no longer holds any fears, residents scattered whenever my camera appeared.

My visit confirmed there was something precious about this group of houses built on the end of a fertile peninsula. At the beginning of the 1960s there were just four people living here, two farmers and a pair of vegetarian conscientious objectors from Kent who had sought out an underpopulated haven after the war. No precise figures exist, but at the time of my visit most locals agreed there were about eighty residents. So on that measure at least it is a success story.

There are two ways to visit Scoraig: you can walk in along a mountainous five-mile path that takes you from the mainland out to the tip of the peninsula, or you can ride in on a boat across the mouth of the peninsula from a small jetty on the other side. I suppose you could also arrive in a private helicopter, but the only local who would be able to afford that is Lady Jane Rice, resident of nearby Dundonnell House, owner of the whole peninsula and estranged wife of Oscar-winning balladeer Sir Tim Rice. (Lady Jane lives a less ostentatious life than her husband, so helicopters are there none.) The boat was a fiver for outsiders like me, but free for locals. However, my repeated phone calls to Jethro the boatman yielded no reply; it was the busiest time of the year, and suspected tourists no doubt took second place to genuine locals with important shopping trips. So I never experienced the journey, though my luggage did. Later I found an Edinburgh University academic thesis describing it: 'sailing across the loch, houses appear in front scattered over the hillside, each one with its own wind turbine, and as you grow nearer you can see the many thousands of trees which have been planted over the last 40 years ... On arrival you will find neither signpost nor reception desk, but very friendly people always happy to stop, chat and help when needed.' I would find that this was the secret of Scoraig: no community facilities but a community set-up and spirit nevertheless.

I parked at the Dundonnell end of the footpath and walked in, carrying my video camera, stills camera, a large Parka in case it rained, sandwiches, fruit and two litres of water. After 500 yards the last of the electricity poles disappeared behind me, and I was set for a truly off-grid day. After the first mile under a bright sun I began to feel the weight of my bags, and sweat formed underneath my Parka. I had climbed to the highest point on the walk, but the houses at the other end of the peninsula seemed just as far away. I stopped to transfer some of the weight from my pockets to my stomach and stared down at the water lapping the rocks a thousand feet below. The smell of heather on the fresh wind was intoxicating. Refreshed, I set forth again, ignoring the chafing of my bag straps, and covered another two miles before running into a local coming the other way. We exchanged good mornings and I learned that she had recently rented a bothy, as the little cottages on the peninsula are called. She was walking the path for the first time, having always taken the boat until now, to see if it was wide enough for a 125cc scrambler bike. I had seen one in the car-park and assumed its owner was responsible for the deep ruts along the path. I continued walking, reflecting that what made Scoraig special was its inaccessibility, but that was also a problem for residents, especially newcomers.

By now I was passing a gushing waterfall, still a mile from the first of the houses I had seen from the other side of the bay. Presumably this distance prevented the residents from harnessing the flow of water into a hydro-electric scheme. Another half-hour's fast walking and I passed the first house – it was deserted – then the second and the third. Still no sign of anyone, friendly and happy to chat or otherwise. My bags were exceedingly heavy now, and it was still another two miles to the house of the person who had invited me – Hugh Piggott, world-famous wind turbine expert.

The path I was on runs along the centre of the peninsula, the land sloping down to the shore on the left and rising up to a ridge that runs the entire length of the peninsula on the right, so before long I could see the community laid out below me like a 3D map of Lilliput. There were some cultivated fields, but the peninsula was mainly a series of houses and gardens, many with vegetable patches. The houses were dotted about higgledy-piggledy, some down near the shore, others between the path and the ridge, facing south-west. There were another half-dozen dwellings over the other side of the ridge, looking north-east, which I did not visit. The tip of the peninsula was more densely popu-lated, with houses close together. 'It's like suburbia,' one of the residents remarked.

When finally I arrived in the only part of the peninsula that could be called in any way a high street, I found another resident. The

Hugh – master turbine builder.

schoolteacher looked startled as she answered my knock on the door. Friendly, but not happy to chat, she gave me terse directions. At last I arrived at Hugh's house, separated from the water by a narrow field and a few trees. A wind turbine was spinning furiously, and from his door I could see the tips of several others turning madly against the bare sky.

Although a handful of the residents are claiming dole or tax credits, the vast majority work, and they have a huge range of skills between them, from violin-making to computing. Some commute to the mainland, others work remotely via Internet or phone. One woman grows Apothecary roses; a coffee jar full of the petals topped up with vodka makes a rose tincture which sells for hundreds in posh health centres. So, on balance, the community is financially self-sufficient, generating more wealth than it actually requires to function. 'Making a living here is just a question of intelligence and imagination,' Tom Forsyth, one of the original community members, told me.

There are wild deer, pheasant and rabbit, and farm livestock including sheep, goats, pigs and cows, all on the common grazing land. But these days the residents of Scoraig are not technically allowed to slaughter the animals themselves. There is a vegetable growers' group, and one resident makes up vegetable boxes comprising locally grown and imported food which she delivers around the community. Highland Whole Food in Inverness supplies most of what they do not grow themselves. 'We don't like Tesco around here – they are too greedy,' said Tom, who gets all the energy he needs from a single solar panel, plus wood and coal which is brought over in a small boat. It sank on one recent trip, Tom reported, carrying half a ton of the stuff.

I met Tom on my way out of Scoraig. I had lost a toenail on the walk in and I could not face carrying the bags back over the mountain. The solution was provided by the founder of modern Scoraig, Alan Bush, a jovial white-bearded farmer who had arrived in 1961, just as the last of the original residents was leaving. He recounted those early times in *Escape to Scorraig*, his self-published memoir, dwelling nostalgically on the era of acid-taking that was the 1960s. Alan had dispatched his daughter in a boat to drop the bags on the other side of the water; all I had to do was walk the five miles back across the mountain in the rain and drive ten miles around the loch to the post-box where they would be awaiting me. No biggie.

Relieved of my load, I felt like I was floating rather than walking as I retraced the route under darkening skies. I had not yet passed the last of the houses when I saw an infinitely old man who looked like Ben Gunn from *Treasure Island* with his mound of white hair and huge white beard. But he was gentle and level-headed when we spoke. This was Tom Forsyth, the second person to settle on Scoraig after Alan Bush. We had only a brief conversation, discussing among other things the threat of trail bikes to the delicate ecology of the peninsula, before I had to hurry on my way because of the rain. 'Yes, there's a bit of dampness coming,' Tom agreed. I even managed to fit in a brief visit to Lady Jane in Dundonnell House as I drove back. I learned that she was anxious to sell her land to the locals, but there were no takers. Everyone was happy to pay her rent of £10 a year and let her deal with the boring admin.

The long journey to Scoraig was well worth it. I learned more there than I had on any other visit – about renewable energy, about the best way to organise an off-grid community, and about how to find land if you are looking to go off-grid. I will return to the subject of Scoraig in later chapters.

An hour south of Scoraig was the site for Dylan Evans's Utopia Experiment. I had last seen Dylan in his university laboratory in Bristol, but since then he had ended his relationship and academic life for good, sold his house, given away most of his possessions and thrown himself into building his Utopia on land lent to him by an old university friend who ran a farmhouse B&B adjoining the site. Dylan and his main 'crew' member, Adam, were already living in yurts they had built in a sheltered dip.

Dylan looked fresher, happier and healthier than when I'd last seen him; Adam was a commune-dwelling hippy from central casting. In his mid-fifties with a beard, a ponytail and strong Australian accent, he was like some wood-nymph, dancing and pirouetting about as he spoke. During my visit he was usually dressed in khaki shorts and a poncho made from a British Airways in-flight blanket. Adam spent his time waiting for conversational openings into which he could insert a mention of his devout belief in the Great Spirit. Every time I was about to write him off as a total loony he would do or say something that made me think again. Both the yurts, for example, had been built by Adam, according to his principle that you must never measure or plan any building work

– the Great Spirit will provide. 'This saw,' he said, holding up a perfectly ordinary saw, 'is the best saw in the world. It is the perfect saw. With this saw I can make anything. I need nothing else.' The maddening thing is that the yurts were perfectly solid, roomy and warm. For the two days of my stay, Adam was at work on his next structure, so I was able to see for myself that he was telling the truth about his woodworking technique.

Adam and that blanket.

My conviction that Dylan was largely sane and rational in his approach to the experiment was dented by meeting Adam, but perhaps Dylan had his scientific reasons for recruiting this strange fellow, who would probably seem just an oddity once other volunteers arrived. Time would tell. They were both living off-grid at least part of the time, and once a few more elements, such as a solar panel, were in place they would be completely self-sufficient and could stop using the adjacent B&B as their refuge. New volunteers were emailing their details regularly, and Dylan planned to invite them twelve at a time, changing the cast every few months. We talked for hours in Dylan's yurt about the possible collapse of civilisation upon which his experiment was premised. When would it happen, and why? And what would count as 'collapse'? Suppose you are ready and prepared for chaos; what do you do about others roaming the countryside looking for shelter? Do you fight them or feed them? The Utopia Experiment may provide some answers.

Rural squatter

No sooner had I set off from Dylan's Utopia than a sight caught my eye that had to be investigated further. Set back from the road on a lovely patch of green grass, I spotted an ancient static trailer painted with black bitumen and surrounded by trees on two sides, with a steep railway embankment behind it. Next to the van was a car, parked exactly parallel to it, and a few yards away a washing line was strung up between some trees.

The tough-looking guy – let's call him Pete – who came to the door of the trailer was not pleased to see me, but I soon calmed him down and explained my research mission. Could I write about you? I asked. 'You can't,' he replied in a gentle Scottish accent. 'It's a whole saga.' And then he proceeded to tell it to me. 'About the time I parked here another caravan moved in a few hundred yards away. The farmer came to see us and told us he'd had a letter from the Highland Council.' It was the same letter they sent to everyone who had a caravan or two parked in their fields: it said that these vans were illegal and had to be moved. 'It looked all official, like,' said Pete, 'but I asked the farmer, "Have you showed this to a lawyer? Are you sure it's kosher?"' No, he had not. To cut to the chase, Pete didn't move his van, and he never heard from the council again. Eventually, the owners of the land applied for planning permission to build a house there, but it was turned down on a technicality. So Pete just stayed. He'd been there over a decade.

'So why don't you just try to go legal?' I asked.

'No,' he replied. 'I'm working class. I'll just lose the case and be blacklisted [by future employers].'

He invited me into a sparse, tidy bed-sitting room with a battered old sofa and matching armchair. A copy of that day's *Sun* lay on the sofa alongside the *I Ching*.

I wanted to know how he lived without any water or power, on the dole with a millionaire's view out of his window. Neatness and discretion were the key. The place was always tidy and there were few visitors. Pete was worried that the recent paint job was a bit shabby as it had started raining during the redecoration, so he was planning to do it again. He chose the spot not for the view but because there was a brick-built underground cesspit there, with a proper underground toilet. He thinks it was dug during the war when British special forces used the area as their training ground. Pete kept the whole contraption covered with turf and vegetation, like a survivalist. He used to be in the army; he talked about how he had learned to parachute. Hanging up on the washing line were three pairs of fatigue trousers – he was wearing a fourth – and three pea-green jackets. As for power, that was why he had the car, to lug the Calor gas bottles from town for his stove and heater. He had a battery radio and a torch, but that was it. Drinking water, from any tap he comes across, was stored in twelve-litre containers, and other water needs were satisfied by rainwater and a nearby stream.

Incense burned in a tray. Pete made me a cup of tea as he talked. We warmed to each other, this writer from London and this shaven-headed, gangling thirty-five-year-old. Did he hunt? No. Deer made for fantastic food, but he would only be able to eat a couple of pounds as he had no fridge. Oh, and the ruling class thing again. He'd be banged up for it.

I thanked him for the tea and drove on towards Glenelg to visit the first and, as it turned out, only architect-designed off-grid house on my tour. The light was fading so I turned off the main road and spent the night by a waterfall. The moist earth smelled richly of fungi during my walk the next morning, and as I looked down I could see them all around, mostly the classic red toadstool with flecks of white in it – psychedelic mushrooms. But it was 6.30, I was alone, and I was working. I left the mushrooms where they were and found a well-hidden spot to use as a loo.

Designer eco-house

After breakfast in the wood I set off for Glenelg, following my directions through the village and down a lane past two old towers, each of which looked like a rook chess piece. I found Neil's post-box and walked up the steepest path I had yet climbed.

The house was a superb design, built of wood with large areas of glass to maximise the sun's heat, black floor tiles to retain that heat, and turf roofs interspersed with solar panels. It was mid-morning when I arrived, and the air outside was already close and muggy from a combination of damp and sun, but the interior felt cool and airy. The house was on three levels because it followed the contours of the hill, and, Neil admitted, 'weather conditions are often extreme so a certain amount of "digging the house in" was necessary.' It struck me as a fine example of sympathetic modern architecture incorporating all the latest

Neil Hammond and Amy Flowerree.

eco-thinking – and the lifestyle of its owner. 'I have spent my whole life sitting around in kitchens so I wanted a big kitchen,' said Neil. Consequently the house is centred around a friendly kitchen with a huge table. From there a few steps lead down to a little TV room, and more steps lead up to a ground-floor guest bedroom. The other bed-rooms and the bathroom are upstairs on the second floor. In that Italian marble-tiled bathroom there was a composting toilet that did not look like any composting toilet I had seen. Instead of being wooden and earthy it was white and sleek, but a composter all the same. And it had 'been a bit temperamental', according to Neil. 'It is very user-friendly but sometimes the liquid doesn't drain properly into the septic tank.' There is a four-foot drum underneath that he empties every six months. It works better indoors because it is warm so the waste dries more quickly. 'It never smells apart from when it gets bunged up,' Neil assured me.

There is solar water heating (the water itself is from a spring), and the solar panels feed into a battery bank. While the three-bedroom house was being built, Neil lived in what is now the big shed that stores his equipment and batteries. The original version of his wind turbine went through a few iterations. 'It took a lot of input from me to keep it going. It was one of the very first Proven 6s. They had not tested it properly, so lots of blades needed replacing. It gets ridiculously wild up here sometimes.' Now that the systems have all been tested and ironed out, Neil has a low-cost existence – except for fuel. The hot water and underfloor heating are gas-driven, and the price of propane has nearly doubled since Neil moved in, so his annual bill is now approaching £500 a year. He spends another £100 or so on red diesel for the generator, and a negligible amount ('except for a lot of my time') on maintaining the gennie, the batteries and the wind turbine. The TV signal in the area is non-existent, so Neil paid for a Sky subscription when he moved in, even though he only watches the four terrestrial channels. Despite the advent of Freeview, he has not got around to cancelling it yet.

Neil and his Chilean girlfriend Amy Flowerree also grow a lot of food, in two large polytunnels below the house. He barters some of the food for beer. Their land leads down to a river where Neil has chosen a beautiful spot to place a little wooden shack sauna.

After six years of living there, Neil has absolutely no regrets. He and his architect, Neil Sutherland from Inverness, had to push hard with the planners, though. It was the old story. 'The local planner was not very happy with the idea of this type of house, halfway up a hill,' Neil told me. 'He was not interested in the environmental aspect – he was a white bungalow man.' It had not been expensive by UK standards, because Neil did some of the work himself, but he would never have reached first base without his architect.

It was a short visit, but I left feeling certain that there could and should be many more houses like this all across the UK, if only the planning community would permit it.

The cowshed and the turbine

Neil Hammond is one of the first of the new off-grid generation – capitalism with a heart and a moral compass. Roy Fountain, seventy, from Kirkby Malzeard in North Yorkshire, is one of the last of the old wave. And he did things the old way, without advisers or experts to steer him through the new regime of clipboarded health and safety visitors and suspicious planners.

I arrived at his place mid-afternoon to find what appeared to be a three-car family, with Roy's daughter and wife hurriedly leaving in one of the

Roy on his land.

Normobiles. Roy looked like a retired rock star or actor, with a mass of curly grey hair and a quiet, gentle Yorkshire accent, but he was a hard-working country smallholder whose outer good looks reflected a gentle inner beauty.

'We had no inheritance,' he reminisced. 'We made our own way.' So it was a bitter blow to buy the twenty acres and then be refused permission to build. He came upon the land ten years ago when he was taking the dog for a walk. At first he thought he had been there before, but in fact he recognised the place literally from his dreams. As a boy he'd entertained the fantasy of a piece of land gently dropping down to a rivulet at the bottom of a valley, with trees just where these trees were and a ridge just where this ridge was. Eventually he bought the land. Then, 'because I told the truth in the planning application', he had to wait ten years for permission to rebuild the old cowshed. Even though the tumbledown building had a hearth and used to be a house, Roy wrote honestly that it was currently used as a cowshed. This meant he was applying for a change of use from agricultural to residential – a complete no-no in planning terms.

There was just one loophole. If he could prove that he could run a sustainable business there, permission to restore the farmhouse would follow. But the word 'sustainable' means different things to different people. Gardeners and farmers would take 'sustainable' in the sense most of us use it these days – somehow ecological and non-damaging to the soil. In planning-speak, 'sustainable' simply means that it makes a profit, provides a living, and above all does not draw undue resources from the rest of the community.

Roy made numerous proposals to his local council, but they were all rejected. After several more years he finally came across a use for the land that the local planners accepted would require his presence on site. He heard of a young local cheesemaker who was supplying posh restaurants in London and who had been featured in the *Sunday Times*. He went to see the man and suggested he start making sheep's cheese; Roy would supply the milk. Sheep milking has never been huge in British agriculture, but Roy's plan to sell sheep's cheese appealed to the cheesemaker, and to the council. Eventually it proved to be a sustainable business in the sense that it made money. For the next decade Roy made a living selling the sheep's milk, until new EU regulations put an end to it. 'The amount of alterations we would have had to make were over the top for the amount of money we were making,' Roy explained. 'It would have been about £30,000. So we had to stop the milking. We still rear the sheep, fatten lambs for the market.'

Roy's planning permission problems continued long after he received clearance to build his house. He is in an area of outstanding natural beauty (AONB), and the local council refused permission to erect a wind turbine. This was despite support from the authorities controlling the AONB. After another three years, Roy received permission. When I visited in the summer of 2006 his diesel generator was charging up twenty-four batteries, each of two volts, and he was hoping his turbine would be online by the end of the year. I'm glad to report that it is now, indeed, up and running.

I walked down the lane that went past Roy's house, a dead-end serving one more farm. A few cows were wandering in the field, but otherwise all was still. A place of complete tranquillity; a bucolic rural scene. There was nothing stupendously special about it, but I found it hard to tear myself away. I could happily have parked there for a couple of days. But I had places to go and people to see, and with a final, regretful look back, I was on the road again.

Eco-pimp my ride

The first thing I noticed on my arrival in Townhead was a bit of a pong. There were enough composting toilets there to service the twelve terraced houses in this hamlet near Sheffield, but they were not the source of the smell.

The houses faced one another on opposite sides of a wide garden which was largely a play area for the kids. Behind one of the rows of terraces was a huge vegetable patch, or market garden to be precise, where the residents grew every kind of salad and green vegetable along with tomatoes and garlic. There were bits of old stuff everywhere – vans that no longer worked, building materials that someone could not bear to throw away. Townhead would certainly fail the Lizzie Purchase test. There were perhaps a dozen working cars parked around the place, so unlike Allaleigh these residents were not purists or idealists, or perhaps it was just that they had no planning issues to contend with. They were mainly former road campaigners who had moved in to what was an existing squat when the previous occupants fell out with one another.

Eventually, after a few hours, I stopped noticing the smell – which turned out to be the local farmer spreading slurry on nearby fields – and the slightly unsavoury first impression was dispelled as I realised this commune of eighteen adults and seven children was a success. Most of the adults had been there for eight years, since the place was relaunched. When they moved in there was nothing but the shells of terraced houses in two rows, in the middle of nowhere, with no roofs, no plumbing and no electricity.

I spent most of my visit with Piet Defoe, an agile, wiry little man from Bradford. In his former life as a road protester he handled media relations for Swampy. He had his own personal power supply because he used so much, and he managed the communal power supply and the commune shop, whose profits went into buying more wind turbines and solar panels. He also ran an embryonic renewable energy company. I had finally given up on Bert Hagley, so to Piet's excitement I asked him to fit a solar panel on the roof of the Bus. He brought out a new Kyocera fifty-watt panel, which for the genuinely knockdown price of £200 would sort out most of my needs.

Solar panels are expensive. The power they produce is scarcely worth the money they cost, which is why many solar panel owners will tell you they are not doing it to save money, but for the good of the planet. But why should a solar panel not fulfil both functions – helping to save money *and* saving us from global warming? If you are starting from scratch, with no other power sources, and if you are prepared to rearrange your life so that you reduce your energy consumption by up to 80 per cent, then panels (plus batteries to store the power) are cheaper than a generator, and have lower ongoing costs. If you include other external factors such as energy independence, then the case for panels becomes even more compelling. Unfortunately most people decide they need a generator for back-up when the sun does not shine, and this tends to tip the whole idea towards being uneconomical. The high cost of PV (i.e. solar) cells is partly because world demand for panels, or rather the silicon used to make the panels, is at an all-time high, and increasing. The solar industry is expecting to consume more silicon in 2006 than the computer chip industry, for the first time. But according to noted architect Bill Dunster, there are also some shenanigans going on. He says the price of renewables components in Britain has been kept artificially high by companies buying up any Chinese suppliers that showed signs of undercutting them.

Next, Piet and I drove to the local town and bought a lorry battery for £35. He clamped it into place in one of the storage lockers on the floor of the van. He also decided to wire the new battery into the engine alternator, so that when I was on the move I would benefit from the power generated by the alternator. This might increase fuel consumption but it turned out to be a good idea because the electric fridge (the standard three-way installed in all campers) had proved to be an energy-hungry beast. Piet swarmed around the van, running a wire from the alternator under the chassis to the battery in the back, and mounting the panel onto the roof. He drilled a hole through the seam of the skylight so as not to affect the integrity of the roof, or the insulation material, and ran the cable through that to a £20 regulator, a small box that would stop power from the panel coming in when the battery was full. This ensured a long-lasting happy battery.

Then Dave from Townhead gave me a great tip on the use of vegetable oil instead of diesel in the winter months. The Renault Master runs on a Peugeot engine, and comes with a heated oil filter. The veggie oil can just be poured straight in during the summer, but in the winter I knew I would need to fit a special conversion kit: the cold thickens vegetable oil, and additives are needed to thin it down. But there is another way. 'I keep the tank nearly empty all the time,' said Dave, 'then when I want to fill it with vegetable oil, I run the van for twenty miles first to warm the engine, then pour in the veggie, but I make sure that by the end of my journey it's run out and I've put a couple of quids' worth of diesel in again.' In a couple of minutes Dave had revealed information that could be worth millions to a group of car users.

I had little in common with the residents of Townhead – mostly they rejected mainstream society and had created a place that ran according to different values, whereas I wanted to be in both worlds – but they did bring me back to the idea that the best way to live off-grid is in a group. Not necessarily a commune like Townhead or Allaleigh, but an alliance of like-minded people, a buying co-operative and a skills bank. Scoraig had shown me that you do not need to live communally to have a successful community. Townhead showed me that at its best, a good off-grid community survives for the same reason as any community: people help each other, and there is a reasonable mix of skills, and something approximating a common set of values.

In the shadow of the towers

As I drove south, back to London, I found myself passing the power station I had seen from across the valley as I sat in Tony Marmont's car. There was a turning marked Radcliffe Marina, and on a whim I followed it, past some shanty caravans and tumbledown houses to the water.

At Radcliffe on Soar there were both mains moorings and, for £75 per month, moorings without services. You could park a boat the size of a large studio flat next to this monstrous power station and be off-grid. The notion tickled me, so I stopped at the café, housed in a Nissen hut next to the boatyard, where I met some fairly eccentric boat owners. The area was abuzz over a recent sneak-thief invasion. Thirteen boats had been burgled out of about a hundred, according to Gary, a

Off-grid irony.

twenty-five-year-old who had lived there for three years with his wife. They had a dog so they'd been left alone. Another man, a retired council worker with a moustache like Hercule Poirot's, had left his new narrowboat moored in a nearby backwater where it was set on fire and sunk by kids. The problem with living on a boat, it seems, is that you dare not leave it unattended for long. On the other hand, you can take it with you on your travels, as long as you only go by canal or river.

I parked close to the water for the night, as far as possible from the vast power station buzzing away across the field. Nobody had mentioned it, or even glanced at it. When I referred to the chimneys the boat owners had reacted as though I'd told a tasteless joke. 'I hardly notice it except as a landmark when giving directions,' said the Poirot look-alike. 'There is some condensation, sure, but it's just steam,' claimed another resident. 'Nothing to worry about. No emissions.' Later I discovered that the power station had been shut down at the time, for annual maintenance. Yet it had definitely hummed all night.

I woke the next morning on what was to turn out to be the hottest July day on record, so it felt appropriate to pop in on the house with more renewable energy than any other in Britain for another peek at the interior. I was received by Tony Marmont's wife Angela, who was less of a green convert than her husband. 'I don't know what a lot of these buttons and things are,' she admitted over a glass of ginger cordial. 'I'm told not to touch them as it messes up Tony's experiments.'

This inability of wives to maintain the household's off-grid systems would strike a chord a few days later when I caught up with Fiona at the Port Eliot Festival. She had a gig at the crossover music, literary and arts festival, drawing a nude live on stage. The audience camps in the grounds of the stately home in Cornwall owned by the Eliot family. There are multiple events all day long and through most of the night, ranging from authors reading new books to post-modern burlesque.

Urban eco-cottage

But I had one more call to make in London before I headed back onto the open road. Although I had not found a single off-grid house in the city, I wanted to explore the idea of being 'off-grid ready' a little further. Tony Marmont is doing this on a grand scale, and we city dwellers could emulate him. Without cutting off from the grid, those of us with gardens or an allotment could prepare for a time of limited or non-existent power and water. Even if it never happens, the exercise is still worthwhile. It means collecting rainwater from the roof and finding a way to pipe it from the water butt to the bath, shower or kitchen. Without going as far as buying a solar panel, it might be worth making sure you have the rudiments of a twelve-volt power system – a car battery charged up, wired to an inverter and preferably a few ultra-low-energy lights. You might want a Freeplay DAB radio, run off the battery or powered by the wind-up handle when all else fails. Another worthwhile precaution might be to ensure you have at least one solid fuel heating source which can double as a cooker.

Donnachadh McCarthy was the only city type I came across who is already doing all those things and more. A former accounts clerk, he has slowly installed all possible eco-features into his cottagey two-up-two-down 1840s brick terrace home in Camberwell, south London. He has become well-known as a result of radio and TV appearances and he can now make a living speaking and carrying out environmental audits for organisations wanting to know how green they are.

'What I have been trying to do with my house is show you can live in the inner city and slash your emissions from waste and water use,' he said as he sat in his little home office. His own carbon footprint is light to the point of invisible. With his accounting background, he calibrates and measures every aspect of his green existence. 'My household waste is a total of a ton per year,' he told me – an eighth of the European average. 'I was the first person in London to export my electricity to the grid. I am a net exporter . . . 20 per cent more than I import. My mains water usage is sixteen litres a day, compared to 160 litres for the average person.' Donnachadh has energy-saving bulbs that reduce consumption by 80 per cent, and he uses a single LED (light-emitting diode) when he is working on his computer at night, 'just to light the keyboard for two to three hours. That's one watt.' Donnachadh's obsessive devotion to reducing his energy consumption is a real problem when he has visitors. 'When I had two house guests from the US last summer my stress levels went through the roof,' he told me. 'Especially when they took a shower.' Perhaps you have to be like that to want to blaze a trail for home ecology.

I pondered my conversation with Donnachadh on the train down to Liskeard to join Fiona and Caitlin, who had driven the Bus from London to the Port Eliot Festival. It struck me that what we had in common was a horror at the fact that so many alternative energy advocates, from sales people to lobbyists, do not live the low-energy renewable life themselves. 'Probably the reason we haven't got as far as we should have got is the environmental movement has not put its literal house in order,' Donnachadh told me. 'I continue the work on my own life, but until the people conducting these eco-summits have done it themselves, for example, the meetings won't mean anything.' At a Department of Trade and Industry-hosted event attended by 150 people from the renewable energy industry, including Donnachadh, to launch the government's renewable energy initiative in 2006, one of the speakers asked the audience what measures they were taking to reduce their use of hydrocarbons. Only three had solar panels, three had solar hot water, and two had a wind turbine, and one of those was Donnachadh himself. I would learn later that four British Energy executives engaged in decommissioning ageing nuclear plants had kitted themselves out with both panels and turbine against what they regard as the certainty of future power cuts. So the nuclear industry is more off-grid ready than the renewables industry, if you believe the results of this informal survey.

The world is their sitting rooom.

By the time I arrived at Port Eliot, the Bus was not in its best state. The fridge had been left on and the leisure battery was out of power. The remains of a little dinner party the night before were stashed in the cool box, which was about to flatten the main battery. Caitlin had been crawling around scattering the neatly stored gear, so it took me a while to locate the final back-up – a foldaway solar panel from Unipart with its own battery pack, which I kept for emergencies. I plugged the cool box into this new power source and started the engine to keep the battery charged up. Mistake. A B&Q gazebo that had been stored under the chassis instantly melted onto the exhaust. The only place to recycle that was the nearest bin.

An off-grid energy supply is always a delicate balance, and whether you are in a house or a bus, it is something you have to be aware of at all times. Fiona had been treating it like an on-grid supply; I would have to find a diplomatic way of educating her in the fine details of battery life and the limited power available from solar panels. And when a baby is added to the mix, the ecology of a camper van is always going to be under threat. Everything has to be meticulously stored or else there is chaos. The answer was less stuff. Like most city dwellers – no, like most people in the UK – Fiona and I were in danger of becoming slaves to our possessions. The only way to prevent Caitlin from turning the interior of the Bus into something resembling a jumble sale was to minimise our load. I resolved to strip down the contents of the Bus as soon we were next in London.

Stately survival

On the way back to London after the festival we had a couple of stops to make. The first was a stately home whose owner I hoped would be persuaded to take it off-grid. And so it proved.

Tapeley Park, near Instow in Devon, is approached along a landscaped drive that winds steeply uphill. I had been summoned to see Hector Christie, who is not your idea of an archetypal aristocrat (or, to be precise, member of the gentry, since his father, Sir George Christie, owner of Glyndebourne, is an hereditary knight of the realm). Hector has all the charm and self-confidence of an Old Etonian, but his appearance – he is tall and shaven-headed – is more down to earth. The gossip columns know him as a wild-at-heart anti-globalisation campaigner who

Hector – his crazy exterior masks a crazy interior.

usually turns up at demos in fancy dress with his faithful bulldog Bryan. He made the front page of the *Daily Telegraph* at a protest against genetically modified food when he stencilled his slogan of the day across Bryan's forehead: 'No GM in Dog Food'.

Over a cup of tea in the kitchen, the warmest and messiest room in the house, Hector explained that he was 'radicalised during the foot and mouth epidemic of 2001'. He led the fight in his area to stop the culling, and was briefly jailed, although he prevented his own herd from being slaughtered. I was amused to discover that this herd numbered just twenty. There is an American phrase for this, 'big hat, no cattle'; but although Hector is a mass of contradictions, I am certain his heart is in the right place.

Years earlier he'd turned his twenty-bedroom house into a spiritual retreat – for friends, not as a commercial venture – which is perhaps in keeping with the estate's long tradition of radical thought: Hector's grandmother was a friend of William Morris, founder of the Arts and Crafts movement. The main rooms are full of Morris's ceramics, wallpaper and furniture. He has perfectly preserved the state rooms, complete with portraits and statuettes, but has made his own additions, in the form of crudely drawn protest posters which lean against the walls directly below the historic masterpieces. He loves it when he is contacted by a foreign academic or perhaps just a little old lady who is a Morris fan, asking for a tour. He likes to watch their faces as they see his posters, and he tells the visitors that they 'perfectly complement' the older works in the room.

For years, Hector has been practising his own form of egalitarianism, allowing local homeless people and other anti-globalisation campaigners to live there in return for two days' work a week for those living in the house and one day for those in vans or benders in the grounds. From time to time a member of his community falls out of favour and is ousted. Two of the current volunteers have built a couple of eco-showhomes on his extensive grounds. In the same field where Elvis the Ram munches grass all day long, occasionally breaking off for tussles with Bryan, there is a beautiful straw-bale house consisting of a single room plus a toilet and shower. It was built by eco-designer Rupert Hawley, and as long as he is in favour with Hector he will be able to use the place as his weekend retreat. If all goes well, between them they may try to build an eco-village on the estate. Among the trees near the permaculture garden is a wooden roundhouse also built by its current inhabitant, a skilled woodsman who asked not to be named.

It may come as some consolation to the rest of us that not even the rich and privileged are immune to interfering council busybodies: when I was there Hector was expecting a visit from North Devon Council inspectors at any moment demanding he tear down the roundhouse. But he reckoned he could handle them. 'I just talk to them, and I think they understand that what goes on here is down to me,' he said. His greatest fear was that the council would decide that any temporary volunteers who happened to be staying on his land at the time of a surprise visit would have to be registered under new multiple occupancy laws and that he will be liable for huge amounts of council tax. Both the payment of council tax and the building of eco-showhomes hold serious lessons for large landowners considering going off-grid.

Hector's plan to take Tapeley off-grid by 2008 is a form of survivalism. Like Dylan Evans, he believes there is a fifty-fifty chance that civilisation will break down in the next decade under the combined weight of rising oil prices, rising sea levels and other side-effects of global warming. He told me he has a collection of sporting crossbows which are merely trophies at the moment, and he will begin to stockpile food when it becomes apparent that disaster is looming. 'We are readying ourselves for when there is no food on the supermarket shelves and have experts in hedgerow herbalism who are not here at the moment but have "booked themselves in" for when the shit hits the fan,' Hector informed me in a handwritten letter some weeks later. 'We also have "warriors" in the wings who will move in as and when.'

He has plans to build six large wind turbines on his land, and intends to spend all the profits advancing interest-free loans to others in the immediate area who want to switch their own domestic supplies to renewable energy. He already has a constant supply of spring water as well as a river. Tapeley has never needed a mains water supply. We went to see the source of the water, below the house in woodland close to a lily pad-covered lake where all was perfectly tranquil except for the occasional croak of a frog. The only slight intrusion into this paradise was the smell of the cesspit, concealed in the bushes somewhere near the lake. But not even that could spoil the bewitching effect of the cool forest and the sound of water running and dripping all around us.

In the afternoon, Fiona, Caitlin and I took a break from Tapeley Park for a different kind of water – a walk along the beach at nearby Instow. I slid the Bus into a parking spot opposite the Commodore Hotel, a 1960s building of such incredible bad taste that it was becoming fashionable again. Caitlin had by this stage of the journey bonded with Olive; they slept curled up together, Caitlin clutching Olive's tail like a security blanket. Now the pair bounded out onto the beach, and Fiona and I set off after them. By the time we caught up they were playing next to a large yacht that had been left behind by the tide. Its keel was buried deep in the sand, which was keeping the boat upright. A jolly-looking lady was staring down at Caitlin from the deck, and after our baby had softened her up I turned the conversation to off-grid living. Sure enough, she lived aboard what is known in the trade as a 'continuous cruiser' with her husband, a marine engineer. They were in the UK for a few months before setting off for Portugal and then the Caribbean. Maureen Jenkins, author of the book *Lone Voyager* about the first female Atlantic crossing, had left her first husband at the age of forty-five and set off to learn how to sail. She had crossed the Atlantic alone, in a different boat, and was more than happy to talk about the technical details of life on board. 'Whenever sailors get together the conversation soon turns to two things – toilets and electrical power,' she told me. After a decade at sea, there was no question the couple would live this way for as long as their health allowed. They had become separated from the landlubbers' life, and they were not going back.

If they could park their yacht on the sand, we could surely park our camper van on the seafront, I decided, so having bid farewell to Hector Christie we spent the next night on the coast at Charmouth, Dorset. The small beach seemed to have the right combination of low security and high beauty. Just beyond the official council car-park several vans were parked on a small patch of hard flat ground. They all disappeared before dark – to camp sites presumably, as by 9 a.m. they were back again. We had no trouble staying all night. At seven the local dog walkers were all about us, and one of them kindly gave us milk for our morning tea. A visitor centre on the other side of the car-park, with toilets and a café, opened promptly at nine.

All our wild camping experiences had been positive and trouble-free. But we had stayed only a night or two. Perhaps it depends on the location, but I began to believe that the main threat to wild camping would be other people coming and joining you if you stayed too long. That would be bound to attract the attention of the landowners. As Pete in his bitumenised trailer had advised, neatness and discretion are essential.

Agricultural co-operative

We set off for nearby Fivepenny Farm at 9 a.m. By ten we were completely lost. It was the only time throughout the whole journey that I regretted my inability to navigate the GPS devices. Somewhere we had taken the wrong road, and now I was trying to turn from one narrow side road into an even narrower lane. With Caitlin bawling in the seat between us, I shunted the Bus back and forth. There was a solitary house on the corner and an elderly couple slowly emerged, disturbed by the roaring of the engine. Their wearily practised instruction made me realise I was not the first driver to get stuck here, and with their help I finally coaxed the Bus around the corner.

It was then that we heard the sound of shattering glass. I jerked my head round to find a road sign poking through the broken rear side window bearing the legend 'Whitchurch Canonicorum 1 mile'. It was one of those traditional narrow white village signs that symbolise the cosy, orderly regime of the English countryside. In every other vehicle I have ever driven, road signs are out there, separate, for information only, not part of the obstacle course. I just hadn't included the height of the Bus in my steering calculations. The shards of glass were all over the floor at the back. Thank goodness for the Electrolux mini vacuum cleaner, part of my panoply of PR freebies. Praying that its cordless battery would not run down, I set to work. Half an hour later, with no more than a few cut fingers, I had transferred every fragment I could into a series of plastic bags. There were bound to be a few more shards lurking under the seats where only Caitlin could find them, so Fiona insisted I double- and triple-check every cranny where glass may have flown. Then, under the watchful eye of the octogenarians, I had somehow to reverse out of the situation I (or they) had engineered, make my way back up the lane and turn around in a field with an unlocked gate.

We arrived at Fivepenny Farm to find Jyoti Fernandes and her husband Dai Saltmarsh hard at work in the fields. They had a rush order from a local restaurant: two and a half kilos of mixed salad leaves in time for lunch. In 1988 Jyoti joined the Tinker's Bubble commune which had been co-founded by Simon Fairlie, but tired of the communal ethos after five years, by which time she and Simon had become firm friends and business partners, co-publishing *The Land* magazine and running a planning advice service they called Chapter 7 (www.tlio.org.uk/chapter7/). Together with another family, she and Dai

Jyoti – now this is what I call having it all.

bought forty-two acres near Bridport in Dorset on which they proceeded to demonstrate everything they had learned in their years of
campaigning for the right of individuals to live ecological, self-sufficient
lives in the countryside. They started farming within a few weeks of
arriving, then built their cabin. When the council finally turned up they
had their planning application ready to submit the same week. They
easily won planning approval after a fight that went all the way to a
public inquiry – as they had expected it would. The inspector's decision,
which granted them a four-year temporary permission, was everything
they wanted. (See chapter 7 for a more detailed look at the process
they went through.)

Three years later Jyoti and her family and the other family were off-
grid and making a living from the farm, and had just won some EU
money to start an agricultural co-operative in the field outside their
house. They were planning to spend the money on a barn-cum-eco-pro-
cessing store for produce being made by other smallholders in the area;
it was due to be up by April 2007, and I have no doubt that that part
of their business will thrive as well. A spin-off from the off-grid movement is a new approach to farm economics, possibly even the rescuing
of subsistence farming and its restoration as part of the British way of life.

I would see Jyoti and many more small farmers and permacultur-
alists at my next and last stop, the eco-community's largest annual
get-together.

Big Green Gathering

I arrived in the area late at night, two days before the official opening.
Fiona, Caitlin and Olive were on the train back to London, giving me
the opportunity to do some writing in the back of the Bus. The gathering had already begun: tents, tipis, buses and vans were massed on the
site overlooking rolling countryside at the top of the Cheddar Gorge.
The gates had closed at 10 p.m. so there was nothing for it but to park
in a lay-by until morning. The nearest already had a few vans, so I
moved on to the next, well away from the road and, I thought, invisible
in the gathering dark. No sooner had I closed the curtains and begun
to cook a meal than the bed shook from the vibrations of what
sounded like a super-sized diesel truck that had pulled up alongside.

Was it Croissant Neuf, I wondered, the travelling solar-powered circus, or one of the other renewable energy entertainers like Groovy Movie? After a minute or two the engine was still running. Did these people have no consideration for others?

I pulled on some shoes and bundled out to try to politely hint to whoever it was that they weren't alone in the lay-by. A strangely dressed man was in the driver's cab revving the engine. As he climbed out to greet me I saw he was wearing a shawl over a hoodie and a kind of Indian skirt.

'On your way to Big Green?' I asked.

'Yes.' He smiled beatifically. 'There's seven of us. We're from the Hare Krishna Temple in Watford.'

I hurried back into the Bus. After a while the engine was turned off, only to be replaced by the most unspiritual muttering and cursing as the Krishna seven put up their tents in the lay-by in the dark.

I was woken up early the next morning by tuneless chanting. I stayed put for as long as possible. When I did eventually emerge for a pee I thought I would have some privacy between the door and the steep rock face of the Cheddar Gorge, but high above me a lone Krishna was sitting cross-legged on a little outcrop, gazing down as he thought his sublime thoughts. I had my pee anyway and returned to the Bus, averting my eyes from his. It took about thirty seconds for me to stow my stuff and hop into the driver's seat. As a chorus of 'Hare, Hare' swelled behind me, I pulled away.

Fifteen minutes later I was in the Sustainable Housing field at the Big Green Gathering. The Bus, which had seemed so hip and remarkable on the streets of Hackney, was in its element with vehicles of every shape and shade, from a tiny Renault baker's van to a Volvo hearse. There were dozens of giant Mercedes, Bedford horseboxes, a pink Dodge, several converted mobile libraries, and so many horse-drawn vehicles that they had been given their own field. The hundreds who live in horse-drawn wagons tend to be political in at least one sense: they are off the grid of state control. They need no paperwork for their vehicles. It is difficult to remove yourself from all government records, especially if you have children, but not impossible. Many of them have no passport and neither claim dole nor pay tax; they sell craft items for cash or work for their food.

Paul and Susie were there, complete with their blue gypsy caravan. Clive Menhenett from Magrec was already setting up his panels to offer solar cell phone charging at a pound a time. I was given a spot near Jyoti Fernandes and Simon Fairlie, whom I had last seen in his scythe store in Petherton, Somerset. On one side of me were some interns from the Centre for Alternative Technology, and a yurt incongruously representing the Brighton Earthship Centre, which specialises in building houses out of used tyres; on my other side was a home-based eco-bakery from Taunton. A few tents further away, in the permaculture area, were half the population of the Allaleigh and Steward Wood communes. Marcus Tribe and Sarah Harvey turned up at the weekend, and they introduced me to Avril from Kingshill, one of the lowest profile and most successful of the eco-communities. Avril's boyfriend Hedge is one of the master builders of the off-grid movement. He can put up a twenty-foot-high A-frame timber structure in a day and a half for under £10,000.

I had to call on Hedge's help, but not for building work. Two days of playing music, typing my notes and running the twelve-volt lights had drained both the batteries completely. Hedge started the big van he uses as a mobile workshop and scaffold and drove it over to me. 'It isn't a festival till I've given someone a jump start,' he remarked kindly. It is probably a *faux pas* to need a jump-start at a solar-powered festival, but also perhaps the best place for it.

Andy Hope from the Croissant Neuf circus, whom I had met in London when I was beginning my research, was out in the middle of the same field with three vans stuffed full of solar-powered batteries and twelve-volt amplifiers. His job was to provide light and sound for the biggest venue on the five-acre site, a blue and red striped tent capable of holding an audience of a thousand. The day after the festival, the Big Green Gathering featured on BBC's *Newsnight*. The long report included an interview with Andy, who stated that he could power an entire stage lighting rig on 240 watts – less than it takes to run a toaster.

I wandered around, meeting old friends and making new acquaintances, and inviting them to drop by the Bus for coffee. 'It's the Off-grid Bus,' I told them, with a surge of pride at my new identity. Off-grid Nick in the Off-grid Bus. And that's the name that finally stuck. I was inundated with my own invitations to visit more off-grid homes, and second homes. I decided they'd have to wait for the sequel. I had travelled nearly 5,000 miles in two months, and, two flat batteries aside, the Off-grid Bus had taken its bumps and knocks without any major complaints. It was time I scooted home to recharge my own batteries after the long adventure and reflect more on what I had learned.

There was to be one final hurdle. It was 11 a.m. when I arrived back in London and, exhausted, I took another wrong turning and then reversed my absurdly long Off-grid Bus into a huge silver-sided lorry, leaving a large hole in its side. The furious driver leapt out and raced towards me swearing noisily in Italian. I tried to calm him down, but he shouted more loudly, and beckoned someone carrying a clipboard who may have been his driving assistant. I gave them my insurance details and the assistant wrote the words down slowly as I spelled them out. I apologised to the driver, offered him money, anything if I could just get him to stop shouting. With hand gestures and more shouting he ordered me to stay where I was. As his clipboard-carrying assistant watched me suspiciously, the driver disappeared behind his van, per-haps to interview a witness or get some friends to come and sort me out. I would never know, because as soon as he vanished, I started the engine and slowly edged forward. This was the second time someone had stationed themselves in front of my wheels to prevent me from moving. I was becoming accustomed to it, and besides, I was on home turf here. The assistant shouted and banged on the bonnet, but I kept going. I screeched around the next corner and made for home. The Italian would call the police of course, though I had given my details so this was not a police matter. I knew the repair would be expensive and my insurance premiums would at least double next year. But I was too happy to be home to mind. As I drove I remembered the horse-drawn field at Big Green. With no road tax, no insurance and no MOT, the chances they would have to deal with a situation like this were minimal.

The biggest lesson I'd learned as a result of my travels was that the transition to off-grid living would be more difficult than I had imagined in the warm glow of my centrally heated London home. Just making the emotional leap to embrace the idea turned out to be the easier part of the process; as it turned from an exploratory trip into the beginnings of a way of life, all sorts of practical problems presented themselves. Finding land was the most complex. Choosing your set of criteria is partly common sense and partly about coming to terms with the fact that not all your needs will be met. And once you have the will and you have the land (or the means to live a mobile life in a van or boat), you still need the expertise to build a shelter, or the money to have one built for you, plus you must bring in water and energy to your new off-grid home, not to mention earn a living.

I had at least confirmed to myself that I would be able to make money on the road. As a writer and documentary-maker, my most valuable off-grid items were the camera battery charger and the 3G Internet card for my laptop. From researching the price of solar panels to mapping my route to reading the online newspapers alone in my van at night, the Vodafone signal was my lifeline. Near cities it was a broadband connection, but out in the country it worked as an ordinary dial-up modem.

As a human being, perhaps the most important tool of all was the one Ross had handed me in Hay-on-Wye – a spade. If you can dig your own mini toilet wherever you are without feeling queasy, then you have arrived at a different place in your attitude towards the world. I don't know why, but somehow it was digging those holes that made me feel free.

The common thread through many of the stories on my travels was of problems with neighbours or the local council. Not everyone wants to embrace the entire local community, like Nigel at Hill Holt, or become invisible, like Judy of the Woods. Winning over the opposition – politics, in other words – turns out to be key to a happy and peaceful life off-grid. But before you can get to the stage of winning them over, you must have neighbours in the first place.

It was an open secret at the Big Green Gathering that everyone who did not already live off-grid was looking for land to launch every shade of green project. In a year's time many hundreds, perhaps thousands of the campers in those fields will have found their land and teamed up with others, and will be in the act of getting started. Others will still be thinking about it and looking for a way to test the idea with a first small step. A festival is one way of doing that, but with 20,000 people queuing for the loo at the same time it hardly mirrors reality. What is needed is an off-grid training course, one that takes recruits through a gradually mounting series of off-grid experiences, starting with a few days.

Or perhaps even a single night . . .

5

Dipping In,
Dipping Off

*Treat the Earth well. It was not given to you by your parents.
It was loaned to you by your children.*

Traditional Kenyan proverb

I T'S A WARM SEPTEMBER evening in Kensington Park Gardens, Notting Hill. The ornate Georgian houses are the icing on the frosted layer-cake of the property-owning classes; huge homes, each with stone steps leading up to a raised ground floor. Through the front door and down the back stairs are kitchens stretching forty feet or so towards the garden, with every spending option exercised: slate tiles, underfloor heating, the obligatory Aga, marble counters, maplewood cupboards, breakfast bar, dining table . . . The styles range from formal US invest-ment banker through funky metropolitan to Moroccan and English Country, but whatever the design, at the back of each kitchen are French windows leading from the house into the garden.

It is what is through the backs of these gardens that makes these £3 million homes among the most desirable in London – another gate into a shared, private garden square, one of a dozen or so in the area, each square protected by the houses around it, an acre or two of prime property laid to lawn with ancient trees, guaranteeing that the children cannot stray very far. The residents are bankers, writers, recording artistes, management consultants and their spouses and children.

And what are they all doing on this particular Saturday? They are having an off-grid evening. Only they call it a 'sleep-out'. It's been organised by one of the residents, a forty-three-year-old who retired from Goldman Sachs and who now spends his time looking after his sons and planning his next financial coup. There's the singer Annie Lennox with her kid – she's in charge of the barbecue. Here's a senior BBC executive, and a nanny helping a small child put up a baby tipi. Each family has pitched a tent in the private garden. The guy from Goldman Sachs has the best one, with two bedrooms – but then he really is planning to spend the whole night out there with his kids. Some of the other parents will slope off in the early hours to their perfectly sprung memory-foam mattresses while their children are treated to the full off-grid experience. 'It's all rather American,' splutters one of the parents, some kind of a media consultant.

For some, the off-grid life is as transitory as a sleep-out; for others it's a permanent decision. Whatever your reasons, being off-grid need not be a lifetime's commitment, nor even a full-time commitment. It can simply be a device to pull back from the frenetic grind of urban living for a few months, or just a cheap holiday for a fortnight or a weekend. You don't have to be rich or poor, eco or survivalist. You don't *have* to be or do anything. I found that anybody can go off-grid at any time, and go back on-grid again whenever they want.

Mobile Gadgets

I set off on my travels in the Off-grid Bus as if for the rest of my life, with an array of mobile gadgets and home comforts. But I quickly shed many of them, either because they didn't work or I didn't need them.

First to go was the double cigar lighter socket, the acquisition I had originally been the most proud of. It blew a fuse the first time I tried to use it, and I quickly learned to steward my various battery-driven gadgets, charging them whenever I was on the move, one in the front cigar lighter, the other connected to the solar-powered battery in the back. The stills camera, the radio, Caitlin's baby steering wheel and the numerous satnav devices I was still trying to master were powered by rechargeable AA batteries, and I found the Energiser fast charger was the best for the job, when I was on the move and using engine power. It charged four batteries at once, but it quickly drained the solar-powered battery when the van was stationary.

As explained in the previous chapter, due to the elusiveness of Bert Hagley it was Piet Defoe who finally eco-pimped my ride. My first lesson, of course, was in the use of vegetable oil instead of diesel. The next reform Piet introduced was to remove the high-energy-use halogen lights that came with the Bus and put clusters of LED lights in their place. LEDs (light-emitting diodes) are often used in bicycle lights. These clusters are specifically designed for camping or other low-energy uses. They fitted into the same socket as the conventional bulbs they were intended to replace, were almost as bright, and used less power. Many

Piet pimps my ride.

off-grid homes use LED lights for the same reason.

But Piet's main modification was fitting the fifty-watt solar panel. As he worked, other members of the commune stopped by, ribbing him, telling him he was hooking the system together wrongly, questioning his knowledge and expertise. A cold feeling stole over me. I am such an ignoramus when it comes to in-car technology. I suddenly realised I had no idea whether Piet was a Walter Mitty repair man or someone with a natural talent for everything electrical and mechanical. I was 500 miles from home in a strange, a very strange, commune with a man who could easily wreck the electrical system in the Bus with a single mistake. I confess I lost faith in his assurances. But by this time I was in too deep. I could only go to sleep (in the dark because the power was all disconnected) and wait until morning. My fears turned out to be unfounded. By the time he finished, well into the next day, Piet had transformed my Bus into the self-contained home-office I had always wanted. His handiwork proved completely sound, and the total cost was about £300 – slightly more than half the market rate. Once I had road-tested the set-up for a few weeks, I rang Piet to confess my doubts and thank him again. I should have had more faith in him all along. This was after all the person who had introduced me to the South African medical freezer chest, designed to keep drugs at a constant low temperature in the hottest summer conditions using only 2.5 amps of power – a third of my conventional camping fridge. Now I could work comfortably and effectively while on tour. My van was my office as well as my bedsit.

I also learned something about myself. I was clearly not trying to simplify my life given all the clobber I was carting around with me. So what was I trying to do? Find a new way to live? That was part of it. Experiment with new technology? Yup. Live a cheaper, freer life?

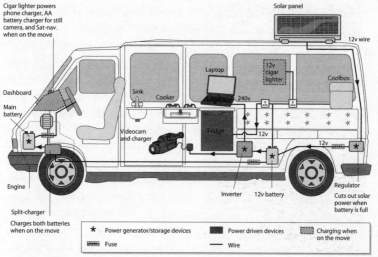

Plan of the van.

Definitely. With few overheads and no fixed agenda I was under no financial pressure, but as had been the case in Majorca, I still needed to earn a living of some sort. And my new battery meant I could listen to the radio, run two mobile phones and broadband Internet, charge camera batteries, and with the twelve-volt lighting stay up working or partying late into the night if I chose.

By the end of my journey, I had learned that you can live off-grid in complete comfort, and at an affordable price. You have to change your behaviour, but only a bit. You have to be aware of your power and water consumption – turn just about everything else off if you want to run the washing machine, for example. But that is better than not having a washing machine, and less effort than doing the washing yourself. (There was no washing machine in the Off-grid Bus, and no need for one.) And I certainly learned which gadgets were worth having and which were not. The Freeplay torch was superb in an emergency. It is always when you need them most that you find the torch batteries are dead. And how do you change batteries in the dark? Winding the Freeplay torch for thirty seconds gave several minutes of adequate light or half a minute of bright light, from near-everlasting LED bulbs. The Energiser head-mounted torch was even better: it appeared to need no batteries, and had an ultra-powerful beam for walking around fields or country paths at night. But the Freeplay radio was simply annoying; it needed to be wound up far too often to be enjoyable. I switched back to my old Roberts, with four rechargeable AA batteries. I charged the batteries via the inverter plugged into the main cigarette lighter when I was on the move. The Energiser battery charger did the job in just twenty minutes but was very power hungry so it was best to use it while the journey was charging the battery anyway.

My two phones were from Orange and Vodafone. Up a mountainside searching for an obscure destination, if one signal died there was always a chance that the other service would still be running. Of the two, Vodafone had better coverage. And having two phones guaranteed my ability to manage the complex logistics of my journey while in remote locations. I was always able to make appointments and change them en route (although that equally meant I was rarely out of touch and completely off-grid). I used the computer and the Vodafone 3G card to look up my destination on Google (www.google.co.uk/maps) and then transferred the map reference to a giant plasticated road map pinned to the ceiling of the Bus so I could keep my eye on the big picture.

I am not a creature of habit, so although I sometimes stayed up all night, I was just as likely to turn in shortly after dark and wake at 5.30 a.m. like a proper country farmer. Then I made coffee on the gas hob with a standard Italian aluminium stove-top espresso maker, the kind with a black Bakelite handle. Simple, effective, and perfect coffee every time. The cooker did not use much gas, but a refill was expensive.

In cold weather, the Eberspacher D3LC compact air heater kicked in, and for the price of a little extra diesel I could stay warm as toast in the sitting-room-style interior. Some enthusiasts buy Renault diesel buses just for the heater and transfer it to their own van.

Van People

Just like me, every van dweller has his or her own preferences and practices, both simple and complex. I came across all sorts on my travels, especially at the Big Green Gathering. That was where I met

Daav, outside a tented vegetarian restaurant where he was head chef for the duration of the festival. He had been van-dwelling for thirty years and has converted three vans in his time on the road, the most recent being a twenty-four-foot-long Mercedes 608. He earns his money from occasional carpentry wherever he happens to be.

Daav (van dwellers rarely give out their surnames) learned early on what Henry Thoreau concluded from his time in the woods, that the best way of life is simplicity. He had slowly pared down the contents of his vans over the years, and had long since scrapped his hot water boiler and tank, though he still washes every day, using a portable camping shower filled with water heated on the stove. He insists on staying clean and smart whatever the surrounding conditions – or at least as smart as you can be when you are fifty-one years old, five feet three inches tall and wear a multi-coloured woollen cap over Rasta dreadlocks. 'I smoke cannabis, but that doesn't mean I have to be lethargic and messy,' he told me as he showed me round the perfectly constructed interior of his van, with cabinets and shelves made from wood he had scavenged over the years. He still uses the same Calor gas oven he bought second-hand in 1972, transferring it from van to van. 'The simpler it is, the less there is to go wrong,' he reasons. It's good advice for a would-be off-gridder.

In a nearby Dodge van, painted bright pink, I found Jim who had a different approach to life. He was messy, he did not shower every day, and he did not, as far as I could tell, smoke any dope. His most important gadgets were a wood-burning stove in winter; a thirty-litre cool box from Halfords, bought in a sale for £30; a dashboard radio/CD player for music and BBC World Service late at night; and a ninety-six-watt wind turbine, which he demounts when travelling. The turbine, a Rutland 913 designed for marine use, is mounted on a metal pole that slides into metal rings welded to the back of the Dodge. A wire runs out of the turbine, under the van and in through a hatch to four big 220-amp Elecsol batteries – not because he needs that much power for himself, but because under the name Sunny Jim's Solar-powered Cabaret he sometimes earns money running the power supply at small festivals. He also has a 110-amp battery for his own personal use.

On the roof of the Dodge there are four 80W Kyocera polycrystalline panels which charge the storage battery bank and one 75W BP Solarex polycrystalline panel which can be switched to charge either the

Sunny Jim about to hop inside.

storage bank or his personal battery. Jim's batteries can power a sound system and lights for an audience of up to 500. If the batteries are full, it's essential for the turbine to have a 'dump load' – somewhere to send the power it generates. The cool box serves that purpose and Jim takes it apart every so often to clean the motor, which will then run for years. The previous one lasted five years. In the end the wires melted from overuse rather than the motor giving out, which is what normally happens.

Off-Grid Tourism and Second Homes

Jim introduced me to Theo Hopkins, a grizzle-headed ex-public school dropout who 'grew up in houses near woodlands' and taught furniture production and design. He 'had bells and long hair' when he was in his twenties, so it must have felt like coming home in more ways than one when he bought his fifty-acre wood in 1988.

Theo's problems started when the local council got involved soon after issues with the neighbours arose. Although they were running a relaxation centre, they were anything but relaxed about Theo living in his bender. Eventually, in 2001, he decided he would take the easier way out and go back on the grid, partly because of the neighbours but also because 'I had some money in the bank and I just made this financial decision that I had to get into the housing market – the prices were just rising so fast. I was forced onto that ladder, or else I would lose out. I could have bought a house and rented it out but I don't want to be a landlord.' Now Theo lives in his house in Devon, sixty miles from the bender, and near his current girlfriend. He only uses his woodland for short breaks. It's become a weekender bender.

It is, as he points out, legal to spend up to twenty-eight days a year there, for the purpose of maintaining the land, which can entail as little as cutting a few branches from trees and making a few fires. He has two white-tarp dome-shaped benders, which he invited me to visit any time I was passing, whether he was there or not. 'It's very nice when your bender is new and white,' he said. 'It glows white at night time if you leave a lamp on. In the day you are surrounded by this whiteness.'

Theo is deeply aware of the moral issues; there are apparent contradictions in being an environmentalist and having a second home. Many of the commune dwellers I met were hostile to the concept of a weekend home off-grid. But the fact is that second homes are a part of the British way of life. 250,000 of us own second homes inside the UK, and another 400,000 have a place abroad. Surely a second home consisting of no more than an acre of land and a bender tucked away in some trees is better than taking up a house that could be a home for someone in need. To me, off-grid second homes of any sort are easier to justify than full-fledged grid-connected country houses or cottages.

Theo has nothing in his bender except a small camping stove and two mattresses. There is a wide stream running through the land, which gives him all the water he needs. When he lived there, he would heat a full kettle on the wood-burner, and have a shower that way. Pete, the ex-soldier I met in Scotland, lived all year round with little more than that. True, his bitumenised trailer was made of rigid materials rather than canvas, and his Calor gas bottles were several sizes bigger than the ones Theo uses. The only other difference was the soldier's alleged ex-SAS bombproof underground toilet, with connected cesspit. Theo just has a plain old hole in the ground, to which he adds a bit of earth every time he uses it, which is not a problem since he is rarely there. 'Every three years I plant a tree on top of the hole and start a new one,' he told me.

Theo arrives for his weekend breaks in a car laden with supplies, and takes them away again when he leaves: water from home for his dicky stomach, 'duvet, blankets, whisky, wine and music, food and tea'. His favourite visit is about three days, long enough to slough off the irritations of village life with its mini traffic jams, nosy neighbours and the tedious admin that falls to everyone who owns a few assets. But three days is not so long that he tires of the dampness and the lack of a flushing toilet. The other benefits are 'no council tax, no insurance, no utility bills, and no oil'. It cost Theo about £300 in materials to move in, and nothing after that. 'I have a watering can for a shower, and a saw and an axe for the wood. I keep it all in a little shed, and I've never had anything nicked.'

I'd heard from dozens of others who have off-grid second homes, I'd met many more at Big Green, and of course that is how I started down this road myself. Yes, it is something of a cop-out if you have a nice safe grid-connected home to go back to, and that is why I restricted my research mainly to full-time off-gridders. But I doubt if I will ever go full-time myself when I can sample the delights of so many different off-grid locations. When I feel like it, a few hours in the Bus will take me somewhere safe and tranquil, and I can go home again when it all gets too much. I learned on my travels that I did not need to own land to set up temporary camp in the Off-grid Bus, especially now I had a host of new friends who, like Theo, had invited me to drop in whenever I was passing. It felt like the national equivalent of the Freedom of the City of London – a licence to stay anywhere, any time.

But even if you set off without a network of friends, it is fairly easy to find spots for a few days or weeks. In the country, I found I could ask almost anyone who looked friendly, in a pub or in the street, and they would advise on the best farmer to approach, or a spot where you may not even need permission. You quickly learn the art of chatting to strangers when you are on the road. One evening when Caitlin, Fiona and I had failed to reach our destination by dusk, I just stopped outside a village pub, and the first old boy I asked told me I could park in his neighbour's garden as they were away. If there is nowhere that is actually free, you will get a positive response from many small farms by offering a fiver for a night's stay in a field. In my experience, most of them also offer a cold water tap and an outside loo. The main tip is to start searching in the morning. Do not wait until it is almost dark. That's all very well in a camper van, you might say, with a wife and a baby, which villagers would find reassuring; some guy turning up alone with only a tent might get a much frostier reception. But I still think the same principles apply, at least when you are not planning to stay long. Friendly and open enquiries will lead to friendly and open advice.

Yes, it is the flexibility of the off-grid life that has always appealed to me. Ross Kennard-Davis near Hay on Wye provides a perfect example. Recently, Ross has not been spending as much time on his forty acres of quarry as he did when I first met him. After years of suffering through freezing winters, first in his caravan and later in his half-finished house, Ross met a girl. Shaking his head in disbelief at his own predicament, he explained to me that Holly didn't drive, couldn't stand the cold, and found the lack of proper toiletary, washing and cooking facilities quite unacceptable. If he wanted the relationship to continue, he had to stay at her place. He still comes out to his spread every week, though, to quarry the sandstone and send it to the customers, and, if he is lucky, to get some work done on his house. But it's fair to say that progress has been slow since he met Holly, who has at least begun to take driving lessons.

But the great thing is, it doesn't matter. The land is not going to disappear. It is not costing Ross anything; there is not even any council tax since his house is still unfinished. The Poles have gone back to Poland and Ross works the quarry on his own now. 'I made a bit of a leap forward in learning how to make bigger tiles,' he told me on the phone. Now Ross can make £500 a day without help, which means his financial future is secure. At some point he will go back to living there full-time – hopefully with Holly.

Bartering, Bushcraft and Foraging

If, unlike Ross, you have only limited opportunities to earn cash, or you just fancy indulging in a real adventure, you can still go a long way as an off-gridder by learning about and practising skills such as bartering, bushcraft and foraging.

Patrick Scott, the former close protection officer in Iraq now ensconced as head of security for a large estate in Northumberland, typified the openness I found almost everywhere I went. After we met in the pub, he became my guide and showed me around the alternative world of country barter. After work, Patrick hunts, fishes and forages in the local fields. Every Friday he arrives at the same local pub with the fruits of his week's extra-curricular activities, and pops down the tailgate on his 4×4, alongside other regulars. 'It's all done casually over the phone during the week, and then you turn up for happy hour and swap everything around,' he said. 'Some of it is just for favours at some time in the future,' he added, but there are also complex deals involving more than two parties. 'Last week I took twenty brace of partridge and swapped it for phenomenal amounts of everything you can imagine – a huge carrier bag of fresh beetroots, a promise of some elderflower wine and some chutneys. There's a deer coming next week to fill up the freezer. I'll get some fresh bread on Saturday made by Trevor who lives in the village. A spring lamb will cost me a few fish. We have had some salmon the past few weeks. A nine-pound line-caught wild salmon is worth a lot in these parts.' Patrick had also been picking sloe berries (used to make sloe gin), and pickling the beet-root he'd picked up.

That is the way it has always been in the country, and I pray it always stays so, allowing romantic figures like Patrick to stay off the grid of roads and supermarkets, even if they happen to have power coming to their house these days. But armies of tax men and accountants who could be tracking down real fraudsters appear determined to stamp out old traditions such as these. 'It's all very innocent and rustic and encourages a paper-free environment, but this can underpin what can only amount to potential income tax, corporation tax or VAT non-disclosure, or even fraud,' accountant Julie Butler, FCA, told Taxation Web, a website for accountants. 'That might sound harsh but it is the hard fact. The dream of a paperless rustic society has to be shattered.'

An accountant speaks. But is anybody listening? I don't support tax dodging, but do we really want to take another bash at the intricate fabric of the countryside?

'Clearly the service or product provided must be at market value,' Ms Butler went on. 'A "contemporaneous" sales invoice must be made with sequential sales/fee invoice number and date. The business records must show how the invoice was settled, perhaps via . . . the settlement of a purchase ledger invoice.' This is fair enough if you are talking about the village butcher doing a swap with the fishmonger, but does it apply to every private citizen who bags a few partridge?

Barter is not exclusive to country communities, of course; it happens in cities and suburbs as well. Painting and decorating work in exchange for motor repairs, for example, or building work in return for legal services. It is just simpler and more direct to work for the things you need rather than to work for money which you then exchange for what you need. Not that you need very much living off-grid. Bills are lower, and there may be no rent; council tax, food and transport are the main expenses. If you live off-grid and barter, you can work less hard for the same standard of living as your on-grid equivalent. And that equals a better quality of life.

Bartering is something you can just do, but bushcraft you must learn, and it too can be beneficial to the off-gridder – not least in terms of providing you with the know-how to use nature's larder and find something to barter with in the first place. I have no affinity with the skills required to own land. From building walls and fences to planting or pruning trees, harvesting and basic DIY, I was a complete non-starter.

I had already been trying to learn some bushcraft when I met

Robin outside the Land Matters kitchen tent.

Robin at Land Matters in Allaleigh. I was looking for a more spiritual approach than I could find on Ray Mears's popular TV series, and Robin was the perfect teacher. He showed me practical skills similar to the ones Mears features – making shelters armed with only a double-bladed knife; skinning a deer, making a plate and a cup from its hide; making fire by friction – but his philosophy worked for me on a deeper level. It was a mix of American Indian wisdom and British countryside common sense. I could not, of course, do some of the things I have seen Robin do, like walk slowly and quietly up to within a few inches of a pheasant. Nor could I survive in the wild by identifying the numerous edible plants and herbs. Conversely, Robin could not survive in a city centre. 'I can't tell which direction the wind is in, I can't hear the birds; I get horribly disorientated,' he told me as we walked through the water meadow at the bottom of the Land Matters holding.

How to build a shelter

In the 'sacred order of survival', as the American Indians call it, shelter is top of the list. You can survive a few days without water, and longer without food, but just a few hours without shelter in extreme conditions spells certain death. In the wilderness, then, the first priority is to build a shelter, however crude this may be. After I had finished my off-grid tour of Britain, I did one other quick trip, to a bushcraft weekend training camp in Sussex. During my weekend at Trackways, Thomas Schorr-Kohn led us out to a dense piece of wood to show us how to do it.

First we had to choose the right site: it needs to be near a tree with a low fork (or anything else that can be the main support of the structure); it should be at the top of any incline to prevent rainwater trickling in; the ground should be as flat as possible; and the shelter should blend in to the surroundings – so build it inside a wood or copse rather than next to a solitary tree. The possibility of snakes was something else to consider, but that threat is absent in certain environments, and in a winter survival scenario.

Next we cast around for a nine-foot sapling, sliced off a seven-foot length using the serrated side of a double-edged knife, then stripped the spindly branches. The design of the shelter is simple: a low-pitched roof with the prepared central branch stuck into the fork of a tree at roughly waist height, the other end sloping down to the ground. Now we had a sloping branch as the central support against which to lean other branches on either side. These form a kind of rib cage for the structure. Without a knife, or preferably a knife and a small fold-up saw, you must rely on your hands and feet to break the wood into the right lengths and strip the leaves.

Once the rib cage is complete, the canopy goes on – wider leaves first, such as ferns, bracken and docks, then moss, and even some dried earth and grass. The covering must be a minimum of a foot thick both to keep in body warmth and to keep out the rain. Starting at the bottom and building upwards reduces the chance of water working its way in, though in heavy rain there will be leaks which you have to patch up by placing more material on top.

Once we had finished the shelter, there was just room for a thin couple and a baby to crawl inside onto the bed of leaves and bracken. It took six of us an hour to build it, and that was in ideal midsummer conditions. On my own it would take at least six hours. In winter, with a bit of rain for company, it would be tough, but not impossible.

With shelter established, the next priorities are food, water and fire. In summer you may not need fire as the nights are warmer and there will be any number of plants you can eat raw. But in winter, with a baby to feed, fire is essential for warmth and to boil tough nettle leaves or cook any of the other plants you might find. A lighter or a box of matches will see you through a few days; otherwise you will need to make a fire using friction. This is a simple technique but difficult to achieve. I shan't describe it here as there are plenty of books on the subject, from the SAS survival manual to Ray Mears's own.

Now that I had a shelter, and some way of making fire, I was more than halfway towards having all I needed. Food was the next item, with Caitlin the priority. The day I spent living off the land with Robin was a satisfying experience, but only because of my guide. I lacked the knowledge to identify plants, and that means I need to take with me a book with good colour photographs. Even skilled bushcrafters find it hard to survive more than a few days in a wood in winter because there is so little to forage. 'You could survive a winter if you had the autumn to gather your nuts and seeds,' said Robin, 'but after November, when the mushroom season ends, you'll be looking for birds and small animals, mainly rabbit.' Finally, I need water. In winter I am unlikely to have difficulty, but I will still want to store it and boil it. In high summer, finding water becomes more of a chore.

So my Crisis Bag, kept ready for any bushcraft eventuality, is filling up: food and a water bottle, a thermal blanket, a strong double-bladed knife, a small cooking pot, a book of colour pictures of edible plants, a reliable cigarette lighter, and fuel.

I treated Thomas Schorr-Kohn's hunting and tracking lesson as a bit of a game when I visited his course, but thinking about it in the context of actual survival, and having to protect Caitlin in the event she was with me, brought home its importance. The part of the lesson I will always be thankful for concerned awareness and the need to use all the senses to the full – smell and hearing as well as sight. And the latter can be extended far beyond its existing confines using a technique called owl vision.

When walking down a street, your natural inclination is to fix your

The basic structure of a bushcraft shelter.

eyes on a point in the middle distance. Owl vision makes you aware of what is happening on the periphery of your vision as well as in front. Start by facing straight ahead and spreading your arms out at shoulder level. Then bring your arms around so you can just glimpse a hand out of the corner of each eye. That is your entire field of vision defined. Now you need to keep watching everything in that field of vision equally rather than fixing on one point or another and being only dimly aware of what is happening on the periphery.

The first time I tried owl vision, also known as wide-angle vision, it was like a light going on in my brain. It is quite simply a very powerful technique for projecting yourself outside your own head, your own space and your own concerns. It is as though you become more a part of the rest of the world; you feel and experience your surroundings more intensely, directly and freshly. As you move around, becoming more used to this new way of seeing, the exhilarating, invigorating feeling and extra dimension of awareness do not diminish.

I use wide-angle vision all the time now. It's just as valid in the city as it is out among nature, and every time I do it I experience the same joyful, almost childlike lift in the spirits, a widening of the eyes and a sharpening of all the senses. (I cannot claim it improved my prowess as a hunter, but I do bump into far more friends as I walk around my area of London.)

The rise in sensory awareness encompasses the sense of smell, the sense we normally rely upon least. Covering up your human smell if you are hunting, or perhaps hiding from other humans, could be the difference between happiness and misery, if not life or death. Woodsmoke kills human scent, as do crushed leaves or a handful of earth rubbed on the body (and on any traps you set).

As well as disguising your smell, you need to conceal yourself as you move. Camouflage does not have to be the conventional khaki to render you invisible. The most important thing to consider is clothes that hide or disguise your body outline. Think cloaks, or if you don't have a cloak, a blanket might do. And they should be quiet clothes, in both senses of the word: mix muted colours (there are no single colours in nature) and make sure there are no tinkling zips attached.

It's essential to avoid giving yourself away through the noise you make in a wood. The final part of my bushcraft education was learning how to walk like a fox – a high-stepping, light-footed padding through the undergrowth. The main trick is to land each foot on the outside edge of the sole and then roll over onto the ball of the foot while maintaining wide-angle vision, staying aware of where your next foot will fall as well as of everything else in the vicinity. You need to move very quietly, and once you have mastered that, you need to learn to move very slowly, which is crucial when it comes to creeping up on an animal unnoticed. It looks almost comical when you see someone doing it, but it is very difficult. I kept practising long after I had departed the weekend course but I still cannot slip quietly through the woods like Thomas or Robin while keeping my eyes on the 180-degree scene around me.

With these simple techniques I feel much more a part of the land rather than being intimidated by it. I am not claiming I would thrive on a few days in the wilderness, but the tips I learned mean I will make a better attempt than would have been possible a year ago.

The foraging expedition with Robin in particular opened my eyes to a new way of being. As we meandered along we found dozens of edible plants within the boundaries of Land Matters. With scavenging, a little poaching and perhaps some roadkill, anyone can live for free off the land from April to October. The English countryside is a profusion of edible and medicinal herbs and plants – if you know what you are looking at. Sceptics say the medicinal properties are all just folklore; I see it as ancient wisdom. And although I had no need for any of the medicines, I did eat everything Robin told me to that day with no ill effects. The stand-out stars of the menu were the honeysuckle flowers – slightly crunchy and tasting of sweet nectar. The flowers, herbs and plants we encountered on that one day in Allaleigh are listed in the box that follows.

Edible Plants, Leaves and Roots

Primrose. Sweet dessert plant. Only eat when you see yellow leaves.

Nettle. Drop in water at night and imbibe the next morning as a power drink, instead of coffee. To eat raw, fold so that sting is inside. But only eat younger nettles as old ones are too acidic.

Honeysuckle flowers. Delicious, sweet, slightly crunchy snack.

Wood sorrel. Like a tiny crunchy salad leaf.

Burdock. Good source of water.

Red Campion flowers and **Lesser Stitchwort**. Adds interest to salads, though bland, 'except for a faint subtle pollen taste', Robin notes.

Bramble tips. 'Absolutely disgusting' raw, says Robin, but, like dandelions, good in a stir-fry with a light soy sauce.

Thistle roots. Add texture, but rather bland taste. Slice into juliennes (short, thin strips), then simmer them. Don't boil, as this toughens them. You might dry-roast them on a hot rock heated in the fire, or just chuck onto the coals, or in a non-survival situation fry in a pan.

Cleavers (also known as **Sticky Willie** or **Goose Grass**). Best boiled; when raw, according to Robin, they 'taste funny due to their texture and bitterness'. Robin also pops them in a jamjar of water overnight along with nettles for a morning power drink. Kids love this sticky plant.

Birch and **Hawthorn leaves**. Can be eaten raw. 'Bread and butter' is the old folk name, as they relied on it in spring. Robin eats birch and hawthorn leaves 'all spring and summer, though by late spring they are harder, more leathery, and don't taste great'. Birch leaves are especially good as a tonic.

Medicinal Plants, Leaves and Roots

NB Only use plants as medicine or food if you are basically healthy. It is safest if none of the plants listed here is given to minors or ingested by pregnant women, unless in the company of an expert like Robin, or after having sought medical advice.

Woodavens, also known as **Herb Bennet**. Eighteen inches high with a yellow starlight flower. It's a treatment for diarrhoea and dysentery. It has astringent and antiseptic properties; you can gargle it for a sore throat. Crush the roots and dry them, then turn them into powder which smells like cloves and put in clothes to use against moths. 'It must have been important in the old days when clothes were made mainly of wool.'

Meadowsweet, Latin name *Spiraea ulmaria*. Grows to about two feet. White flowers when it opens out, but I thought the first buds looked like tiny cauliflowers. Aspirin was synthesised from it until it was produced in the laboratory. It is regarded by some as a general cure-all; old texts say it 'makes the heart glad'. Robin uses it to make tea.

St John's Wort. Delicate yellow flowers identified by holding them up to the light to see if there are perforations – Latin name is *Hypericum perforatum*. Make into a tea in summer and store until winter against the depressing effect of longer nights.

Nettle. Edible as well as medical. Can be made into lotions and tinctures against burns and scalds, insect stings, psoriasis, eczema, and the symptoms of rheumatism. Also called 'the arthritic helper'.

(Greater) Plantain. Long, thin, green leaves low down in pasture. Known in Africa as White Man's Foot because it grows where the soil is disturbed. It's a coagulant – crush and chew, then place on wounds. Also treats haemorrhoids, diarrhoea, toothache.

Staunchweed (also known as **yarrow**). Unique-looking – its many tiny leaves look like a millipede. One foot high, with white flowers. Achilles used it to treat his army's wounds (the plant's name pretty much indicates its properties).

Woundwort. Another coagulant. Three feet high, with purple flowers in a pyramid formation.

Woodsage, also known as **Gypsy Baccy** (it can be smoked and Robin has experienced no ill effects – although that is no guarantee generally) and **Clear Beer** (it was used to clarify cloudy homebrew). Leaf looks like a rough textured mint. Cleans teeth and gums; in infusions for coughs and colds. Known to reduce temperature when patient is feverish.

Foxglove. Four feet plus tall, with distinctive bell-shaped flowers. When not in flower it contains digitalin, an important drug for stroke and heart attack patients (it stimulates the heart muscle). Can be dangerous if consumed in large quantities, but cannot be synthesised.

Betony. Its Latin name, *Betonica officinalis*, shows it was used by 'official' apothecaries. Grows to just nine inches, with purple flowers. Romans used it for hysteria, neuralgia, anxiety, vertigo, asthma, bronchitis. A sedative, diuretic and astringent.

Burdock. Huge heart-shaped leaves. About four feet tall. Use as a poultice for boils and gout. Can be used to treat skin diseases like eczema and psoriasis.

Silver Birch (leaves). Tincture is a feelgood tonic.

Turkeytail Fungus. A bracket fungus. Looks like a semi-precious stone, such as Tiger's Eye. In tea it's a booster to the immune system.

Sorrel. Wood sorrel is rich in vitamins; sheep sorrel makes a good cooling drink for fever. Mild diuretic.

My shuttling back and forth into and out of the off-grid world convinced me that the life is valuable and enjoyable, and a period of reflection after my journey was over did nothing to dissuade me from that view. I knew I could do it for a few days, and my newly acquired bushcraft skills had infused me with a good dose of confidence. Now I wanted to immerse myself a little deeper, and that meant getting into hard facts and some complex details. I had to find the right location, for a start. I felt nowhere near ready to make a permanent full-time commitment, so what criteria should I use in my choice? I could hardly apply to join a commune like Steward Wood as a weekender member. I had to find another way of working it, of making a little off-grid world of my own. Like Majorca, it would have to be quirky and cheap.

6
Only Disconnect: Land and Water

A low-impact development is one that through its low negative environmental impact either enhances or does not significantly diminish environmental quality.

Low-Impact Development, Simon Fairlie, 1996

I WANTED TO LEARN how to choose the right land, what criteria to use, and where to look on this crowded island. Price was key for me, but what else? Should I be looking for a piece of land the size of a large garden or something more substantial? And water is the essence of life; surely a decent supply was integral to the choice of land?

As I travelled round the country, some natural distinctions became apparent: between living off-grid for ideological reasons and doing so simply to save money; between trying to make a living out of the land and commuting or (like me) working on site but not on the land; between those who had struggled for their home and those who had acquired it easily. Hector Christie was granted Tapeley Hall by a family trust; Steve Hardman bought his house and land in Northumberland for a thousand pounds in the 1970s as soon as he dropped out of university. His struggle was paying the mortgage and bringing up his children there, not finding the property in the first place or being allowed to stay in it. But the bender-dwellers of Allaleigh, Tony Wrench in his roundhouse, Marcus Tribe in his yurt – all had a far more complex time establishing themselves. As I had expected, the range of people who have opted to live off-grid is as great as those of us who are still plugged in. Each person had his own issues and reasons for being off-grid, and each held a different lesson for me – even if it was only showing me how and/or where I did not want to live.

As I said, price was key for me, so be warned: going off-grid on a decent bit of land in the UK has become pricey, just like everything else in this country, though it still costs less than buying a house. I shall come to the subject of price shortly. First, let me just say that if you are prepared to look at other parts of the world, whether you are talking about your primary residence or a weekend retreat, what you would pay for a few acres of woodland in the Home Counties is enough for a detached cottage or a large tract of land in many desirable parts of the world, including just across the Channel.

Go Abroad

Increasingly, Brits of all ages and points of view are opting to go off-grid overseas in the same way that the people of this country have taken to buying holiday homes abroad. There is much to be said for simply flee-ing this damp chicken coop of an island, and setting up an off-grid home in the sun, especially if you are young. The 2001 Census found that hundreds of thousands of Brits in their twenties had disappeared from the population. 'Census officials were ridiculed when the overall population figure was a million lower than expected,' reported *The Times*. 'The missing million was blamed partly on young men dis-appearing into the Mediterranean rave culture or students going around the world on gap-year trips.' Some of those 'disappeared' young men are living off-grid in communes, vans and smallholdings dotted around Europe, and further afield. And anecdotal evidence suggests to me that the phenomenon is also tied up with the shocking divorce rates. Many single men living in vans have an ex-wife and kids back home.

My friend Julienne Dolphin Wilding from Hertfordshire decided to move to warmer climes after a fruitless search for somewhere permanent to park her caravan. Knowing she would never be able to afford a country retreat in the UK, she rented a flat in Barcelona and bought some land in Crete. In October 2006, while preparing to emigrate, she bought a twenty-foot-long freight container and filled it with five tons of her possessions, including the caravan. Containers were pioneered by the US Army in the 1950s, and they revolutionised freight transport. Today, over 90 per cent of all worldwide cargo is moved in containers stacked on transport ships. In 2005, eighteen mil-lion containers made over 200 million trips. With each container making over eleven trips a year, they get dirty and smelly, so Julienne had the right instinct when she opted for a new one, even though it cost £1,200. For another £1,600 she had it shipped out to Crete.

When her new container arrived on the Greek island she ran into all sorts of problems. There are rules on Crete about the movement and ownership of containers, apparently designed to prevent people from doing what Julienne was doing. She had to pay off the handlers (€300), the shipping brokers (€150), and the customs officer (€50). As is always the case with second homes abroad, Julienne was rushing to

Julienne kicks back in Crete

meet her commitments before the date marked on her cheap, unchangeable return ticket. The owner of a Caterpillar tractor she needed to make a path to her property sensed the urgency and doubled his rate (an extra €800). The container was finally towed on to her land by a Greek man with a van (€200) who heroically braved the worst rain for 250 years. Once she had finished celebrating her bureaucratic triumph, Julienne adapted the hatches on the container to accommodate windows and a glass front door, and hey presto! An off-grid home. (For great examples of container homes across Europe and the UK, see www.fabprefab.com/fabfiles/containerbayhome.htm)

Thousands of Brits have moved off-grid in southern Europe. Spain and Italy contain entire villages in deserted parts of those countries where literally every indigenous inhabitant had departed until it was rediscovered by foreigners looking to build their own off-grid Utopia. The largest of these communities is probably in Spain, just forty-five minutes from Granada airport, where Leanda Brass from Putney has rented a house. Within a few minutes' drive in every direction there is a total of 500 eco-activists living in yurts, benders, tents and brick-built houses all year round. This is how the alternative movement and the cash-poor are dealing with the problem of British prices and British weather. And though they are mainly British, 'it's one of the most mixed places I have ever been,' Leanda told me. 'There are Chinese, Germans, Yanks, everything.' Leanda is a sound artist from London who has moved there for part of the year to work 'in a place where there are interesting artists and musicians coming and going all the time. Everybody comes into the market in Orgiva [the village made famous by Chris Stewart in his book *Driving over Lemons*] on Thursdays.' She is most struck by the three contrasting communities in the area: a group of yurt-dwelling hippies who were given their land, known as Beneficio, by a mysterious benefactor in the 1980s; a posse of Mad Max bikers and illegals; and a third group of middle-class foreigners who live in houses and integrate with the locals. 'It has no beautiful features,' Leanda added (referring to the village, not her house). 'It's just a strange little place. You arrive here and think, "God, this is really ugly." There is no way that anyone who was driving through would ever stop.' Nevertheless, she took the former rectory overlooking Orgiva with a 270-degree view of the mountains because at €300 a month it was cheaper than renting a studio in the UK, and she could work outdoors most of the year.

The likes of Bert Hagley and other more conventional types have gone a step or two upmarket and bought into normal villa developments in Spain, albeit off-grid. Bert bought a plot near Valencia with a shell of a villa and saved between £50,000 and £100,000 compared with similar properties that have mains power and water. He then spent £15,000 to £20,000 on renewable energy and a similar amount on water management.

If you're planning to buy abroad, be careful to hire the right lawyer. In common with those who purchase grid-connected houses, many find that their dreams of living cheaply and self-sufficiently in the sun go up in a puff of smoke once they examine their land deeds more carefully. A decade after I had begun experimenting with off-grid living in Majorca, I discovered that the land I had bought had been illegally sub-divided from a larger plot and that my land fell below the minimal legal size. Although the deeds had been properly signed by a notary public, he was doing it as a favour to a friend and they would never hold up in a court. One day when I arrived at my hut, a new owner stood there telling me that I could stay for now, but eventually I would have to leave. Only then did I discover that my own lawyer was an alcoholic and had failed to spot a scam. Fortunately I was able to find a new lawyer through the British Consulate in Palma, and I bought some extra land with another small house on it in order to bring my holding up to the minimum legal size. I nearly lost everything, though.

Of course, by the time I decided to take things further and investigate how to live off-grid more permanently, it was living here in the UK that interested me because leisure air travel was beginning to feel slightly amoral. I consulted Julienne about her flights between London, Crete and Barcelona, not to mention the occasional visit to friends around the globe. Her answer was an apparent solution for all who want to live an international life without moral anguish: 'You can offset a lifetime of air travel by planting two trees.' Julienne planted two walnut trees on her land in Crete, after the container was delivered, and plans to plant a further hundred different types over the next few years.

I couldn't quite believe it was that easy (and as it turned out it wasn't). According to online carbon calculator www.terrapass.com/flight/flightcalc.html a short journey such as London–Berlin produces 121.14kg of CO_2. And the website www.coloradotrees.org/benefits.htm says that a tree will absorb 1,091kg of CO_2 in its lifetime. Unfortunately trees absorb very little CO_2 in their first decade so the damage done now is not repaired for twenty years. And I have a family now, so the cost of each journey has tripled. Still, six trees will be no trouble the next time I go to Majorca. I will slip Toni Baloney a few euros to come up and water them, and Fiona will be very happy.

Price of Land

If price is an indicator of demand, then British land must be more desirable than anywhere else in Europe. It certainly has a scarcity value: I have yet to find any worthwhile land I could afford. The Internet is full of ads, mostly at the top end of the price range: plain farmland for £3,000 to £10,000 an acre, sheltered pony paddocks for £10,000 to £15,000 an acre; woodland for £5,000 to £12,000 an acre; or plots where planning permission is highly likely to be granted (anything from £50,000 an acre upwards). That is a big investment if you are not sure what you will do with it. The lower-priced plots I visited all had too many drawbacks: too ugly, too close to the road, or too overlooked by neighbours for my purposes.

In this country, where property ownership is put on a pedestal, it's worth reminding yourself that you can also rent. Back in 1990, IBM consultant David Allender, you will recall, paid less than a pound a week for his sprawling home on the Yorkshire Dales. 'The rent was £50 a year to start with, but I spent a lot of money on the house,' he said. 'Now it's £40 a week, but still less than market [value] because it's so remote.' Had he stayed, the rent would have continued to rise and one day it might have been too much for him. As I knew from my Majorcan property, owning a sizeable area of land around your house is as much a burden as a pleasure. In the end he chose to leave for Spain with no regrets. It might be better to enjoy off-grid property without owning it, but when Louis della Porta and Annette Robinson moved in they had to pay a much higher rent (they did not want to reveal exactly how much). Perhaps that exposes the weakness in the argument for renting off-grid. If you are seeking freedom and independence then you only want the most sympathetic of landlords. The permanent threat of a price rise looming over you is no good for your tranquillity quotient.

Iona in her caravan in Machynlleth is a rare example of a renter who has no fear of price rises. Her £20 per week was fixed six years ago and includes use of the washing machine, shower and landline in the house.

If you were to find a landowner willing to rent you a bare field on a long lease in the knowledge you were planning to live there, then the inevitable planning battle might be worth contemplating. At least the inspector could be sure you were not trying to profit from the planning permission.

The majority of the houses I visited – as opposed to the yurts, boats and benders – had been acquired more than ten years ago. Dennis Potter, Annette's father, paid £70,000 in the winter of 1986 for the windswept and isolated Upper and Lower Heath near Knighton. He found the job lot in an estate agent's window in Presteigne. 'I came back from Wales one dark, stormy night and this was in the window.' He had spent six weeks hunting for 'somewhere isolated' and a few better properties had already slipped through his fingers before this came along. After they had to sell the big house to pay for Annette's horses, they started looking again, but prices had soared too high. Now their neighbours can't find a buyer for their old property. Dennis says land in West Wales is cheaper, but even so it is too expensive for the Potters. One ray of hope is that 'there's a lot of properties for sale last year and the year before that are still for sale now'. They are hoping the next downturn might give them an opportunity to move somewhere with more land.

Most of the people I met who had bought within the past decade had searched for years. Many of their stories had a similar ending: their piece of heaven, when they finally found it, just fell into their laps. They still had to pay roughly market rate, but such prices can soon start to look like a bargain. Sandy Boulanger and Nigel Dodman paid £165,000 for their picturebook house and forty acres in 1998. 'If it had been on the grid,' said Nigel, 'it would have been way out of our price range.' And they had to move fast, making an offer as soon as they saw the place. 'We were the first to see it, although subsequently we heard of a lot of people who had their eye on it,' said Sandy. The property is now worth something approaching £400,000, and that is without the twelve-acre wood they bought.

Once house prices started to rocket, many switched to buying farm buildings. In 2003, the Land Matters commune in Allaleigh shelled out about £60,000 for their forty-two acres of mixed land in Devon in a sealed bid. They were lucky. Sealed bids are sometimes used to test the market, as you are forced to name your top price with no way of telling what others are offering and no guarantee that you will win even if you

Benders at Land Matters – hardy meets solar tech.

are the highest bidder. When they unexpectedly won the bid, the word went out to a network of political and eco-activists, road protesters and anti-McDonald's campaigners, many of whom had been looking for an opportunity like this. 'I was looking at mortgages and things, and then enough people got in touch, and it developed into this mutual purchase idea where we were all going to put in an equal amount,' said Christian Taylor, who founded the co-op. 'Then I realised we were not able to buy the land outright because not everyone could put up the £3,000 we each had to put in. The shortfall was loaned interest-free – about £15,000 in total – by some very experienced people who are not members of the co-op. I call them our guardian angels, fairy god-mothers. One of them was my landlady, and another was my co-lodger in the house when I finally bought the land.'

Also in 2003, Jyoti Fernandes and friends bought their forty acres of pasture in Dorset at auction for £90,000 and borrowed the money from the UK branch of ethical bank Triodos. The bank advanced the loan and took the land as security.

Woodland

Now that land prices have risen sharply, the last alternative is forestry, or a mix of woodland and pasture. Forestry might cost slightly more per acre, but it has the added asset of trees for fuel and building materials, possibly even to sell as timber. Despite the prices quoted on the web, woodland is still affordable, if you buy it direct from an owner. The more remote the wood, the further away it is from big cities, the cheaper it is likely to be.

Judy of the Woods bought her 22.5 acres of woodland and meadow for about £16,000 in the early 1990s. Originally she paid just £15,000 for 17.5 acres, and a year later bought the other five acres, including an overgrown paddock, from a neighbour 'partly to stop the local hunt coming up there'. She had expected to pay a thousand an acre so she was amazed when the seller said, 'I've asked around and the going rate is £200 an acre.' Judy nodded, murmured that she had been expecting something around that price, then virtually pulled out her chequebook on the spot ('So not completely unworldly, then,' I thought). She had only wanted the acre down by the river, but she ended up with 600 yards of fishing rights she never uses.

Theo Hopkins bought his fifty-acre Devon mixed woodland in 1988 for £30,000. 'I like playing in woodlands, I thought it would be fun, and it was very cheap at the time,' he said. 'Recreational woodland is rocketing up in price now – way above the amount that many of the sort of people who would want to live in a bender can afford. That's a big problem.' I am not sure how much of a problem it is, although I envy Theo his good purchase. If you can buy five acres for £25,000, or fifty acres for £125,000 and split it with some friends, then spend say £10,000 each on shelter, water, a track through the woods perhaps, you have spent £30,000 or so for something that would have cost £300,000 had it had a house on it. Assuming you do not have £300,000, this seems like a pretty good alternative.

Marcus Tribe's twenty-year search ended when he met another forester who had managed to accumulate some pockets of woodland up and down the country. The six-acre plot in Devon was growing wild and the entrepreneurial owner had no time to maintain it, so he sold it to Marcus for £9,000 in 1998 on the understanding that Marcus would 'manage it well and keep it as woodland'. These days 'you can pay up to £4,000 an acre for this kind of wood,' Sarah Harvey informed me as we sat close to the wood-burner in the yurt on a damp June evening. She was displaying a charming naivety about the current cost of her partner's sole asset. These days you pay *at least* £4,000 if you buy through an agent.

Marcus earns just £57 per week from his forestry – barely enough to pay the council tax that was levied as soon as his case was concluded – though it does represent a commercial return on his investment. The income is mainly from the sale of charcoal which he burns himself using wood from his trees and bags up for locals who are happy to pay a couple of quid per kilo. He also makes some furniture out of wood from the trees he coppices, as well as teaching people how to make yurts using willow, which he bends into shape by steaming it. Because his right to stay in the wood depends on it providing him with his living, Marcus must survive on the low wage the wood provides. But despite this, he has a high quality of life. He and Sarah do not need much money to sustain themselves and they are happy – or as happy as you can be when the council make you a pet project.

Now Marcus is approaching fifty, and after thirty hard years' forestry he sees the six acres as his retirement fund. It's a pretty modest one, but it will provide him with all he wants and needs once he has it set up so that it is easier to manage in old age. Marcus and Sarah could probably claim all sorts of state hand-outs and tax credits, but they can't be doing with the paperwork, and the same is true of the many woodland grants that alter the economics of buying a wood.

Woodland grants

When calculating what kind of wood you can afford, consider the possibility of grants. Some are relatively easy to apply for (you can even pay a more experienced form-filler to do it for you) and amount to little more than a subsidy for planting trees. Others are complex, and you should discuss them with a forester before attempting to apply. You don't want to be blacklisted for filling in the wrong information.

The English Woodland Grant Scheme is worth a special mention. It's a five-year contract between the wood owner and the English Forestry Commission, and it lists operations that the owner will carry out. There is a points system. The larger the area of new woodland to

Nigel giving me the tour.

be planted, the more points you get. Points are also awarded for local community involvement of the sort that Nigel Lowthrop introduced at Hill Holt. Every year there is a target number of points you must achieve to qualify for the grant. In *The Woodland Way*, Ben Law lays out this scheme in great detail, showing you how to calculate your potential grant and suggesting ways of making sure you can do all the work within the budget the grant stipulates. He also lists several places to apply for loans to cover the cost of buying a wood or improving it, including Triodos Bank, the Agricultural Mortgage Company, and Scottish Agricultural Securities Co-operation.

Crofting grants, to plant trees, can be secured in Scotland from the Crofting Commission and the Scottish Forestry Commission.

Natural England (the new body combining the Countryside Agency and English Nature) gives grants for planting trees where public involvement and long-term benefits can be shown.

Most of the grants listed here are specifically for woodland. A few are more general but are known to encourage applications involving woodland.

The Forestry Commission. English Woodland Grant Scheme (EWGS) encompasses stewardship and creation of woodlands (separate details for each scheme).
Aim: public benefit from existing woodlands; to help create new woodlands to deliver additional public benefit. Tel. 0131 334 0303. Enq: 0845 FORESTS (3673787).

Countryside Venture. Grants for individuals and organisations anywhere in the UK for practical rural skills training where a conservation or environmental benefit accrues. Grant limits: for individuals, course fees up to £350, travelling £50; for organised group training courses lasting more than one day, up to £1,500.

Natural England. Reserves Enhancement Scheme – grants for voluntary conservation organisations who manage Sites of Special Scientific Interest as nature reserves. For five years. **Aim**: contribute to the day-to-day management of sites. Tel. Paul Horswill on 01733 455129 or Duncan Macfarlane on 01733 455138.

Section 35 National Nature Reserve Capital Grants Scheme – grants to Approved Bodies under Section 35(1)(c) of the Wildlife and Countryside Act 1981, where these Approved Bodies are not eligible for the Reserves Enhancement Scheme (above).
Aim: improvement of reserve management, access and interpretation for capital projects.

Enfys. Environment Wales offers five grant schemes to registered projects:

> **Project Grants** – up to £10,000 to help fund project materials, tools and equipment.
>
> **Management Grants** – £1,000 to £11,000 to support new project-related posts. Awarded for up to three years.
>
> **Start-up Grants** – up to £1,000 to help cover costs involved with establishing new voluntary community groups and developing a project.
>
> **Training Grants** — travel expenses, subsistence and course fees up to £400 to help meet the costs of third-party courses or training events for project staff or volunteers.
>
> **Pre-project Grants** – £500 to £4,000 to help cover the costs of feasibility studies, business plans and community appraisals in order to assess a potential project's needs and its chances of success.

Tel. 029 20 48 6969.

Heritage Lottery Fund (HLF). Grants for local groups and national projects: £300 to £10,000 (England), £500 to £10,000 (Scotland and N. Ireland) and £500 to £5,000 (Wales). **Aim**: to bring people together.

Tel. 020 7591 6000.

It's Your Community. Awards to groups and individuals for all types of environmental project anywhere in the UK. Up to £1,000. **Aim**: to benefit the local environment.

Tel. 020 7591 3111.

National Parks Sustainability Development Fund. Open to individuals/organisations. Up to £1,000 (as well as larger amounts, not specified). **Aim**: to change the attitude and behaviour of individuals and communities, enhance understanding of sustainable development and the role of the National Park, promote co-operation and social inclusion.

DEFRA Helpline: 08459 33 55 77.

BBC's Breathing Places. Grants for small groups, £300 to £10,000, must be spent within one year of being awarded. **Aim**: to promote 'breathing places' – green space that benefits wildlife and local community.

Tel. 0845 4102030.

The Mersey Forest. Grants to companies, landowners and non-profit organisations. **Aim**: to establish new woodland and bring neglected woods back into use; to assist new ventures with advice, business planning, machinery.

Tel. 01925 859606.

HLF Your Heritage Grants. Grants of £5,000 to £50,000. **Aim**: to encourage communities to identify, look after and celebrate their heritage.

Tel. 020 7591 6000; contact: 156 High Street, Dorking, Surrey RH4 1BQ.

Nurturing Nature. Grant available to properly registered local groups. Up to £350 for any single event/activity. **Aim**: to assist small nature conservation organisations and groups to organise and carry out their activities.

Tel. 0121 454 8018; enquiries@wmbp.org

The Tree Council. Trees for Schools Fund/Community Trees Fund – grants for schools/community groups, £100 to £700. **Aim**: to undertake well-planned tree-planting projects starting in 2007 during National Tree Week; to actively engage children in the planting of trees.

Tel. 020 7828 9928.

The Co-op Foundation. Grants to local groups and organisations across its trading area, £500 to £30,000. **Aim**: to demonstrate evidence of co-operative values and principles: self-help, equality, democracy, concern for the community.

Tel. 0161 493 4582.

Transco Grassroots Environmental Action Scheme.
Open to secondary and middle schools, conservation charities and
community groups.
Aim: to protect, enhance or restore a natural feature or habitat, or
create a new environmental amenity.
Tel. 01392 84927.

Waterways Trust. Small Grants Scheme up to £1,000; for
projects along the non-tidal River Thames (Teddington to
Cricklade) up to £5,000. Grants normally given to organisations,
community groups and schools. **Aim**: to fund waterway wildlife
conservation projects for communities.
Contact: ljenny.rogers@thewaterwaystrust.org.uk

Action Earth. Grants of up to £50 for groups.
Aim: to enable people to take part in practical conservation
projects, empower them to improve quality of life for themselves
and their communities for the future.
Tel. 0121 328 7455.

Community Champions. Set up by the Department for
Education and Skills (DfES) for individuals. Up to £2,000.
Aim: for volunteers who want to become active and make a
difference in their community.
Tel. 0114 2594113.

Waste Recycling Group Communities Challenge.
Prize fund of £1 million. Organisations can bid for £75,000 to
£250,000 for capital projects.
Aim: to breathe life into rundown facilities or provide new
amenities.
Tel. 01953 717165.

Lloyds TSB Foundation. Grants to charitable organisations
and small community-based charities.
Aim: to help disadvantaged or disabled play a fuller role in
communities in England and Wales.
Tel. 0870 411 1223.

The Ethnic Minorities Award Scheme for Environmental Projects (EMAS). Limited funds for small grants to innovative projects. Up to £500, or advice/funding referral service for projects that can access funds from larger grant schemes elsewhere.

Aim: to spur vital local development.

  Tel. 01286 870715.

(With thanks to the Woodland Trust.)

The classic book *Shelter*, edited by Lloyd Khan and first published in 1973 (www.shelterpub.com), states that 'every seriously operated homestead should contain within its bounds some woodland acres'. Beside the obvious benefits of fuel and building materials, woodlands help stop soil erosion and provide shelter from wind and a habitat for flora and fauna. They can also influence the microclimate of an area, sending moisture up to create cloud cover and therefore reducing the risk of drought. And if you love trees, then woodland-dwelling might be for you. (On the negative side, many find woodlands too damp, too dark, and generally too inhospitable to consider as a living space.)

For historical reasons, woodlands tend to be planted on land that is not good for farming because it is inaccessible (which is why so many woods are on hillsides) or has poor-quality soil. You'll be lucky to find a flat piece of woodland. 'I'd worked on so many steep hillsides in my years as a forest warden,' Marcus Tribe advised me, 'I knew the most important thing was to have land you could manage easily. Especially as you get older.' But in these days of four-wheel-drives and phone masts, inaccessibility is relative.

The location is one thing, but the actual trees growing on the land are another. The trend to grow one kind of tree in cash-crop woodlands may make superficial economic/management sense, but it is not the best idea in the long run. If the trees are all the same they will all be fighting for the same nutrients at the same level below the earth. The best woodland has a mix of trees, evergreens and deciduous, of different ages. This will reduce the chances of blight affecting the whole wood.

Timber has fallen in value over the past decade, but there are signs that the price will rise over the next decade. The UK imports two thirds of its wood and paper products; it would only take a fall in the value of the pound or a rise in world demand for wood to make a forest suddenly more valuable. Even without a rise in the value of timber, careful management of a woodland can bring more profit than can be gained simply by selling off a percentage of the trees to loggers every year. A strong straight pine is more valuable as a pole than as fodder for a saw mill. High-grade logs such as oak are best sold as veneer timber. Whatever you do, never invite in a 'gypsy' logger who will cut down whatever he fancies and steal far more than he'll pay you for.

When Nigel Lowthrop bought Hill Holt Wood he took over a plantation that had been badly maintained for years and was of little interest to the average buyer of recreational woodland. The thirty-four acres are hard by the main A46 between Lincoln and Newark-on-Trent, and the whoosh of lorries is as much part of the soundtrack of the land as the crash of waves are part of living by the sea. 'When I first got here, there was an explosion of brambles and rhododendrons with bits of wood in it so you could not use a cutter. I cleared most of the existing paths on my own by hand. I was looking around for friends and supporters so I contacted the local forest officer and said I had bought the woodland and told him approximately what I was planning to do, and he said, "Well, Mr Lowthrop, you must be a very wealthy man to be able to buy a bit of forest to play with," and put the phone down on me. Even when we did succeed the reaction was "Well, it's a one-off" – from senior forestry people.'

As we know, Nigel chose to involve the local community in every aspect of the wood, from the landscaping to their intention to look after problem kids on the property. There was nothing new about providing amenity access to local people, or selling timber from the woods, or consulting others on how they could do the same, or the way Nigel and Karen joined numerous local committees and steering groups. It was the combination that was unique. Ever since Nigel first drew it to the attention of policymakers there have been the slow stirrings of a long-term policy shift in government thinking. Other woods are now being lined up for similar treatment.

If you are buying a wood in order to become a hermit, then the social enterprise model is not for you. But Nigel's achievement is to have established a viable model for many others to copy.

Scramble for Farm Land

Russian billionaires are targeting the UK property market; City bonuses are piling up; and 'horseyculture', as the practice of buying up agricultural land for horse paddocks, is becoming ever more fashionable. As well as this tsunami of big-money deals forcing up prices for everyone, more and more middle-class people are looking for second homes in the country. 'Agriculture can be outbid by all other land uses,' Simon Fairlie pointed out to me. 'This is what has led to the suburbanisation of the countryside.' All of which makes it ever harder to find a nice place to go off-grid.

The new EU single-area payment system awards grants based on what was farmed on the land between 2000 and 2002, whether or not there is any farming currently. So stewarding the land for amenity or environmental reasons suddenly has a decent payback. As a result, there is little replenishment of farming land at the moment. In the long term this may turn out to be a mistake. What happens if food imports suddenly become more expensive, either because of increased global demand for food or reduced food production as a result of climate change?

Most of the Land Matters' forty-two acres is agricultural, although there are also a few acres of wood. Christian Taylor, the commune's founder, had been looking for land for only a few days when he heard about the site at Allaleigh. 'I saw the photo and thought, "This is what I have always dreamt of." I wrote a handwritten note, saying that if the [sealed] bid was successful the land would be used for sustainable farming, and the main emphasis would be the production of local food for local farmers' markets. We would keep it in its traditional state. That's paraphrasing; I didn't even keep a copy of the original letter. I had to give it to the estate agent who handed all the letters to the farmers who owned the land. I thought it was a very remote chance. By the time the estate agent rang me at work,

I'd forgotten about it. He said, "Are you willing to proceed? You've won the bid." '

That's when Christian began spending a lot of his time communicating with friends and solicitors – so much so that eventually he lost his job. 'It got to the state where my tea and lunch breaks and weekends were full time on this project for more than a year. I felt a lot of responsibility and stress.' Three of the fields they were buying didn't have proper land registry titles. The land hadn't changed hands for so long that the paperwork had never been done. There was no evidence of who owned it and it couldn't be sold until the ownership was legally established. But the stress was caused more by the need to conceal who was actually buying the land. 'We got so worried about whether we were finally going to own this land or if someone would gazump us. Almost a year after we had first met we were still meeting in town and we were slightly worried that the estate agents might feel shy of a whole group. So I conducted it [the negotiations] myself on behalf of the group. The focus was my own name, Dr Taylor. We felt there would have been a bit of resistance if it was known there was a group.' Then, when everything was ready to be signed, 'Dr Taylor' simply told the vendors' solicitors that the contracting party would be Land Matters rather than him personally.

'It was a big relief when we finally exchanged. It was a glorious May day in 2003. We all went up for a long picnic, and had a toast. It was a very moving occasion and a great relief. The whole co-operative went up, and our fairy godmothers [who loaned the co-op the remaining money to purchase the land] – Pat, Angela, Adrienne, Jenny – rather wonderful people who have the inclination to think this is a very wonderful project, which is rather lovely.'

I found Christian's story as depressing as it was 'lovely' – not for what it said about him, but for what it meant to me. Basically he had lucked out with his original bid and then managed to complete on the deal only by using a certain amount of deception and by being the beneficiary of some valuable financial help. If that was what you had to do to get your own little patch of heaven, well, it was too much for me.

Still, Sandy and Nigel in Wales had needed no deception to come by their off-grid farm, just luck and the sense to take an opportunity when they saw it. They are both beneficiaries and victims of the horsey landowners in their area. Nigel makes his living from them as a horse vet, of course, but when they began searching for a house they found the horse-owning classes had driven prices beyond their reach – even in mid-Wales, which is cheaper than many areas, and which they both loved. 'We thought four acres, forty acres, no difference,' said Sandy of their forty-acre farm. 'We were just being naive really. We thought we would make a profit on the farm, which we finally did last year.' Nigel immediately contradicted her, and after some discussion they agreed they had made a loss every year since they bought the place; it had been Nigel's vet income that tipped them into profit the previous year. Sandy is a good farmer and they are growing their income from the cattle, but they may never see a profit and they just accept that as a price for their quality of life.

The house itself is adorable. The setting is private and sheltered and it must warm their hearts every time they step out of their front door and look at the ancient trees surrounding their small lawn. But it was the way they found the place that interested me most – through reading the local newspaper ads. 'Instead of looking at houses with a bit of land which we had been doing until then,' Sandy explained, 'I happened to look on the farming page. It was advertised as an organic farm, so that caught my eye. It was a nice enough picture to make one

Alan Bush, daughter-in-law, wife and daughter.

go and see it. We decided then and there, the day we saw it, that we liked it so much that we ought to just go for it.'

I tried to follow their example, but the property landscape has altered since 1998. Big city bonuses and the terrorist threat to cities, to name only two reasons, mean everybody (it seems) wants isolated houses with acres of land.

Eventually, however, I learned what may be the secret of reliably finding land – and it was so obvious. I was in Scoraig, visiting the founding father of the township, Alan Bush. 'I'd been looking for an island,' he told me, 'but all I could afford was the end of this damn peninsula.' But it was not the piece of property he had chosen that excited me, it was how he had come by the land – through the extremely simple and time-honoured method of advertising for a small farm in the classified section of the *Oban Times*.

Agricultural grants

DEFRA's Environmental Stewardship Scheme is probably one to look at first to see if you are eligible, as it is designed for effective environmental land management. There are entry-level grants, high-level grants for high-priority areas, and organic grants. Some of the other grants are more specific, so you should read through all the 'Get the details' links on the DEFRA website before proceeding. If you are thinking of buying land *and* moving, it would be worth finding out which areas and situations DEFRA consider 'high-level' to ensure you get the best possible funding.

Environmental Stewardship
Organic Entry Level Stewardship (OELS). For land registered as 'fully organic' or 'in conversion to organic farming' with an organic inspection body *before* the application. You must achieve your points targets on your OELS- and ELS-eligible land. £60 per hectare per year (for all OELS-eligible land); £30 per hectare per year (for all ELS land). Aid for converting conventionally farmed unimproved land and established top fruit orchards (planted with pears, plums, cherries and apples, excluding cider apples) also available as a top-up to OELS payments. £600 per hectare per year

(first three years of an OELS agreement for areas of top fruit orchards); £175 per hectare per year (first two years for areas of improved land). For more details contact Natural England. A list of contacts can be found at www.naturalengland.org.uk/contact/default.htm. Or contact your local Rural Development Service (RDS) offices (a list can be found at www.defra.gov.uk/erdp/schemes/oels/handbook/appendix6.htm).

East of England
Bedfordshire, Cambridgeshire, Norfolk, Suffolk, Essex and Hertfordshire.
RDS East, PO Box 247, Cambridge, CB2 2WW
    Tel: 08456 024094 Fax: 01223 533777
    e-mail: bdce.genesis@defra.gsi.gov.uk

East Midlands
Derbyshire, Leicestershire, Lincolnshire, Northamptonshire, Nottinghamshire and Rutland.
RDS East Midlands, PO Box 8296, Nottingham, NG8 3WZ
    Tel: 08456 024091 Fax: 0115 9294886
    e-mail: bdcem.genesis@defra.gsi.gov.uk

North-East
Northumberland, Tyne and Wear, Durham and the former county of Cleveland.
RDS North East, PO Box 578, Newcastle-upon-Tyne, NE15 8WW
    Tel: 08456 024097 Fax: 0191 229 5508
    e-mail: bdcne.genesis@defra.gsi.gov.uk

North-West
Cheshire, Greater Manchester, Merseyside, Lancashire and Cumbria.
RDS North West, PO Box 380, Crewe, CW1 6YH
    Tel: 08456 024093 Fax: 01270 754280
    e-mail: bdcnw.genesis@defra.gsi.gov.uk

South-East

Greater London, Berkshire, Buckinghamshire, Oxfordshire, Hampshire, Surrey, East Sussex, West Sussex, Kent and Isle of Wight.

RDS South East, PO Box 2423, Reading, RG1 6WY
> Tel: 08456 024092 Fax: 0118 939 2263
> e-mail: bdcse.genesis@defra.gsi.gov.uk

South-West

The Scilly Isles, Cornwall, Devon, Somerset, Dorset, Gloucestershire, Wiltshire and the former county of Avon.

RDS South West, PO Box 277, Bristol, BS10 6WW
> Tel: 08456 024098 Fax: 0117 9505392
> e-mail: bdcsw.genesis@defra.gsi.gov.uk

West Midlands

Herefordshire, Worcestershire, Warwickshire, Shropshire, Staffordshire and West Midlands.

RDS West Midlands, PO Box 530, Worcester, WR5 2WZ
> Tel: 08456 024095 Fax: 01905 362888
> e-mail: bdcwm.genesis@defra.gsi.gov.uk

Yorkshire & Humberside

North Yorkshire, South Yorkshire, West Yorkshire, East Riding of Yorkshire and North Lincolnshire.

RDS Yorkshire & The Humber, PO Box 213, Leeds, LS16 5WN
> Tel: 08456 024096 Fax: 0113 230 3790
> e-mail: bdcyh.genesis@defra.gsi.gov.uk

Or you can contact the **Rural Payments Agency** customer service centre in Newcastle:

Customer Service Centre, Rural Payments Agency, Lancaster House, Hampshire Court, Newcastle-upon-Tyne, NE4 7YH
> Tel: 0845 6037777
> e-mail: customer.service.centre@rpa.gsi.gov.uk

Aggregates Levy Sustainability Fund

For any individual or organisation. Aim: to minimise demand for primary aggregates, promote environmentally friendly extraction and transport, and reduce local effects of aggregate extraction. ALSF Team, Area 2D, Ergon House, Horseferry Road, London, SW1P 2AL

e-mail: alex.j.comber@defra.gsi.gov.uk, or
oyenike.noibi@defra.gsi.gov.uk

Land Purchase Grants

Natural England grants to voluntary nature conservation organisations to acquire and manage important areas of land. Grants are normally 5 to 25 per cent of the purchase price of land; up to £50,000, but normally in the order of £10,000. Contact your local Natural England offices – numbers and addresses can be found at www.naturalengland.org.uk/contact/default.htm

Hill Farm Allowance

Supports beef and sheep producers farming in English Less Favoured Areas (LFAs). Requirements: minimum of ten hectares of eligible forage land; minimum of 0.15 livestock units per hectare (or less if there is an acceptable environmental reason for stocking at a lower rate). Details for applying will be confirmed later in 2007. Check for updates at www.defra.gov.uk/erdp/schemes/hfa/default.htm

Parish Plans

Grants, up to £5,000, available to support local consultation to produce parish plans that identify needs and set out how these might be tackled. DEFRA funding available for England only. Parish council would be expected to apply for the funds. A Parish Plan Steering Group (involving a wider range of local people) will then be set up to produce the parish plan. Contact ACRE (Action with Communities in Rural England) at Somerford Court, Somerford Road, Cirencester, Gloucestershire, GL7 1TW

Tel: 01285 653477 Fax: 01285 654537
e-mail: acre@acre.org.uk

Agriculture Development Scheme
Grants for industry-led measures in England to improve marketing
performance and competition.
Marketing Grants & Consumers Branch, DEFRA, Area 4C, Nobel
House, 17 Smith Square, London, SW1P 3JR
   Tel: 020 7238 1205 Fax: 020 7238 5728
   e-mail: ads.mailbox@defra.gsi.gov.uk

The Importance of Water

You can live without gas and electricity, as long as you have the means
to make a fire, but the availability of water is one of the most important
considerations when choosing your land, almost regardless of how long
you plan to be there. You can carry in drinking water, but you are
unlikely to want to do the same for washing and cooking water. My first
thought when I arrive at a new piece of land is to see if there is a spring,
a well, a stream or even a tap within walking distance. If not, can I
make do on rainwater? This, of course, requires large storage tanks and
places to site them, and roofs with gutters that transport the rain into
the tanks.

Water purity is another essential consideration. Local councils have
a statutory duty to ensure that drinking water conforms to minimum
standards. Ben Heyes, agent for the Bolton Abbey Estate and therefore
responsible for the spring water at Louis and Annette's), told me he is
constantly fending off what he sees as busybody council inspectors.
'Frankly, the water coming to my house is beautiful, and as far as I'm
concerned, better water than I will get anywhere. If it's got a few bits
and pieces in, then it's probably keeping our resistance up. We feel quite
put upon by regulations, but of course we are forced to meet them, at
considerable cost.'

As well as its uses for drinking, cooking and washing, water is a
potential source of energy. Judy of the Woods is lucky with the water
from her springs. When we met she was in the midst of reconfiguring
her system, which has the dual function of supplying her domestic

water as well as micro hydro power. She knew about one of the springs on her land when she bought it – that had been a key factor in her decision. 'I shared the water rights of the first spring with my neighbours. When I moved in, I carried water in jerry cans on a cart and filled up a barrel on a stand to have running water, but a few years later I bought back the rights because they never used the water anyway. Once I had the rights back, I installed a manual stirrup pump in the spring and pumped the water to a holding tank a little higher to let it run to the caravan by gravity through a medium-density polyethylene pipe I laid.' Working slowly and methodically over many months, Judy then hand-built a hydraulic ram pump to raise the water to the same tank. Hydraulic ram pumps are a time-honoured technology that uses the energy of a large amount of water falling a small height to lift a small amount of that water to a much greater height (see www.lifewater.ca). Although ram pumps are inexpensive and use no power other than the energy of the water, they can only make use of a small fraction of the water passing through them, and much of the water used to power the machine is then wasted. So Judy started looking for a better system. 'I found a spring high on the hillside at the top of my property, and made a small dam, fed the water into a storage tank just below the spring, and extended the pipe to bring the water to the caravan by gravity.'

There was also a river at the bottom of the land. Judy had looked into making it a source of domestic water as well as energy, but in the end the river was just a landscaping feature rather than a usable resource. The cleanliness of river water can never be guaranteed. 'Also, it was too far, and below the level of need,' Judy said. 'Pumps use power, they can break down – unlike gravity – and they are an unnecessary expense when avoidable.' If Judy had decided to take her water from the river, that might have been a reason to build her home down in the river basin; but it would have been too damp, and a 'frost pocket' in winter, susceptible to flooding, and too shady. 'The best sites are halfway up hillsides,' she told me, 'as it's also best to avoid cold, windy hilltops.'

Judy had one of the most efficient hydro-power set-ups I encountered. Over the years she found another stream a few hundred feet further away from her collection of shacks and is planning to try to harness that as a back-up power source.

Judy and her Waterbaby hydro-generator.

While Judy is working alone and with little funds to maintain her minimal water supply, millionaire property consultant Simon Marr-Johnson has developed a far more luxurious, and complex, approach.

It was not always so. When he and his wife Katherine bought their seventeenth-century cottage thirty years ago, the only water was from a well, lower down the hill. They simply lowered a bucket into its depths and poured the clear drinking water into jugs to hand-carry up to the kitchen. Five years later, Simon installed a sink and waste pipe. 'Can you imagine it,' he recalled nostalgically, 'a waste pipe! We were so excited.' Next came an inlet pipe and the kind of foot-pump used in boats and caravans to bring water from a well direct to the sink. Baths were taken in a tub placed on top of an open fire range, and with friends visiting frequently 'each one was a performance'.

The water supply leapt forward when Simon bought an adjoining field, with 'an intermittent spring' crossing his land which feeds into four 2,200-gallon tanks, each costing about £1,000 and spread around where he can make best use of them. When there is a water surplus, the tanks overflow into two ornamental ponds. The total amount of water gathered depends on the weather, but 'we really have stacks, even with watering the two veg gardens almost daily in hot, dry weather'. A quarter of a century later the couple still pay no water rates, and the storage has expanded to another four tanks which take rainwater harvested off the roofs of the house and newer outhouses. Each of the tanks is capable of supplying top-quality drinkable water, largely thanks to the German Wisy filters Simon found on the web (www.wisy.de; the UK distributor is Rainharvesting Systems at www.rainharvesting.co.uk). The simple, ingenious gadget is inserted halfway along the downpipe from the roof. Using the natural surface tension of the water, as it passes over the fine filter the dirt separates out and is sent back into the main pipe and down the drain; the clean water goes off at an angle to one of the tanks. Key to the success of the system is that each tank is independent of the others. 'It's very important you don't have everything linked. You don't want a small grandchild to leave a tap on and drain the entire system.'

For drinking water, Simon also has 1,800 gallons underground in a concrete tank, and a separate 1,000-gallon steel tank, both of which feed into a clay filter beside the kitchen sink. 'It doesn't taste too wonderful when the flow is right down,' Simon confided. 'We had it passed with flying colours last year by the water inspector lady from Brecon, but she did say it was a snapshot and I think we should get it checked every other year.'

This complex system has grown over the years, and Simon is probably the only person who fully understands it. For an altogether simpler approach I consulted the aptly named Roy Fountain.

His place came with a spring at the bottom of the land which provided water for the sheep. But as his water usage increased, Roy realised he would have to act to ensure a constant supply of water in the summer, and he decided to spring for a borehole. He invited various locals around, and between them they decided where they thought the water would be. Next task, find a drilling company. Some charge by the hour, others ask for a 50 per cent deposit plus the balance of the flat fee if they find water. The drilling company must have lost money on their deal with Roy because 'it took him till eleven thirty to finish on a misty November night. Once they hit water, at about a hundred metres, they pumped compressed air down the borehole to flush all the rubbish out, and all this grey mud flew into the air.

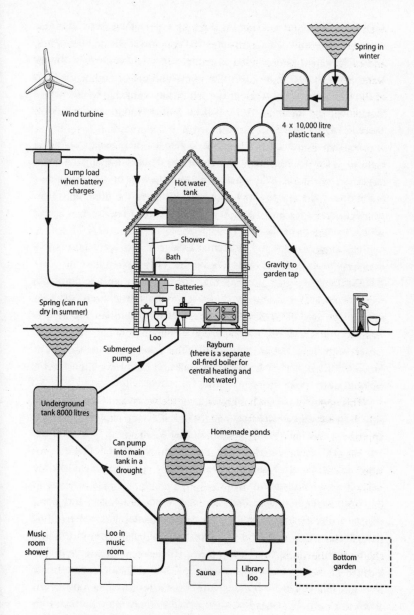

Simon Marr-Johnson's water system.

Luckily they had the wet gear on, but we were scraping the mud off the caravan for months after.' Because the hole was so deep they had to weld the water-carrying tubes together. It must have been a strange sight, with the men in their wet gear and the arc-lights throwing shadows on the night-time fog. The whole job cost £5,500, including a steel lining and a pump. 'We've had no bother with it. It's been down there nearly ten years.'

For non-domestic use a borehole owner will still have to pay water rates to the water company. This applies to farmers and anyone growing on a commercial scale, whether it's food, flowers or hay for animals. But it does not apply to simple domestic water, so it is possible to have access to water for only the cost of finding and extracting it – as long as it is solely a domestic supply.

At Land Matters, the residents decided to go for a borehole a couple of years after moving onto the site. They looked into the possibility of bringing water up from their stream with hydraulic pumps or even mechanical ones, but concluded it was impossible. Eventually they applied for Lottery funding. This was thanks to Christian Taylor, who had become head of science at a Steiner School in Totnes and began to bring his pupils up to the land for a two-week nature course. Permaculture hippies may not need grants for their water, but the Big Lottery Fund could see why a group of schoolchildren would need a borehole, and £4,000 was allotted to meet the cost quoted by a local firm. First a track had to be built so that the drilling equipment could be brought up the hill. Finally, in early August 2006, the drilling company arrived, and after two false starts they found water at 160 feet. This, however, left the problem of how to pump it up – a problem that has yet to be solved at time of writing.

With hosepipe bans a common occurrence in London and global warming threatening to dry out the nation's capital (if it doesn't flood first), I decided to investigate the possibility of a borehole in the tiny, inaccessible back yard of our house. There are only a few drilling companies doing this sort of work, and they are overwhelmed with demand. HD Drilling in Buckinghamshire was prepared to consider my request for a hole, but before they would even give me a quote they wanted me to pay the standard £250 to the British Geological Survey (BGS), which will look up your map reference and tell you what chance you have of finding drinkable water under your property. The BGS normally sells 400 of these contracts a year; it was about 800 in 2006, and they reckon about 2,000 boreholes were actually drilled in that year.

In my case the omens were good: the park across the road had a borehole at a depth of fifty metres which had once been the water supply of the East London Power & Light Company. There was a thin layer of clay near the surface which meant that the drilling would be easy and that the water table nearby is protected from local pollution. That is good news because 'shallow water round there would be dominated by mains and sewer leakage', the man from the BGS told me. The local water would also be high in iron content. 'It's not thought to be a health problem, but it tends to stain – laundry, for example, and plates.' To treat it you have to aerate the water by cascading then filtering it. So my borehole would also have to be a water feature in our Lilliputian yard.

When the estimate finally arrived, the costs were high. I had warned the company they would have to bring in the drilling equipment over a high wall, but neither that nor an allowance for London hassle explained the discrepancy between their quote and the price paid by Roy or Land Matters. HD wanted £5,000 for digging a ten-metre hole and an extra £90 per metre thereafter. If they did not find water my costs would be halved. Assuming they did, there would then be the extra cost of installing a metal well casing inside the hole. This was included in the £6,000 cost of installing the pump, but there would also be an additional cost of £95 per metre for every metre over ten. It was a useful exercise, but with our water use expected to cost £200 a year if metering was introduced, the £18,000 estimate did not make financial sense. Had I decided to take it further and haggle with the supplier I would have asked them to install a hand pump rather than the electrical one they recommended. And I would have chosen the one adopted as standard by the Intermediate Technology Group (www.practicalaction.org), the India Mk2, which is the Ford Escort of water-pumps in the developing world.

The recent series of droughts are still a worry, though, and we have decided to go for the far cheaper option of harvesting rainwater from our roof in London. A rainwater harvesting system is becoming a necessity for gaining planning permission in some new buildings. A system from the roof of the house or outhouse can be used for most domestic purposes apart from drinking. A typical roof size might be eighty square metres and this is the surface area that will trap your rain and run it off to storage tanks. If you are on the grid it's the essential preparation for the coming age of water metering, together with water-saving measures like showers instead of baths.

We will run a spur from our roof gutter to a recycled plastic tank, chosen to be narrow and tall for ease of storage. For reasons of space, Rainharvesting Systems suggest draining the water from a typical system into an underground storage tank, but this entails the use of an electric pump to bring it back up again, adding to installation cost and running expense. I remembered Judy's advice about simplicity. If you can site your tank high enough to use gravity to at least feed the ground floor and garden, then you can avoid the underground tank and the consequent need for an electric pump. Water tanks are available free (or very cheap) at most recycling centres. Some guttering and pipework and a bit of help from a plumber may be all you need to connect your rainwater to the right parts of the system.

If you can't gather a lot of water, either due to little rainfall or a small roof, then a standard-size tank is bigger than you need (www.water-tanks.net has tanks of all sizes). If you go for a purpose-built kit, Rainharvesting Systems will quote for off-grid systems based on the roof area of the house and how many loos/sinks you have. A system will cost you £1,500 to £2,500 plus. They tend to suggest you buy a pump, because most of their customers are on-grid, but they are helpful if you explain that you want a system that does not require a pump. Where drinking water is also needed, water can be sterilised using ultraviolet radiation and carbon filtration. You may want to make sure the rainwater does not come into the kitchen, and/or perhaps install separate drinking water taps. You may even have the opportunity to design your rainwater tank into the mains water system for the house. This could be because it is a new build or because you have a site for a large tank which is high up and therefore able to feed the whole house.

The Green Building Forum (www.greenbuildingforum.co.uk) has a useful section on rainwater. For figures on how much rain to expect in a month in your area, try www.meto.gov.uk/climate/uk/averages/ 19712000/sites/wisley.html.

A Word About Toilets

The water closet was first introduced into the language, if not the culture, in 1755. Cutting-edge off-grid toilets are still based around the idea of a free-standing closet, but water is not required. What you need is space, and possibly a power source.

I am ashamed to admit that for my first few years in Majorca I used to drive down the mountain track most mornings to the local four-star package tour hotels, the ones with swimming pools, to use their toilets, showers and indeed their pools. But with the help of Toni Baloney, my plumber neighbour, I now have a flushing loo, installed before I had ever heard of some of the alternatives listed below. If I had my time again I would do things differently. I can talk gaily, as I have done, about using a shovel to dig a hole and then covering it up again afterwards, but nobody could face doing that all the time, could they? Well, apart from Ross Kennard-Davis. Over the months in the van I slowly became more comfortable with the idea, but for most of us, most of the time, it is absurd. So, what are the options? Assuming you are prepared to make the investment, there are four: the digester toilet, the outhouse, the chemical toilet and the composting toilet.

The digester toilet is a fantastic piece of science which uses special microbes to digest your waste. The eventual result is some clear, clean, odour-free liquid which can go on the plants. The only problem is that it uses electricity to operate an aerator to oxygenate the waste. For some, that may be reason enough to omit it from consideration. And it can be expensive.

An outhouse is really just a glorified hole in the ground. The advantage is that, like the chemical toilet, no preparation is required, and waste gradually degrades in the pit and seeps into the soil. The pit eventually fills and the outhouse must then be moved. The initial cost depends on what materials you have to hand. It could be as little as £25. It consumes no power, is easy and inexpensive to build, and requires no pipes or water; neither does it have any moving parts.

The disadvantages are that in summer you can be guaranteed an unpleasant smell, and more seriously, it might contaminate ground-water in the area.

Next to be eliminated is the chemical toilet, which is relatively odourless, except for the smell of the chemicals, which can be dangerous to children. And where do you dispose of the waste once the toilet is full? You can hardly pour chemicals into the ground.

The toilet of choice for most sophisticated off-gridders is the composting loo. The way it works requires more space than the others, but if space is not an issue – or even if it is – the results can be very good. The space is required partly for the drop between the seat and the bin where the waste is stored, and also to allow room for the pee to go out a separate way. The principle of the composting loo is that the waste dries and becomes first-class manure.

When there is only one person, or even one family, using a composting loo, they seem to work well. There was not the slightest smell from Judy's shed, and Marcus's composting loo was calm and clean, with a beautiful view. But the ones in communal situations like Allaleigh or at the Big Green Gathering were a bit stinky. Whether this was because of the greater use or because of improper use I could not tell.

I met one of the country's leading experts on composting toilets while at the Big Green Gathering. Dave Wood runs the Thunderbox company in Devon (www.thunderboxes2go.co.uk). His thunderboxes are designed for 'easy production of friable compost'. And Dave will chatter away for hours about his product. 'To create safe and useful compost,' he told me, 'the material needs to either spend considerable time composting away from human contact, thereby breaking the pathogens cycle, or by rapid "hot composting". Oxygen-loving bacteria are present almost anywhere. They

Judy again – kindly posing on her privy.

do have specific requirements though. Just like a fire they need oxygen and fuel in the right condition. The "fuel" in this case is our "deposits" plus "soak" – usually sawdust or straw. This produces a mix of carbon to nitrogen of around 30:1. A cubic metre of fresh compost will reduce by one third in a month and a further third in three months, with turning once a week. It can get to sixty degrees Centigrade. This will kill all known pathogens to humans in hours.' It takes between six months and two years for compost to be available, depending on how dry it is in the loo. During the summer, if the composter is indoors for example, six months is plenty, but if it is outdoors in a damp spot, it might take well over a year.

Dave sells single composting loos from £800 and doubles from £1,000. By definition, a compost toilet produces compost, not waste, and many choose to have a double chamber installed so that when the first fills up and is still composting you can switch to the second. Dave supplied a couple of these double loos for use at Big Green, tucked away in the eco-homes section, and they were infinitely less unpleasant than the rows of chemical loos on offer. They had high steps, about five feet in height, and consequently a long drop from the loo to the large compost container below. This allowed for a larger container and made for fresher air in the loo.

Your off-grid toilet is a decision that will affect happiness for those few minutes per day, every day. It's also a political statement, because if you deal with your own shit instead of refusing to think about where it goes, you are very much in charge of your own life.

Neighbour Problems

I felt I was at least beginning to understand how to find the right land, and what to do once I had it, but it was still hard to see how an outsider, a city dweller like me, could make a success of the rural off-grid life. From what I'd learned on my trip around the UK, high on the list of skills required was the ability to manage your nearest though not necessarily dearest.

Once he had established himself there, Alan Bush looked around Scoraig one day and noticed he had almost no neighbours. There had been a population of five before he arrived; Alan, his wife and three children now contributed to a population of seven, the only others being the very old and eccentric pair of Kentish vegetarians on the other side of the peninsula. They used to delight in tormenting poor Alan, phoning the local council and complaining about almost everything he did. They literally made his life a misery, and he worked as hard as he could to recruit others to come and live at Scoraig as a kind of counterbalance.

Nigel Lowthrop and his partner Karen had the opposite experience when they moved into Hill Holt Wood. With industrial farmland on one side of the wood and a fast road on the other there was never any local opposition other than bloody-minded officials.

But Marcus Tribe and Sarah Harvey can trace their problems almost entirely back to their neighbours. They moved into their wood as soon as they bought it, living in a tiny caravan for the first year. But shortly after they built their yurt they had an altercation with a local farmer and within a few weeks the couple had a visit from the local council enforcement officer, which was swiftly followed by an enforcement notice. An enforcement notice from a council is a serious thing; you cannot just ignore it. The council use it when they think there has been a breach of planning control, either because of a change of use (such as from agricultural to residential) or when a building has gone up without permission. (For a clear explanation of enforcement notices, see www.planning-applications.co.uk/enforcement1.htm; and see chapter 7 for more details about planning permission and how to deal with it.) You have just twenty-eight days to appeal, and there are many grounds for doing so. But whatever your case, the notice is the heavy reality that shows your off-grid activities have come to the attention of the authorities.

'You want to be polite to neighbours,' Simon Fairlie advised me, 'but if they aren't polite to you, if they are going to be prejudiced against you, then you have to just ignore them. You get problems with neighbours everywhere, but unless they are remarkably powerful the planning system will ignore them. Never worry about them getting in a tizzy. Some of them will come round and some will live in a great big sulk for the rest of their lives.' Simon has only ever seen one appeal when the inspector paid any attention to the neighbours. 'At the

[Tinker's] Bubble we had 144 letters of objection to our first appeal, but the inspector still recommended in favour. Five years later it was down to twenty-seven letters of objection. When we renewed last time, there were no letters of objection. Once you've been through that, you think, "I can't be bothered with these people." '

That may all be sound advice, but it's hard to follow when you are right in the middle of a battle, with the hostilities and paranoia that induces. Whether it was the commune at Steward Wood getting jumpy because I parked my car too close to the neighbours, or Emma in Brith Dir Mawr welcoming journalists of all sorts to help publicise her struggle and the wider principles at stake, or Marcus Tribe doing his best to get on with the locals, the natural tendency when you are under threat is to be extra pleasant to those around you, even if they are nasty back.

Bad neighbours cut both ways. No doubt they can cause all sorts of stress over the years, but every once in a while the neighbours could be the reason the locals are leaving a piece of land alone. After all, if you find a fantastic wood on the market at a cheap price and you think, "This is too good to be true" – well, it probably is.

By the time Judy of the Woods bought her second tranche of land, she had already fallen out with her other neighbour – or rather he had fallen out with her. Shortly after she moved into the woods, still staying in her camper van, he told her she had no right of way up the only track that led from the road to her land. He was an 'incomer', a Londoner who had bought his piece of countryside and did not want to share it with anyone. He had, Judy told me, the mind-set that allowed him to think she was merely a woman who would know nothing and obey him. Judy ignored his opening gambit, so he dug a ditch in the way of the track. She filled it in. Then he positioned his cattle feeder so that the cows would stand in the road to feed, causing maximum damage. She complained to the council and he had to move it, which just stoked his already smouldering resentment. By then he had complained about her filthy off-grid habits, but a planning control officer remarked, 'If I had to remove every hippie and hermit from a woodland I would never do my proper job.' The neighbour took to driving his tractor up and down the track, both churning it up and occasionally delaying Judy if she was on her way to or coming back from town. 'Finally he moved away two years ago. Nobody round here liked him. A lot of people talked to him so as not to have too much hassle.' Now, over a decade since she moved out of her caravan and into her first self-build dwelling, Judy has a very settled life.

To some extent, then, dealing with bad neighbours is much the same thing as standing up to bullies. The analogous situation in an urban environment is moving to a crime-ridden, dirty street and toughing out the problems for a few years until the area improves.

Over in Hay on Wye, it is likely that Ross Kennard-Davis's neighbours – given their well-publicised tussle with the previous owner, his uncle – discouraged knowledgeable locals from bidding for the place, thus making it more affordable. Ross's neighbours are the sort who only get on with other hill farmers, and perhaps not even with them. One visited Ross soon after I first met him to tell him he should just leave. 'Sell the land, and fuck off' were the exact words used. Another wrote to his bank to tell them he had cancelled the contract for commercial right of way that allowed Ross to carry the stone across his land, in the hope that this would cause Ross's mortgage to be withdrawn and force him to sell, but that backfired. 'The bank was quite supportive,' Ross told me. 'They put it to the solicitors at Barclays, who said because [the neighbours] had accepted payment from me they waived the right to complain about breach.' He added, 'I went to see the neighbours to ask them whether they would leave me alone if I stopped the parties, but they said no.'

Ross decided to circumvent his contract problems by bringing his stone out via an old bridleway, but other neighbours complained to the council that Ross was building a road, though he maintains that all he was doing was repairing the bridleway where it had been damaged by cattle. He immediately started to make contingency plans. 'I'm not going to roll over and let them beat me on this one,' he said. 'I have a very good 4×4 lorry I could use.' His plan was to drive the stone across his own land and onto a public bridleway. But 'the route via the bridleway is very challenging. I would need to prepare sections of it where it will be very difficult in the winter.' And the ancient bridleways are overseen by a group called the Grazers who have already sent Ross a letter saying he 'may not build a road across the common'.

Ross mining his sandstone.

So Ross will stay with his girlfriend in winter and work the land in summer. And he will continue to have 'a couple of hundred people for bank holiday parties'. The police don't mind about them as long as they hear from Ross in advance.

He may not think so, but on one level Ross has cracked it. His neighbours hate him, but the bank is on his side and the police are on his side. He's got 200 friends who are prepared to travel to this wild, inhospitable mountainside for the pleasure of his company. And he can make £500 a day whenever he wants.

The problem for anyone trying to establish themselves off-grid is that the balance of power is too far in favour of neighbours. One complaint can ruin your off-grid life for ever.

Nigel and Sandy cross all kinds of social boundaries; they're 'in' with both the horsey set and itinerant traveller types. They invited one van dweller to live in the twelve-acre wood they acquired along with their farm, but because their guest parked near the side of a footpath, someone complained. 'It was a footpath that used to join one railway station to another,' Sandy explained, 'and the footpath goes alongside the old railway. Someone got this proprietorial thing – just nosey neighbour stuff. The council came to investigate two years later, and now he is going to have to leave and go back on the road after seven years.'

I was becoming used to these kinds of stories: off-grid dweller doing no harm causes huge offence to local busybody, shock horror. The hapless van dweller is moved on, the community loses a member. The complainant feels he has halted the decline of the area and reduced the chances that travellers will end up on his own land. But, Sandy pointed out passionately as she tried to make a common-sense distinction between property speculation and looking for somewhere one can call home, 'They must understand when they walk through the countryside that there could be something else going on there. To have these strictures about how the countryside should be used and that footpaths have to be in straight lines between places that nobody ever goes to because that's the way they have always been – well, it's not the way real people live. People live in funny little shacks and they always have done, and then they leave and the shacks all fall down. People should relax. You use your common sense. Anyone could see our chap was not trying to put up a block of flats. If our neighbours had just relaxed a bit they would have realised he was beneficial for the area. Everybody in the village knows he is living in the wood and has done for years. Tramps and gypsies were around here for years and they were very useful.' They are an extra pair of eyes, better than any CCTV camera, and they could traditionally be relied upon for odd jobs. 'If they stepped out of line they were soon moved on.

'It's the difference between the person trying to make money out of the countryside through property development and the person who just wants to live in the countryside,' Sandy concluded. I said the law found it difficult to distinguish between the two, and had to ban the latter in order to prevent the former. But Sandy disagreed with the way her local council, at least, went about it. 'There's a place near Rhyader called the Peod. For the last twenty years people have been living there in vans, shacks, houses – a farmer allowed them to park up there in tents and tipis. Powys have spent £10 million in the last twenty years trying to kick them out and finally they have had to give in because one person got residency. So all that money was wasted.'

Communes and Communities

The superior resources of a group, whether in terms of chipping in for expensive lawyers or because they comprise a confusing mix of different household units, repeatedly allow larger settlements to run rings around local councils in ways single households have not achieved. There are between fifty and a hundred off-grid communities in the UK with populations of between a dozen and a couple of hundred, and many more currently searching for land. All communes are communities, but not all communities are communes. The difference is that communes have a group decision-making structure, sometimes but not always formalised into a constitution or shared legal ownership.

Dylan Evans's plan for an experimental commune is focused on seeing how the rules of the group are formed. He started with a few base rules: obey the law of the land; Dylan is the only permanent resident; all volunteers can stay a maximum of three months. All other rules were up to the residents to agree together, and they would be subject to change as they learned from experience, and as specific individuals came and went. Would work become compulsory, for example? Would there be cooking and cleaning rotas? Dylan was expecting the experiment to run for up to eighteen months before he had any conclusions.

Communities like Tipi Valley in Wales and Scoraig in Scotland have no rules. They are looser groupings of single households which are more or less autonomous. On Scoraig, it was Alan Bush who had the guts to move to a deserted area and start farming it. Others followed. So the first lesson is that you do not need to gather a group around you in advance of starting a community or a commune. If the conditions are right, if the space is available, the group will follow, whether the impetus comes from a communard like Dylan or an anarcho-agriculturalist like Alan.

The history of the development of Scoraig's community is revealing. In 1961, Alan found he had unwittingly arrived in a dying farming community, a decline that was to be repeated all across Britain. But he did not have to wait long before another pioneer appeared on the scene. Tom Forsyth, the figure with the wild white beard I had met on the path during my visit, had learned about Scoraig through a chance meeting in 1963 with an American agricultural equipment salesman. In a stirring example of salesmanship, the American had taken a tiny boat across the peninsula to sell Alan some new-fangled farming implements.

By late 1963, Tom was living on a separate croft near Alan, so both of them had control of a strip of land perhaps a mile wide leading down to the water's edge. Under crofting law they had the right to subdivide it. They put the word out via friends and families, and began to offer sections of their land to anyone who was willing to turn up and work for a few months in order to become acquainted and make sure they were suited to the lifestyle.

At the time, Tom was on a fully fledged sixties spiritual quest. His striking looks and enthusiasm attracted the attention of local nobility. 'Ursula, Lady Burton, wife of the owner of part of Loch Ness, walked onto the peninsula with a couple of friends,' Tom recounted to me. Lady Burton was an Episcopalian, and the bishop had asked her to visit Scoraig and report back. Others who took an interest were the Duchess of Hamilton, who invited Tom to Lennoxlove, and multimillionairess Jane Owen, who paid Tom some expenses for eco-projects elsewhere in Scotland. But it was Lady Burton who was soon entertaining Tom at her husband's baronial hall. 'We were sipping champagne' and hatching plans to start a community, said Tom. Lesson number two, therefore, is to find yourself, if you possibly can, some highly placed and preferably wealthy benefactor who will sponsor your commune or community. In these less class-ridden days, your sponsors are more likely to be city traders working off the guilt of their huge bonuses than members of the aristocracy, who are either too impoverished or too selfish in my experience. And whereas in the sixties the idea of a community was enough, especially if there was a bit of sex and drugs involved, in these post-Kyoto days it needs to be an eco-community, preferably constituted in such a way that donations are tax deductible.

Scoraig's population may now be approaching eighty, but it is not without its critics. Tommy Beavitt, who grew up on the peninsula, was one of a group of younger residents wanting to build a 'local power grid'. He was opposed by Hugh Piggott and others on the grounds that 'the rest of the country is on the grid, and if you want to live on the grid then go and live somewhere else'. The arguments became intense and personal, as they are prone to do in isolated communities, and Tommy left in 2006. Living off-grid 'tends to accompany and even encourage what I would describe as a survivalist mentality', Tommy told me when we spoke on the phone. 'It is firmly linked in the minds of those who espouse it with the obnoxious doctrine of self-sufficiency that has permeated the drop-out movement from the 1960s to the present day. The baseline rationale is something like "If I can't do any good, at least I can go somewhere where I won't be doing any harm." As a child I was totally in thrall to this guiding ethic of my parents' generation and it has taken me a long while to realise why this attitude is so offensive. The trouble is that it allows its adherents to adopt an "I'm all right, Jack!" attitude to the looming energy crisis. I have lost count of the number of times I have heard wind-farm nimbys state that they are all in favour of local, small-scale, stand-alone installations but that they object to the "inhuman scale" of the pylons and turbines. To me this is an extremely short-sighted and selfish attitude which totally ignores the global scale of the challenges facing us. I would like to say that Scoraig was immune to this kind of thinking, but actually I have recently come to believe that it constitutes one of the most egregious examples.'

The rows over the use of motorbikes along the narrow mountain paths have crystallised into another battle between young and old, the young wanting the technology and the old-timers arguing that they can find grids and motorbikes everywhere else in the country, so why on earth would they want to come here, the one place that does not have modern technology, and insist on introducing it? 'I studied botany,' cried Tom as he railed against the trail bikes. 'I am a great lover of plants. It hurts me to see the land being chewed up and plants being damaged.' Not that Tom is any sort of Luddite. Now seventy-six, he is delighted with his new wind-up LED torch, an £8.99 Dynabrite from Task Tools in Kingston on Hull. It runs for over twenty minutes if you wind it for one minute 'and fits nicely in the hand'. But he is just as at home making a brazier 'out of the knots in a pine tree'.

This generational conflict, however, is not necessarily unhealthy, which is the third lesson I learned from Scoraig. Its success is in part due to the fact that it does not have any overarching rules, other than each man for himself, or rather each house for itself. There are no endless meetings around the campfire about the rights and wrongs of trail bikes on the path; no debates about Kyoto; no measurement of carbon foot-prints. People just get on and live their lives, and if they don't like it there any more, they leave. Just like most other places in fact. Anyone can go and live on Scoraig these days. In the 1960s you had to pass an interview with one of the original residents who owned the crofting rights, but these have been subdivided so many times that a free market now exists. 'It's totally anarchic,' Tom explained. Each individual person who has been granted crofting rights by the Crofting Commission can agree to subdivide their croft, as long as they can get permission from the commission and the landlord. They can then give their land away or sell it.

The Scoraig experience provides a model I think many could follow, as long as they have land and existing locals do not prevent them from setting up. At Townhead near Sheffield there is a contrasting ethic. The group sets rules for most of what goes on outside the individuals' own homes. Whatever you might think of this, it works in the sense that the place is successful, thriving and growing. Decisions are arrived at by majority if a consensus can't be found. Most often members of the group lobby one another to achieve a consensus before any major decision is taken. The residents are all members of a co-operative, which means each owns shares in the organisation Lifespan, which in turn is the official owner of the property. Group meetings take

Piet and his 50s-style control panel.

place in the courtyard between the two sets of houses, in the communal space, or in the pool room where Piet Defoe and I had sat drinking beers during his marathon stint on the Bus's electrics. Sometimes lone dissenters (usually Piet) are over-ruled. 'I don't want to stop things happening, but I don't do group-think,' Piet told me. 'I would rather agree to disagree and let the majority get on with it, as long as my objections are noted.'

Before the current residents arrived, Piet explained, the commune was going through a sticky patch with the wrong sort of members, many of whom were 'into bad drugs' and uninterested in maintaining or improving the land and buildings, 'more into profiteering from the place'. Piet and his friends arrived in 1998 and set about revitalising it. Many of the dozen or so adults were friends before they moved in to the group of terraced houses out in the middle of open countryside. They had met on road protests and now they were looking for a more stable base. Some came from other communities when they heard Townhead was attempting a fresh start, and a couple of the members had been living on travellers' sites. About half of them remain, and others joined over the years. The numbers continue to grow slowly.

Some of the eight children on the commune are collected by a school bus during term time while others are home-educated. It was midsummer when I visited and there was decent money being made from an honesty box at the front gate selling berries and vegetables. That was spent buying implements, seeds and fruit trees. Some of the members claim the dole, but most work, either on the commune's own land or in nearby towns. Piet himself makes a low-wage living from his renewable energy business, Raisystems, and computing activities. He personally lives on 'about £25 a week – that's for food and general living'. Other members of the commune make between £3,000 and £10,000 a year, he told me, but 'I turn over more; it's just most of the projects I run are not for profit.' One of these 'projects' is the commune shop whose profits go to funding more renewable energy resources and providing Internet access for the group. There is a mixture of private and shared renewable energy at the houses. Piet has his own supply, and each household has its own solar panels and, in some cases, mini wind turbines, but there are also several shared wind turbines. Most members of the commune are vegetarian, but there is 'everything from avid carnivores to full-on vegan. The communal kitchen is vegetarian – milk and eggs allowed, but no meat.' There is no rota for cooking, cleaning or gardening, and there are 'non-compulsory work weekends'.

This is only one template, but communal life generally is not for everyone. Jyoti Fernandes tried it for years and never settled into it. She was at Tinker's Bubble with Simon Fairlie and left at roughly the same time as him because the conditions were just not right for long-term enjoyment. 'It's underneath a lot of trees at Tinker's and far away from the growing area, so it's dark there, and I mostly wanted to be growing,' Jyoti explained. 'If you wanted to nip out to do a bit of garden work you would have to go all the way down the hill and then all the way up again. I wanted to change the layout, zone it according to common sense and permaculture. There was great resistance to that. It's hard to change the way things are done in communes. I wanted it to be more like a commercial farm and have more control over running the place.' Her patience with group consensus decision-making exhausted, that was when she, her husband Dai and their three children teamed up with another family and founded Fivepenny Farm. They have joint ownership of the land with the other family but don't make joint business decisions, nor do they have the shared mealtimes of commune living to contend with.

At Brith Dir Mawr, the original founders also concluded that communal life did not suit them, though the later joiners are still happily living in the converted farm outhouses. Julian Orbach, who bought the place, has moved out, of course, and Emma, Tony and Jane have separate holdings elsewhere on the same land where they are not governed by group decisions. So now both systems are operating, and arguably it's the best of both worlds as a result – a community with a commune at its heart. There are half a dozen households in the commune ranging from two parents and two children down to single guys, living separately but sharing the main farmhouse as the group eating area and garden. Tony and his wife have their roundhouse in a separate field, next to their market garden; Emma has her area of twenty acres or more, with its collection of sheds, huts, yurts and tipis. The three groups co-operate on practical matters like stacking hay, and maintenance of paths and fences.

As my journey progressed and I saw more off-grid groups in action, I decided I would not live in a commune of any sort. Even the loose arrangements of Brith Dir Mawr would probably be too much for me – if I failed to recycle some of my rubbish, for example, and had to run a gauntlet of disapproving stares. And the frequent impasses would I'm sure prove too much for my patience. At Land Matters I noticed that the development of the agricultural base was being held back because of disagreements over whether to keep livestock – disagreements

Dynyn – every country house could be like this.

between vegans and meat eaters. There were only two vegans, I was told, but there was no mechanism, or perhaps no enthusiasm, for simply overruling a minority view. I expect in the medium term that is what will happen. A similar log-jam developed over the plans to draw water from the new borehole. The price had included installation of a £700 electric pump, but that was still sitting unused some months later. The problem was the expense of providing electricity for the pump, which needs four times as much power to start it as it requires once it is running. This entails a large investment in wind or solar power, and batteries. A volunteer had offered to build a hand pump, but not until some time in 2007. Some members of the group wanted to return the pump and get their money back; others – especially the mothers – wanted to use it temporarily. But that would mean its resale value was reduced. So three months after it was sunk, the borehole had yet to provide any water for the commune. It was another example of group decision-making slowing down progress.

Some communities are run by a single leader who chooses who comes and goes. Dylan Evans, for example, selected his ideal cast list from the volunteers for his Utopia Experiment who all contacted him in response to media coverage; Alan Bush and Tom Forsyth decided who they would allow to set up crofts at Scoraig (and who they would turf out once their probationary period was over). In both those cases, once they were in, the new members had roughly equal rights with the old. The same is not true at Tapeley Hall, where Hector Christie is sole arbiter of who can live there.

Hector is a giant personality. The first time I saw him, he was striding out of the kitchen door, eyes fixed on some visitors who had just arrived. 'Ah, the serfs!' I could swear he had cried, but when I saw them pulling surfboards out of the car I realised he must have been greeting 'the surfers'. If his life had gone in a different direction, Hector would be living with the usual set of paid staff – secretary, butler, cook and housemaid; instead he has a retinue of ex-homeless volunteers. He has only one full-time member of staff as well as the two-day-a-week volunteers, and that's the gardener who works in a huge walled garden beside the house. His pay is covered by the surplus products sold locally – maize, asparagus, artichokes, carrots, beans, spinach, peppers, grapes,

Hector and the north wing of Tapeley.

and fruit from the old apple and pear trees. There are also three poly-tunnels next to the little plantation where I parked the Bus, producing several bushels more food, mainly greens. And there is no shortage of mouths to feed. Up to twenty people stay there in the summer – they tend to be 'vaguely hippy types from all over the country,' one of the locals told me – though in the winter the population is smaller, older and more local. With house prices rising faster in Devon than almost anywhere else in the country, stress and homelessness are rising too. Many of the guests would be homeless if they were not at Tapeley, either because they have alcohol problems or because they lost their agricultural job and the house that went with it.

Later I spoke to a woman whom Hector had ejected, and I felt grateful I had not been drawn in further. She had been accused of stealing and was asked to leave. The theft was nothing serious – not one of the William Morris ornaments Hector keeps in the formal wing of the house, with museum-like equipment monitoring the dampness levels. It was someone else's duvet cover. Hector told me that he had quelled a mini-rebellion among the guests, who thought they could run the place better than he. Now they had been caught stealing, he said, his eyes widening. 'Can you believe it? That's the way they thank me.' Of course I believed him. I was fascinated at this apparent insight into the prob-lem of a commune run by a benign dictator. 'It was a feudal system under the disguise of a community,' recalled the woman.

For me, as I've said before, the attraction of the off-grid life is freedom and independence. I knew I would never be able to submit to a higher authority, however benign. That was exactly what I wanted to avoid. I considered the possibility of becoming the leader myself, but having followers is a grave responsibility. And so I could cross this approach off my list. I had learned the downside of democratic communal decision-making. Yet again I returned to Scoraig as a model I personally might be able to adopt: a close community with the strength in numbers that brings, no hostile neighbours, and a relatively supportive wider community. If only it was somewhere less isolated.

However, there was another possibility, one that combined the options, allowing isolation at times but also a coming-together with others when you felt like it.

Caravan Park-Ups

A boat, a van or a caravan provides the off-gridder with a self-contained autonomous unit in which one can be as free or as integrated into a community as one chooses. Thanks to the Bus, I had already tasted this lifestyle, and it worked for me. Now I only needed to find a community of like-minded van dwellers parked in a field where everyone had a large space and complete autonomy (as long as they didn't interfere with anyone else's autonomy, of course).

Paul and Susie, in their gypsy caravan in Somerset, know all about the semi-mobile existence I had in mind. The second time I met them was at the Big Green Gathering, to which they had hauled the very same caravan. They were by now relatively long-term residents on the farm where I had visited them. Susie worked in the farm shop, and they had become good friends with the farmer and his wife. I had no doubt that Paul's farmer landlord was a reasonable man, but with the example of Hector Christie still fresh in my mind I felt I had to be able to park the Bus in a field of my own where I would never be dependent on someone else's decisions.

Paul and Susie had picked up a cheap nearby orchard at an auction a few years previously, but as Paul explained to me, they wouldn't risk their future living there because they were 'not passionate about growing vegetables'. They could go for planning permission under the rules that allowed sustainable agricultural development, but 'we know a lot of friends who have done that and ten years later their backs are aching, but they have no choice, they have to keep going.' Paul's research had taught him that much of the land off-gridders would find desirable is sold without ever reaching the open market, in private deals between farmers who meet on market day and 'shake hands as they lean on the Land Rover outside the cattle auction'. Even if I could do a deal with an old-boy farmer, how would I sustain ten years, or even ten months, of agricultural work?

Perhaps I would have to stay mobile, a few weeks here and there, thus never becoming dependent on any one scene. I remembered writing an article about a twenty-five-year-old van dweller called Charlie Danger (he changed his name by deed poll), who spent most of his time in and around London, living full-time in a 1986 Ford Transit van he bought for £150 and had customised himself. 'It was a minibus originally so it has windows all the way around,' Charlie told me. 'When I'm parked in a field it's like sitting in a conservatory.' Charlie used to be an educational consultant working for the Royal Institute for the Blind, among other clients. 'It was the stress of the job, and sharing a flat with people that didn't pay their bills' that led him to the van. 'I'm quite proud of the way I live and it shows there's an alternative to the normal rushing-around-paying-bills sort of living. I built a little bed along one side and a sink and a cooker on the other side. It is a very small space but I think of it as being my bedroom and the world is my living room.' Parking in a city can be difficult, so he keeps 'lists of places I parked that were successful. One thing you have to watch out for is cambers in the road. You can fall out of bed or wake up in the night crammed against the windowpane.'

On second thoughts, I had already experienced the van on my travels, and although it was delightful as a break from the reality of living in a three-storey house, I did not think I could do it for too long. I need to feel that I can close the front door, and in doing so close out the external world. On one level that is what makes a home. This feeling was confirmed to me when I heard from Charlie again many months after I first tried to re-contact him. It was a short email, but it told me all I needed to know. 'I don't think I'll be of much use to you any more since my van and its contents was stolen (not while I was in it),' he wrote, 'and I've had to resort to living in bricks again. I did get another similar van but it was stolen before I even started to convert it. The van-dwelling life isn't very compatible with London.'

I'd never had the Bus so much as tampered with, despite leaving it parked for weeks in a yard in darkest Hackney. If I was depending on it as my only source of shelter, how hard would it hit me if it was so much as vandalised, never mind stolen? At least with a house you can be pretty confident it will still be there when you get home. The city was now exposed as a nest of faceless enemies. But the country seemed to me to have its own dangers, mainly from neighbours whose identities one knew only too well. Where to go? What to do next?

Maybe a canal could provide me with the cheap off-grid existence I was seeking. In fact, it proved to be not as cheap as it was a few years ago. In the past five years or so, Renee Vaughan Sutherland explained

Off-grid in the city – at a price.

as we sat on her boat moored in the middle of Springfield Park, the price of canal living in London has doubled, under the influence of the land-based property market. People are paying up to hundreds of thousands, not for the boats but for the moorings, which are in short supply. There are a total of 25,500 British Waterways moorings, most of them grid-connected, but around 3,000 do not have mains power and water. As a result there is a long waiting list, administered partly by British Waterways and partly by individual private marinas. Once you are granted a mooring, usually on a twenty-five-year lease, you have limited security of tenure as long as you keep paying the fees. If you want to travel in the vessel you also have to buy an annual waterways licence which varies in price according to where you want to go. But Renee does not have a mooring, which is why her boat was so cheap in the first place. Instead she paid for a different class of licence, called 'continuous cruising', which means she is allowed to stay in one spot only for up to two weeks. If you stay a bit longer, then nine times out of ten nothing happens. But 10 per cent of offenders are fined. British Waterways say there are about 2,000 continuous cruisers in the UK. Renee's favourite places to stay in London are Angel Islington and on the Regents Canal near Camden. These are pricier areas than Springfield Park, but there she feels less at risk from gangs of kids who are the bane of boat owners everywhere. There are other advantages. The flats and offices overlooking the canal all have wire-less broadband and sometimes she can surf the web for free from her deck. The Angel stretch of the canal also has a famous tunnel where Renee sometimes shows her films, projected onto the curving brick walls.

Renee has an extraordinary ability to make the most of her surroundings – the reason why she can make life on a boat work while so many others can't. Plus, as she told me when we met, she loved water and wanted to live close to it.

Off-Grid Space-Hunter's Checklist

My tour of Britain had introduced me to a varied collection of mini-country landowners. It had taught me that owning land was difficult, it could be expensive, and it could even lead to back-breaking commitments. Occasionally I had come across someone who had managed to live quietly and contentedly, but they were the exception rather than the rule, as were the beautiful and affordable pieces of land I had visited.

The moral of the tale appears to be that you should not hold out for that perfect piece of countryside as it may never arrive. Instead, aim to get something that will allow you to do most of what you want. You are unlikely to find the ultimate beauty spot any more. And you have to be prepared to pay: an acceptable piece of land will cost much less than a house, but much more than a car.

By the end of the journey I had put together my checklist:

❖ Beautiful

❖ Legal access

❖ Cheap

❖ South-facing (or if not south-facing then at least having sun all year round)

❖ Tolerant neighbours

❖ Quiet

❖ Local council with good record on eco-projects

❖ Good cell phone reception (landline access?)

❖ Well above sea level (flooding has become more common)

❖ Mixed use – pasture and wood

❖ Good general condition – not over-harvested, not left to go wild

❖ Sheltered but with an exposed area for siting a wind turbine

❖ Water supply from spring or well (to supplement rainwater harvesting)

❖ Road access all year round (check the winter conditions)

❖ Access to local amenities such as shops and pub

❖ Outside but on the edge of a local development area

Others no doubt will have different priorities. Without question, my own list puts beauty first. I could not imagine going to the effort of living off-grid without a massive reward right up front from the sheer joy of getting up each day and looking around outside at a magnificent view. That does not necessarily mean a panoramic vista. I would be just as happy with an enclosed landscape including a few beautiful old trees. Legal access, however, goes without saying. My own experience and that of countless others, including Ross in Wales, showed that you must eliminate the negative possibilities or you might end up regretting your purchase.

So, be prepared to compromise, and remember, the main aim should be to enjoy it now, not at some indefinable time in the future. If you are taking on a long-term project requiring lots of work, then you must expect to enjoy the work. Otherwise you might as well get a shed from B&Q, or a camper van you can drive to half an acre whenever you feel like a break. And I have to say, this last idea was really beginning to seem an attractive solution to me.

7

Gimme Shelter
– from Benders
to Barns
(and even Houses)

*A country house should face slightly to the south-west. The dining
room should face east . . . in the depth of winter, when the sun rises
in the south-east, you will get sunlight at breakfast. The main living
rooms, where most of the day is spent, should be filled with sunlight
and therefore face south; the warmest room in every house is the
kitchen which therefore needs less sunlight . . . Larder and store-room
need to be kept cool so they should face north.*

The Countryman's Weekend Book (1944)

I F YOU ARE LUCKY enough to secure a good piece of land, or if you feel comfortable renting, you will soon want some sort of a shelter. It might just be a lean-to shed or a tent. It might be a barn or a yurt or an old bus. Whatever you're planning to put in place, here's a truth to live by: if you are off-grid you have to think about the sun. Where is it today? Where will it be tomorrow? Is there enough of it to heat your water, power your batteries and warm the damp air? If there is not enough sun, your shelter will still have to be capable of keeping you warm and dry.

Yurts, Tipis and Benders

The yurt and its cousin the tipi have become media favourites: a school in a yurt near Bath; a couple living in a yurt pitched in a back garden in Oxfordshire . . . It has become a symbol of our yearning to live more freely, to be less tied down by mortgages, or by conventional assumptions about what a living space should be. And because they tend to be round, yurts bring another dimension to the experience of free living: circles have a special place in our consciousness, echoing the shape of the earth, the sun and the moon.

The yurt was brought to this country by a few backpacking apostles, Brits like Hal Wynne-Jones, who came across them on the Anatolian plains, and Stephanie Bunn, a Manchester University academic and felt-maker. The Mongolian originals were made of felt. The design has hardly changed in the past millennium, but these days they come in a wide variety of materials including canvas, and can have an over-cover of the same shiny synthetic material that bags of animal feed are shipped in. The yurts, or *girs*, are designed to be completely mobile so that their occupants can shift home at will and still remain warm and comfortable. Large swathes of the Mongolian population still live in them, much as they did back in the time when the nomads of central Asia travelled widely to find food for their cattle.

In his book *Yurts, Tipis and Benders*, architect David Pearson lists some of the advantages of the yurt. It is strong, economical, long-lasting, portable and self-supporting, and it can even be moved fully built. It is easy to put up and take down, does no damage to the ground it is placed on, and its relatively low domed ceiling makes it less visible and therefore lower-impact than most houses or even bungalows. The circular shape is aerodynamic and deflects the wind. It is easy to heat and keep cool, and it can be made from cheap, local, environmentally friendly materials. If you want a yurt, you might be able to persuade Marcus Tribe to make one for you, if you tell him Off-grid Nick sent you. But Marcus is fearful of becoming a yurt production line, so his answer would depend on what mood he is in. You are on safer ground asking him to teach you how to build one yourself, or try commissioning one from Woodland Yurts of North Somerset (www.woodlandyurts.com).

The tipi (or tepee) is a different design, but with some similarities. It is circular, and it is made of canvas with a frame made of saplings, but it is more elegant than the yurt. In North America the tipi was the equivalent to what in Europe became the bender, as popularised by road protesters – the shelter for those who have no shelter. Benders are based on a design that has been traced back to prehistoric times: bent saplings covered in canvas, grass, moss, leaves or whatever comes to hand. They can be simple and crude or elaborate and delightful, and are often made of medium-weight white cotton canvas – not for reasons of price or ideology, but because the light looks good during the day.

Caravans and Mobile Homes

The classic caravan, with four wheels and a few small windows, is such a staple form of shelter in the countryside, seen so often behind hedgerows, in fields and gardens, and next to barns, that it has become almost invisible to all except planning officials. But as property prices continue to rise, so does the importance of the caravan as a shelter for those with limited funds who perhaps cannot get their head around the idea of living under canvas. I have already described Iona Sawtell's caravan and explained how Julienne Dolphin Wilding exported hers to Crete. There does not seem much more to say about the old definition of a caravan. These days, however, a caravan does not have to be anything you would see being pulled along the motorway behind a car.

From his pitch near the farm shop in Somerset, Paul Score has been working to perfect a design for an eco-home that fulfils the legal definition of a caravan but which offers all the benefits of a fixed house. For the past year he has been attending county shows and green festivals to muster support, investment and clients. Wherever he goes he draws a crowd, partly as a result of his natural charm and salesmanship, but also because the design is truly attractive.

Paul's eco-home is a transportable bungalow, designed to face south-south-west and to run off renewable energy. It harnesses the full range of eco-techniques, from solar gain through south-facing windows to its method of construction and the materials used. And it provides a large, comfortable, attractive space that legally conforms both to British Standards criteria and to the definition of a caravan, and therefore has benefits over a house, especially in planning and building control terms. Planners limit mobile home size to sixty-six feet by twenty-one feet, with no more than ten feet between the top of the floor and the bottom of the ceiling. Mobile homes also have to be easily transportable, 'so ours will be built on a steel chassis, designed to be anchored to pier foundations,' Paul tells his audiences during presentations at events like the Royal Bath and West Show, a major event on the annual West Country agricultural community calendar where the design attracted the interest and support of the Country Landowners Association.

The units Paul is planning to build will be forty feet by eighteen feet, which seems an easily transportable size. 'The timber framework will be constructed of 150mm x 150mm [six-by-six] locally grown Douglas Fir, and built using traditional mortice and tenon pegged joinery,' states the publicity material Paul hands out at fairs. 'The floor joists, rafters and studs will also be of Douglas Fir, and the cladding will be made from Western Red Cedar. All the insulation will be as eco-friendly as possible. We will probably use flax insulation, and wood fibre boards, in a breathing wall system,' says the leaflet. 'We expect our insulation levels to meet house building regulations, rather than mobile home ones. The units will be double-glazed throughout, with generous eaves overhangs, and high-level ventilation to prevent overheating in the summer. Some want to have living sedum roofs on their eco-homes, because these have ecological and energy-saving benefits, but standard sheet roofing material could be used instead. The steeper pitched roof is designed for solar collectors, both water heating and electricity generation. The units are designed with self-build in mind. We are thinking that most people will buy the chassis, frame, cladding and roof, and do a lot of the work themselves.' Paul reckons that the completed home, ready to move in to, will cost £40,000, or £25,000 for the kit you can build yourself. If the land you put it on has cost, say, £20,000, that is one affordable home. And you could borrow a portion of the money from a funder like Triodos, based on the value of the land, as long as you had a plausible plan for repaying the loan.

Self-build Shack/Cabin

I learned from Judy of the Woods that the main requirements for building your own house, or at least a cabin, are bags of determination and plenty of time. Judy had learned 'from watching builders in the first house I owned', she told me as she showed me around her woodland buildings.

There are two major structures next to each other in Judy's wood. The first she built was made of vertical logs. It was intended as a workshop, then she decided to live in it, but her favourite elder tree grew over it, casting it into the shade. The construction method of having the curved edge of the logs facing outwards means the rain runs down the outside of the logs and rarely finds its way through the cracks. That building measured about eighteen feet by twelve and cost Judy about £300 for the tongue-and-groove floor and a corrugated roof. The gaps between the logs are filled with clay from the soil and 'half a bag' of lime. 'The ceilings are quite low so I never had to go on a high ladder,' she told me, 'just a chair for the ceilings and a small ladder for the roof.'

Next, Judy built the one-room bungalow she now inhabits. It sits on nine concrete blocks to allow air to flow underneath and it has 'a wrap-around shed and conservatory to act as a buffer against cold in winter, as well as being built against an earth bank on the north side to protect it from the wind'. Originally the conservatory was intended to have a big overhang, but, inspired by the design of Earthships (www.earthship.org), Judy built a slanting outside wall running from the eaves all the way down to the ground. 'But it's an awkward space to use,' she confessed, and she plans to go back to a gable roof and a very large window. In addition, she has an American-style front porch for sitting out and for storing food in winter (in outdoor cupboards to protect them from animals). The total cost was much more than the first shelter, but still 'less than £2,000', and that includes about £300 worth of sheep's wool for a four-inch-thick insulation of the walls and six inches in the ceiling.

Judy emphasised the need for your building to match your capabilities as much as possible, which for most of us means keeping it small and simple. 'Doing it bite-size' makes the whole project easier to handle, and keeping the buildings smaller makes them harder to spot. Judy's small laundry building, for instance, is set in the recess of a steep bank, just below the toilet. 'I like buildings to blend in with the countryside,' she said. 'It's much nicer if the building looks like it's grown out of the ground. And I don't like to be intrusive.' There are, of course, 'a few tricks', such as the use of levers and pulleys to make heavy lifting manageable, but 'I did not bring in a great deal of materials', Judy told me. 'The log cabin was made from wood I cut here. And the bungalow came in one van.' The windows were picked out of a village skip. A double-glazing company had obligingly thrown out several of them.

While Judy gave me a lesson in slow building, Jyoti and her husband Dai were a study in how to throw a wooden cabin up in a matter of a fortnight, as their planning permission strategy demanded (see below). Their home had a wooden studwork frame, prepared off-site using Douglas Fir from Tinker's Bubble, which they felled and cut themselves using the on-site steam-powered log saw. They hammered the frame together in a couple of days, then put up the outside wall, made of planks which had also been cut at the Bubble. Most of the five inches of insulation was 'recycled wool off-cuts from a carpet factory, plus our own sheep wool'. The exception was the roof, for which they bought expensive treated wool. One of the walls was a straw-clay infill, but that was a painfully slow process they chose not to repeat. Then they hammered the inside wall onto the frame. The pitched roof was also made from Douglas Fir.

Straw-bale houses on Hector's estate.

Straw-bale Houses

Another quick, cheap house-building technique is to use straw bales, like the house Hector Christie showed me during my tour of Tapeley Hall. It was built as the first stage of a planned eco-academy where students would be trained in green building techniques as they toiled on the estate, but also to house Rupert Hawley, its designer and main builder, an MSc graduate in Human Ecology from Edinburgh. He was living in the house when I visited and had just shown it to a local parish councillor. Clive Menhenett from Magrec in Okehampton was due to arrive to teach a course in the straw-bale house, on 'sculptural lighting using solar panels'.

'I'd rather be living here than in my house,' Hector remarked as he showed me around. It was certainly warmer than Hector's mansion. In fact, the one-room building just felt good to stand in. The wall facing into the field was almost completely made of glass, and we had a good view of Elvis the Ram enjoying a head-to-head butt-fest with Hector's politically active bulldog Bryan. The heat trapped in the other three walls compensated for loss through the windows. The walls went up in a day and a half. Rendering the straw with lime took a few weeks, only because they knocked off during bad weather. Preparing the ground and foundations added another week. Rupert plans to market the house as a showhome for eco-builders.

Straw-bale buildings have low material costs but high labour costs. They are straightforward to build, recyclable (they can be used to build another house or can simply be reabsorbed into the environment), warm (the walls absorb the sun's energy during the day and leach it slowly into the building at night, reducing heating costs) and naturally sound-proofed. There are two types of straw-bale building: 'load-bearing', like Rupert's, and 'infill', meaning the bales are used as insulation around a load-bearing frame. Foundations can be concrete, flint and lime, brick or timber pillars, or car tyres with rammed earth (foundations don't need to be as deep as for brick houses). Roofs can be live earth, slate, tile, corrugated metal or bitumen, shingle or thatch. Floors can be con-crete, earth or floorboards on joists. The bales are laid with each course offset, like bricks, with hazel stakes pinning the bales together. Smaller bales can be made using a baling needle. Recycled materials can be used, including timber, doors and windows. Frames can be inserted during the wall-building process, and doors and windows can be fitted later. You can self-build entirely, preferably with a little help from friends, or get professional help with plumbing, carpentry or electrics.

Once the straw bales are in place, around a basic wooden frame, the whole structure is held together with lime, the building material that was largely replaced by cement during the twentieth century. Its manu-facture still involves heating, though the temperatures required are not as high as for cement, and lime does reabsorb the CO_2 it produces, making it carbon neutral. It is also breathable (any water that enters a structure through a crack can escape, which isn't the case with cement), and soft and flexible (if a building moves slightly it won't crack, like cement, and let water in). Also, with cement mortars, the only way moisture can escape is through the brick, which can begin to erode.

You can go through the whole process and slake your own quick-lime, which means making it into lime putty. To slake lime you need a big container like a bath. You need water and lime in the ratio of 3:1. Add the lime to the water, and not the other way round, as it could cause an explosion. Rake the mixture continuously for ten minutes to ensure that all the lime is slaked. There will be a violent reaction, and heat and steam are given off. After slaking your quicklime and allowing it to cool, you are left with lime putty, which is the basic constituent of lime mortar, render, plaster and limewash. The lime putty can be stored in plastic buckets indefinitely as long as there is a layer of water on top. Quicklime costs around £8 plus VAT per 25kg bag, which represents a price of around £2.50 for 25kg of lime putty if you slake it yourself. You can buy it from www.lowimpact.org/acatalog/lime_putty.html.

Mortar: one bucket of lime putty to four of sharp sand. The older the mortar the better. It can be kept in airtight bags and 'knocked up' when needed.

Exterior render: one part lime putty to three parts sharp sand. Ideally, spray the wall with a weak limewash the day before to provide a key. Two coats to be applied with a trowel or by hand (wearing rubber gloves).

Interior plaster: first coat, one part lime putty, three parts sharp sand, plus horsehair, to bind the plaster; second coat, one part lime putty, three parts silver sand (washed and finer), with horsehair again, cut into 20mm lengths.

Slurry: one part lime putty, one part sharp sand. Paint on with a thick paintbrush. Cheap, wonderful texture; will cover anything.

Limewash: one part lime putty, two parts water. Can add pigments. Can apply up to six coats (one a day), and coats of limewash can be applied very quickly.

(Lime instructions and recipe thanks to Low-Impact Living Initiative website, www.lowimpact.org.)

Remember, all lime products need to be applied to a moist surface. Moist lime has the advantage of settling into its own cracks before it dries.

Log Cabins and Other Kits

Nigel Lowthrop's cabin in Hill Holt Wood was made from a kit supplied by Finlog (www.finloghomes.co.uk) which cost £41,000 including VAT and delivery, though that price does not include the concrete foundation, plumbing, electrics, insulation, or the final finish. Moreover, all the materials and the building equipment had to be brought down a long track and around several tight corners, which added significantly to the cost. Nigel was a bit hazy about the details, but 'the bottom line for everything including excavation of the lake, the little separate chalet, the garage, the barn, and the greenhouse was about £120,000.'

However, the two-room, two-storey house on the other side of the lake from the main home, where Nigel's daughter now lives, cost only £2,000. It's made of trees from the wood and recycled materials, and it was built in about two weeks. It has an outside staircase and a covered veranda overlooking the lake, but the main costs were the new windows, the recycled doors, and 'a little treated softwood where the bottom of the building comes into contact with the water'. The insulation is a mix of fibreglass and some cellulose wood pulp left over from other jobs. 'We took a building down somewhere and salvaged the fibre,' Nigel explained.

I heard more about log cabin kits from a surprising source – the elusive Bert Hagley, who finally turned up in my life again just as I completed my travels. He was back from Thailand, where he told me he'd been selling solar panels door to door, though he was now no longer in the 'sowlar business'. He had become an eco-property developer: he bought plots of land, built off-grid log cabins, and sold them.

You may ask why I am still wasting space on this absurd person. Well, because he represents a widespread social type in this age of the New Silicon bubble. Wherever there is money to be made you will meet many, like Bert, with a superficial plausibility to them. He was now telling me about log homes, planning permission and building plots, and I was still listening.

He had, he said, sold his first off-grid housing development 'last Wednesday'. It was a two-storey log cabin without mains water or power. He had bought the plot and immediately gained planning permission from the council. I was fascinated. I wanted to know which council, and how he had gained the permission. It was 'the other side of Worcester – between Telford and Whitechurch', Bert told me. 'In some areas there is no problem at all having log cabins. If you say, "It's only for a log cabin" they give you permission; but it has to blend in to the natural background. So if it's in the middle of a wood you can't paint it red.' I phoned several councils in that area, including Worcester and Telford planning departments. None of them admitted to any such policy. 'Some areas you can have a log cabin but only for seven months in a year,' Bert went on, incorrectly, illustrating to me the vital importance of choosing the right adviser before you start out down the off-grid road. 'Why should we pay council tax with no water or electric or dustbin collection? This is the argument I am having with the councils. Some councils say eleven, some say six months. It's a new clause the government has got for gypsies and other travellers.'

The cabins themselves sounded equally dodgy. With a 45 per cent discount, the two-storey log cabin cost Bert £23,500. The wood is from Sweden; the manufacturers are in Holland. His materials are certainly not ecological. The cavity walls of his cabins are filled with polystyrene and fibreglass insulation material. The logs themselves were 150mm cross-section, with a 'double active skin' – 'treated for fire woodworm on both sides, but you need to paint it'. Bert was now looking for as small a plot as possible – a quarter of an acre, if that – as plots of one to two acres can gain planning permission for twenty or so houses and are therefore too expensive.

I asked Bert for a photo of his log cabin, but of course it never arrived.

Architect-designed

A step or two up from these sorts of homes is an architect-designed luxury off-grid house. I mentioned Neil Hammond's house in chapter 4, with its big kitchen and multiple levels. While I was there, his girlfriend Amy made me a cup of tea and brought it to the wooden table that could comfortably seat twenty-four. 'It went to the planning committee and we had the support of our local councillor, which was important,' Neil told me. 'Our architect is respected in the community and he pushed it through the committee.'

Actually, the house is no luxury pad, but it is built to a high standard. The main innovation is its 'service core' – a concrete tube running up the building. 'Sustainable houses have to be fundamentally adaptable, extendable, repairable,' said the house's architect, Neil

At last – designer off-gridness.

Sutherland. So he grouped 'all the essential service transactions – water, power, sewage, ventilation' into a concrete core running from the ground floor to the first-floor ceiling, where they are hidden away but very easy to access. After all, it is these aspects of a house that tend to get changed/upgraded the most.

The build cost was £120,000 all in, Neil Hammond told me, though 'a lot of the labouring was done by us. It would have cost double if we'd had builders do everything. Most of the finishings are hand-built. All the wood is locally sourced Douglas Fir bought in logs and I machined it myself up here.' Neil Sutherland added, 'Materials were generally natural and sourced as close to the site as sensibly possible. Windows were made in the Highlands and are as high a spec as we could source. The roof system is a Norwegian proprietary grass roof system, quite low-cost and self-buildable. The floor slate was a bit of a mistake as I believe it came from somewhere far off, when we were told it was Spanish; it's very difficult to get something from this part of the world. The insulation is a mix of sheep's wool and cellulose fibre – a recycled product.' Plus Neil Hammond already owned the wind turbine and the battery store, which would be another £25,000 now – although it cost him half that with grants and special deals.

Finding the right off-grid architect can be difficult, especially if you need one with a good relationship with the relevant planning authority. Try the Association of Environment-Conscious Building (www.aecb.net), which has a fairly large and searchable list of green architects. Another option is *Building for a Future* magazine (www.buildingforafuture.co.uk) and its associated discussion forum, www.greenbuildingforum.co.uk.

Instant Eco-home

I had already seen first hand that you really can turn up on a piece of land and build yourself a shelter. But despite my repeated lessons in how achievable it is, I still lack confidence in my abilities to put up my own dwelling. If, like me, you need help, and you can pay for it, then my advice is to go for something a little better than a bender or a shack.

You could contact Hedge at the Kingshill Community near Shepton Mallet (who gave me a jump-start for my van at the Big Green Gathering). He will turn up ready to erect an A-frame timber house, and as long as you have a clear patch of land for him and his crew to work on, he will have the whole frame up in a day. The next day it will have roof slats, and the wooden walls will be in place. That leaves you to sort out doors and windows, insulation and roof-tiles. The cost is £5,000 to £8,000, depending on size. For £8,000 you get something that is about twenty feet by fifteen feet, and eighteen feet high – 'large enough to include a mezzanine'. And it can be built just about anywhere that is more or less flat. Hedge pre-cuts the wood before arrival, and even if the land is not flat, he says it is cheaper to adjust the design of the frame than to take on the work of levelling the land.

Hedge is a former supervisor for Exmoor National Park, so the advantage of working with him, apart from the fact that he is a terrifically nice guy, is that he understands everything about land, woodland and, above all, planning permission. In fact he considers it part of his job, and part of the price quoted above, to contact the local planning department if you want him to, to negotiate the planning application. There is a limit to the number of hours he can spend working on it, of course, but he is very flexible. And you should never under-estimate the value of a little bit of expert or insider knowledge when it comes to the tangled thicket that is planning permission in this country.

Planning Permission

There are now thousands of people who have either managed to gain planning permission to live off-grid on agricultural land or woodland, or are living quietly without permission – because they are only there part-time; because so far their neighbours have not reported them to the planners; or, in rare cases, because a friendly planner has turned a blind eye to them. Nevertheless, exceptions aside, council planners can be the enemy if you are trying to live off-grid.

In this section I'm going to explore the planning implications of low-impact living, whether that's in a straw-bale house (or any other form of eco-housing) or a caravan. Much of the content applies equally to a full-scale off-grid house, including a newly built one, but I'm assuming that if you have £150,000-plus to spend you already have a number of advisers. You will need to extrapolate what is said here for your particular circumstances.

Of course, this section cannot teach you how to win planning permission to live off-grid, mainly because even a book would not be able to do justice to the tedious obscurity of the process, and the complex mesh of national and local issues that have to be borne in mind. This is partly because there is a hierarchy of rules, some enshrined in laws and legal precedents but others issued as 'guidance notes' from central government – notes, moreover, that have recently changed significantly. Planning laws have been altered many times since 1947, when the Town and Country Planning Act was passed (there were precursors, in 1909 and 1925, but the 1947 Act was the one that switched power from the freeholder to the state). There are fresh Acts of Parliament with each change of government, but the basic principle remains the same: to balance housing demands with environmental ones and allow decisions made by local councils to be appealed to the Secretary of State for Communities and Regions, and in the case of issues of principle to the House of Lords. The current law is enshrined in the Planning and Compulsory Purchase Acts of 2004 and 1990, together with guidance notes issued by government with names like PPS1 or PPS3. These guidances are not binding and are open to many interpretations.

Dealing with planners

In the future, the majority of those hoping to live off-grid will be buying bare landholdings or agricultural buildings, or squatting on common land because they simply can't afford houses. The new policies and grants promoting the diversification of farms offer some support, but also have the effect of encouraging farms to become property opportunities. So redundant farm buildings are now out of the financial reach of most.

The main obstacle to living off-grid, however, is not the price of land but the closely related issue of planning permission. You see, although many exceptions will be discussed here, it is not really possible to gain planning permission in the UK for a nice little eco-home in open countryside.

Sometimes, instead of helping their customers – us – through the maze of planning regulations, council planners regard their job as being as obstructive as possible. The planner Nigel Lowthrop encountered when he first moved into Hill Holt Wood was typical of the stories I heard. 'We immediately applied for planning permission, and the officer said, "Absolutely out of the question – over my dead body." He just had a closed mind, which was so often the problem, and still is the problem.'

How you get on with your planner is the big issue when it comes to gaining planning permission. Most can be persuaded to provide a service if you approach them in the right way. And even if they are rude, incompetent or even deceitful, we are the supplicants in the relationship; we just have to smile sweetly and take whatever they hand out. I have to say up front that I have no personal experience of the British planning system and am relying 100 per cent on stories I have heard from those who have won or lost planning permission, and some advice from experts. But my instinct if the time ever comes for me to apply for permission will be to present as bland a face as possible to the council planning department. Don't disturb them, don't give them any particular reason to notice you. If they take exception to your scheme, your main task will be to ensure that the battle never becomes a personal struggle.

Many off-gridders try to sidestep the planning system, ignore its existence and hope for the best. And you can try to move onto the land you've selected unnoticed. But beware: every beautiful piece of land has some beautiful local residents who love it, cherish it and notice every little thing that goes on in and around it. So whatever you do you will always need a strategy for dealing with the planners, prepared in advance and thought through to the end, even if you never use it.

Dealing with the system

You must apply for planning permission when you build certain kinds of structures on agricultural or forest land, or when you change the use of land or buildings (for example from agricultural to residential), or when undertaking certain kinds of 'engineering works' such as digging a trench for cables or water pipes, or putting up a pole for a wind turbine.

Some off-grid building is outside the reach of planners. If you bring a caravan or a container onto your woodland site, for example, and only use it for storage, that is not development; but if you live in it, that is development because it's a change of use (from woodland to residential). If you build a playhouse in your garden and it's only for domestic use, that is not development; but pitch a tent in your garden and live in it for a year and you would have to apply for planning permission. If your garden is big enough, you would expect to be able to invite a guest to stay in a caravan, like Iona Sawtell, or to put up a yurt-like structure as a workshop, like Luca did. Although you would probably not be stopped, in fact it is not as simple as that. Nothing is quite as it seems in the Alice-in-Wonderland world of planning permission. I was surprised to learn, for instance, that private landowners *can* decide what is done on their property, as long as it does not 'cause unacceptable damage to interests of acknowledged importance'. The principle is still enshrined in British law via the Human Rights Act even though the Labour government omitted it from their new guidance notes in 1999. But as I discuss later, that is not the end of the matter.

Not only are planning restrictions a form of over-control against off-grid living, they contradict other stated priorities of current British life: to protect the environment and reverse global warming; to provide low-cost, affordable housing at a time of soaring property prices; to preserve skills and communities that will die out unless we do something about it. It seems iniquitous that you can be stopped from living a low-impact, sustainable life on a plot of land you have bought, or rented. As long as what you do does not disadvantage others, surely owning land ought to give you the right to do with it as you will? That is still a basic principle, often overlooked by planning officials, but again, it's not as simple as that. The planning authorities might well wish to allow low-impact dwellings on farmland, but there has to be equality of law, so if rules were loosened to allow sustainable development, that could become a property developer's charter to despoil the countryside. One planner, while giving his reason for refusing permission for an innocuous little mud-house, said, 'If permission were granted for an earth-sheltered structure on land which was not allocated for development, and the building was never built, then that site would carry a history of planning consent which could be misused at a future appeal.' Whether or not he was right in this assessment is another question I will return to later.

The problem facing the off-grid movement is how to apply the laws so that they work in favour of off-grid developments. Just as professional property developers use every legal tactic to make a profit on their activities (and quite a few illegal ones), so the off-grid community needs to be clever to achieve its goals. As long as you are not expecting a long-term financial outcome from your off-grid activities, if you just want to enjoy the off-grid life as an occasional break from your normal existence, you may choose to put up a cheap, temporary structure on land you have bought or borrowed for the purpose. In England and Wales, putting up a temporary agricultural structure will only work if you inform the council about it before they catch you. The law says that certain kinds of work-related structures are 'permitted development' (see below). But agricultural permitted development requires you to inform the council first. The risk is that if they decide to go after you, then by informing them you will only have succeeded in tipping them off. Catch-22, or what? There are other issues at play here, unless, as I said, you get clever.

Whether they owned farmland or woodland, whether they were thinking of a building or just a caravan, many people I met had had to decide if they should apply for planning permission in advance of moving in or wait until the council found them and then apply retrospectively. The reason for opting for the latter is that if the council refuses your application before you move onto the land you are in a much weaker position than if you are already living there. And there is always the chance that the neighbours will not shop you and you can live unnoticed for a few years. If you do manage to stay in a building for four years without receiving an enforcement notice from the council (or ten years in the case of a caravan), you can apply for a Certificate of Lawfulness of Existing Use and Development (CLEUD), and you are home free.

Brig Oubridge, the founder of the Big Green Gathering, is also the founder of Tipi Valley in Wales, a group of about a hundred tipis, vans and caravans that have successfully defied the Carmarthenshire County planners for over twenty years. Brig is a charismatic leader. He loves attention, and his appearance alone ensures he gets plenty of it. He has a beard down to his sternum, swept-back dark hair and piercing deep-set eyes under thick brows. He had been living and breathing his legal battle with the council for those two decades until he finally won his permission to stay in 2006. He could quote me detailed rulings, and recall the name of every judge, secretary of state and planning inspector who had ruled on his case. 'Nobody thought we needed any sort of planning permission because it was just a bunch of tipis moving around fields,' he told me with great glee, 'until autumn 1984. That's when the council served enforcement notices on part of the valley saying there

Typical Tipi Valley dwellings.

had been a change of use from agricultural to residential.' In 1985 Brig and his Tipi-ites won a public inquiry, but the Secretary of State 'called it in' – meaning he decided to examine the case himself because it was an issue of principle. 'The decision stayed on the Welsh Office shelf for two years until Peter Walker came into office in the summer of 1987. He overturned the inspector's recommendation and gave us twelve months to get off.'

It's worth repeating that enforcement notices are a serious thing, and have to be responded to within twenty-eight days. What made Brig a hero of the off-grid movement was the trick of moving the tipis from field to field. 'The council found that because people kept moving around and because in law they had to give us twenty-four hours' notice before they came onto our land, they couldn't pin down whose tipi was which,' Brig told me. 'And because some were on land covered by the enforcement notice and some were on land that wasn't, they never managed to summons anyone for being in breach of the enforcement notice.' However, a warning to groups hoping to imitate Brig's approach in future: new statute law aimed at preventing the subdivision of land into tiny plots may have the side-effect of preventing new Tipi Valleys from forming. The huge, unsatisfied demand for a place in the country has led to many unscrupulous schemes where property companies buy up a bit of unwanted land and sell it off a quarter-acre at a time for many times what they paid. Local councils are now wise to the scam, and there is not a hope of winning planning permission. The new law withdraws all permitted development rights from such schemes.

In early 2006, Wales's First Minister Rhodri Morgan wrote to Brig to issue him with a CLEUD for his three tents and gypsy caravan, although a lean-to porch was refused permission. It was victory, of a sort, but Brig wasn't celebrating. Who wants to give up part of their life to masterminding this kind of operation? Brig said he had not been offered any apology over the length of time the case had taken, or any sort of compensation. He said he doubted that others in Tipi Valley would follow his lead and apply for retrospective permission to put the community on a lawful footing. 'I can't see anyone in the community being encouraged to do so after what has happened with my case.' Carmarthenshire Council said it was looking at the assembly government's ruling. 'This matter has been ongoing for over ten years and demonstrates the complexity of regulating temporary dwellings,' said a spokeswoman.

Meanwhile, just a few miles away, Reuben Irvine's lawyers were doing all they could to stop the council demolishing the house he built with his own hands. From my conversations with Simon Fairlie and others it seems that councils rarely demolish (except in the case of gypsies), but Reuben's great error was to do nothing when the enforcement notice arrived five years earlier. Friends who lived in Tipi Valley told him to ignore it, but what worked there was never likely to work for Reuben, who was living on his own land in a permanent building. Tragically, the beautiful home he has built, which can be of no harm to the community or the environment, may well be pulled down in the long run, and the argument against wrecking a home and a family's life may never be heard, for Reuben has managed to get only limited legal aid. The magistrates' court has to decide on only two things: did Reuben receive his enforcement notice, and did he appeal against it within the time limit.

Many local authorities are unwilling to enforce to the point of eviction, especially where families are concerned, so if you are on legal aid you can sometimes continue to appeal all the way up to the European Court of Human Rights, until you are finally turned down. But be warned: a lax policy on enforcement could change at any time. All it needs is a directive from the Ministry for Communities and Local Government. 'It's all power politics,' said Reuben. 'They are doing it because they can. We can't afford lawyers like Tesco can, and we aren't campaigners like the people you hear about [e.g. Brig at Tipi Valley]. We don't want anyone coming to our door and looking around.' In fact, Reuben was a victim of Tipi Valley twice over: in the first place he received bad advice from the tipi dwellers, and he was also powerless and therefore an easy target for the same Carmarthenshire Council to hold up as a rare victory. Reuben was right: Tesco and Brig might be able to run rings around the council, but a single household has much less chance.

Still, Reuben might have a case. Because the Irvine family moved their caravans onto the land in 1991 and did not receive the council enforcement notice until 2001, as long as they can prove the caravans were used as dwellings all that time . . . but that is not always easy to prove. Simon Fairlie told me of one case where a caravan dweller proved his case only when he was able to produce a photo of his caravan which showed someone who had died a decade earlier. Tony Wrench wanted to use a similar approach at Brith Dir Mawr: he took 'index prints' of Emma moving in to her roundhouse, and filed a set with the laboratory that developed the negatives. This allowed their barrister Stephen Cottle to persuade the inspector to give them an eighteen-month stay of execution on their enforcement notice (although there were other issues involved).

When Jyoti Fernandes, Dai Saltmarsh and another family bought those forty-two acres in Dorset, they had already decided exactly how they would go about winning planning permission for the homes they intended to build. They had considered applying for planning permission before living on the land, but, said Jyoti, 'once we got a feeling for what the villagers and the planning department were like, we knew that if we applied and they turned us down it would have been a complete disaster.' Their success is a textbook example of how to buy non-residential land in the country and then live on it, so it is worth studying in some detail.

The first thing they did was to start cultivating the land. Well before moving in there, they erected four polytunnels (two each) bought second-hand for a few hundred pounds. The plastic sides were secured with concrete footings to withstand the strongest of gales. They planted beans, lettuces, tomatoes and nasturtiums – relatively high-value, high-yield crops that they planned to sell to local restaurants as well as in the Saturday farmer's market in nearby Bridport (a market that did not exist until they pioneered it). Their aim was to be able to prove at the inevitable planning hearings that they were working the land in an ecologically and economically sustainable way. In other words, that they would be able to make a living from the land.

Then they applied retrospectively for permitted development consent from the council. They were fairly confident it would be granted because these were just polytunnels; the only change the council might order was a move to elsewhere on the land. In the end the planning official who came to inspect the site was happy with what he saw. He arrived early one morning to find Jyoti working the field, still wearing her stripy M&S pyjama top. But it didn't occur to him that this was because she had just got out of bed. And he failed to spot the two tents and the yurt where the families were living at the time.

Only after the first shoots of the first vegetables appeared inside the polytunnels did they risk building their cabins on the land. By then they had already assembled the raw materials for their two homes. 'We got everything up onto the land – all the straw bales, all the materials – and then we built it all within a week before the planners could say anything,' Jyoti told me when I visited her two years after the event. The houses were already partly built in panels that bolted together. The aim was to 'ensure that our houses were kind of established, so if the council issued an enforcement notice, it would be when we already had a place to live'.

The entrance to the land is in the furthest corner of the top field, from where it slopes gently downwards with a commanding view of the surrounding area. The best place to site their house was near the entrance, by the hedgerow, where it would be sheltered from some of the winter weather, but Jyoti and Dai decided this was a bit too visible, and likely to annoy the neighbours, so they built further down the field.

In the end it was about six months before the planners arrived – much later than they had feared. It came as little surprise when they were ordered to move out and take down the buildings on the grounds that they were in an AONB. They weren't worried. Reading between the lines, said Jyoti, 'the attitude of the local council was "oh, we're going to lose this but we have to make them do something" '. If she was right, then it seems to be another example of the same old thing of the council spending ratepayers' money on seemingly unnecessary legal battles, presumably without having sat down and thought through what exactly it was they were fighting about. Within a week Jyoti filed the retrospective applications for temporary planning permission they had prepared months earlier.

Local opponents argued that there was no need to build a 'new settlement' on the land in order to manage it, and that their neatly built wooden cabins were a blot on the landscape. At a meeting packed with their supporters, the district council planning committee voted unanimously that there was no agricultural need for the two families to live on the land in order to work it. The parish council added, 'We do not want the fields covered with buildings. We are concerned that more people might join this settlement.' This was at a time when gypsy encampments were in the news.

So far everything had happened as expected. Now the main part of the plan kicked in. As she left the court meeting that day, Jyoti shouted for the benefit of the press, 'You realise you are evicting five children from their homes?' In one shrewd sentence she had begun the process of wooing public opinion in the neighbourhood, and reminded the council of the cost to the community of rehousing the two families. 'It was a lot of work,' Jyoti recalled as we lazed in the sun outside one of the polytunnels while Dai set off in their shiny 4×4 to deliver the day's crop of nasturtium leaves. 'We caused a stir in the papers and on TV. We made quite an issue of it, getting people writing in, because it's important that people have the right to do what we're doing. There's no reason why what we're doing should be illegal, and basically it is. Fundamentally it's a good thing. It's bringing employment to the countryside, young people to the countryside, keeping it all alive . . .' They even marshalled the neighbours, who agreed with their stand, and persuaded them to give interviews to the local media. 'Villager Chris Roper said the food the couples were producing in the style of TV chef Hugh Fearnley-Whittingstall was what was now wanted – a view shared by Lyme Regis greengrocer and former mayor Mike Hartley,' reported the *Dorset Echo*, which followed the case closely.

The council planning committee gave the couples six months to leave the land. Nearly eight months later they were still there, because they had taken their case to the next level – an appeal to the Planning Inspectorate, a national body that sends an individual inspector to the area to see for himself. He can overrule any decision made by a local council. The council sends officers and/or representatives to the inspector's hearings to put its case for refusal, and the residents put their side of the argument.

In this case, the council also appointed an 'independent expert', a land consultant from Reading who said he could see no reason why anyone should need to live on the land. 'I am not of the mind that just because you can't find a house right on your doorstep that is affordable, that you can build a house in the middle of the countryside,' he said. He added that all the arguments put forward by the families for need-ing to be on the land – looking after propagating seedlings, hatching chickens, pest control, charcoal burning and lambing – could be answered either by temporary accommodation, such as that used by shepherds at lambing time, or by living between fifteen and thirty minutes away. But under cross-questioning from Jyoti's barrister during the two-day hearing, he conceded that there was a need for one worker to live on the land, although not for two dwellings and two families. The council's planning officer, in his evidence, was forced to concede that although the two couples could live within thirty minutes of the farm, the only local property on the market for under £115,000 was a one-bedroom flat, so it was inaccurate to suggest the families could live nearby on an agricultural income.

Jyoti had Simon Fairlie advising her through the process. At first she did not think it was worth having a barrister, but in the end they retained one at the last minute. Jyoti was pleased they did because she would never have cross-examined the hostile witnesses as effectively, and he provided a level of objectivity and professionalism they needed.

The inspector decided that both families should be given temporary planning permission for four years. He said the council's agricultural expert had based his assessment of agricultural need to live on the land on conventional farming methods. 'Assessment of need for the presence of the appellants on the site should be based upon the enterprise as it is, and not, as the council suggests, upon a theoretical use of the land for conventional farming methods,' he stated. 'I consider that, whilst the degree to which the appellants embrace self-sufficiency in their home life may be a matter of personal choice, the form of agriculture they have chosen to adopt is not. Against the background of government advice, the choice of this type of farming is no more an expression of merely personal preference than the choice of anyone who decides to pursue more conventional farming methods.' He then quoted government policy for rural areas, which says that promoting sustainable, diverse and adaptable agriculture should be encouraged 'where farming achieves high environmental standards, with minimal impact, contributing to the rural economy, and providing products the public wants'. However, the inspector did order Jyoti's cabin to be re-sited from its spot next to the polytunnels – to near the entrance, by the hedgerow, exactly where she and Dia had wanted it in the first place.

Jyoti was cock-a-hoop with the outcome. 'I particularly liked the bit where he said, "The time is long past when such an approach could be regarded as eccentric or utopian and a modern approach recognises that there is room in agriculture for farms embracing both approaches,"' she said. The result came through in August 2005, so they've got until late summer 2009 at the very least. If the council refuses to extend the planning permission she will appeal again, which will take until early 2011. But most find that the longer they are in place, the less opposition there is. Once they have overcome people's fear of the unknown, the neighbours will probably settle down and stop worrying.

Jyoti, and most of the off-gridders I met with planning permission on agricultural or wooded land, had managed to win because they were working the land – growing food in the case of Jyoti and Dai, harvesting wood in Marcus Tribe's case. These were both examples of eco-farming and subsistence living. Roy Fountain had to wait years for his planning permission, until he could come up with a more conventional proposal, albeit a very imaginative one, that convinced the council he would indeed be making a living from the land. Even the commune at Land Matters is planning a permaculture farm as the means to win their planning permission, though the occupations listed in their planning application (including video maker, musician and teacher) do not strengthen their case. More compelling is the information that there is at least one building on the land that was once a habitation.

But what if you are trying to live off-grid on a small patch of land and you do not want to commit yourself, your family or your co-owners to ten years of back-breaking work? How do you win planning permission if you cannot show that you intend to manage the land sustainably? What if you are not planning to manage the land at all, you just want to live there, do a bit of gardening, and make your money some other way – perhaps using the Internet, or even commuting? That requires even more creative use of the current planning regulations.

The planning inspector

I needed to go back to the source, and talk to a planning inspector. I wanted to find out how their minds work and how they come to their decisions.

Robin Bryer is a chartered town planning consultant based near Yeovil. His work has included being a consultant planning inspector, paid by the National Planning Inspectorate to adjudicate in disputes. He packed it in because 'I hate to say no to people', which must be a large part of your job if you are a planning inspector.

We spoke on the phone, and as we were introducing ourselves Robin mentioned in his clipped, rather plummy accent that he had recently hosted a hunt meet on his lawn. This told me all I needed to know about the size of his lawn and where his overall sympathies lay. (I have no idea if he is typical or representative of inspectors, although I suspect he is.) Robin was not unsympathetic to the idea of living off-grid in principle, but that did not mean he approved of it in practice. Quite the opposite. 'The fact that you are back to nature does not actually mean to say you can flout the planning laws,' he began once I had explained what I wanted to know from him. 'We don't want houses in the middle of nowhere because that is unsustainable. The doctor's got to go to your home and the postman's got to go out there.

'I've backed people in planning appeals where somebody's working in a wood and needed to live there to maintain it, and there are exceptional circumstances, like farmers get farmhouses if they have young stock to look after twenty-four hours a day. In exceptional circumstances the planning laws allow for forestry dwellings if you can make a case. But not because you are holier than thou, greener than thou – that doesn't wash. Why should you get a site on the cheap when the rest of us can't?' My rejoinder to that was to point out that off-grid development was not everyone's cup of tea. If I only put up a shack, and if the planning permission is restricted to me personally, then surely it is equitable that I bought the land for less than if it had permission for a conventional house. 'No,' said Robin. 'You perhaps shouldn't pay as much council tax, but if all you want is a shack, that's your look-out. You could argue that you are better off with something like that these days.'

Robin was becoming quite worked up now, in a restrained, polite, English way, and had seemingly categorised me as some sort of closet property developer operating under eco-credentials. ' "The world owes me a living ... I'm doing no harm" – it doesn't wash,' he exclaimed again. The 'triumph' of the planning system, for Robin, 'is not in what you do see, it's what you don't see. If one or two idealists cannot go out in the sticks and do their own thing, that is unfortunate, but a small price to pay . . .'

What about low-impact dwellings? I asked. I was aware that Robin would not have the latest thinking at his fingertips, but his answer was useful, and it made sense: 'The fact that a development is not visible and has minimal impact is not a reason to approve it, because it could be repeated time and again and cumulatively cause a lot of damage.' I could imagine the residents of Allaleigh hiring a good lawyer to hammer home that point at the public inquiry. Land Matters itself may be low-impact, but another carbon copy next door, and another down the road would eventually add up to more than the sum of its parts.

'However,' added Robin, 'under the four-year rule, if you have lived somewhere with no-one noticing you or complaining about you then in some sense you are having a minimal impact, and after four years you can apply for a Certificate of Lawful Use.' Robin wouldn't condone this 'bypassing the system', he told me, but it was possible. The planning laws allow for exceptions. If there is someone who has some exceptional case then it is open to him to prove it, but he has to prove that the exceptional circumstances tip the balance. Then statutory policy can be outweighed. If you had some outstanding system of living which is highly sustainable and you are a trailblazer who is pointing the way to the future,' then a case can be made. At last I felt we were getting somewhere, if this representative of planning's orthodoxy was prepared to accept 'trailblazing' as an 'exceptional circumstance'.

Planners need to be reassured that a project that starts out low-impact stays low-impact. They fear that every eco-home is the thin end of a wedge – perhaps because they see so many proposals from greedy speculators coming across their desks. But are there no weapons in the planning armoury specifically designed to ensure that low-impact buildings remain low-impact? Well, yes, there is one. Planning officials, and planning committees (of councils), can grant permission subject to pretty well any conditions they consider reasonable. This might include a restriction on car-parking or ownership, or on what can be done in certain parts of the property near existing neighbours, or a commitment to plant trees to screen the new residents from the old. Planning inspectors have the same power. In fact inspectors nearly always ask the council to suggest some conditions that could be imposed on the householder if their appeal is allowed, though these conditions must be 'necessary and appropriate'. They can, if they want, ensure the entire planning permission is solely for that individual and their family only. This is called making the permission personal and it removes the potential that the land could later be sold to a developer who would use the residential permission but dump the eco-dwelling in favour of an imported prefab villa. Marcus Tribe's permission, when he finally won it, was for him personally.

The expert on planning permission

A few years into his long battle, Marcus became a little more confident – enough to put up his woodshed. He and Sarah had hardly finished celebrating their permission for the yurt in 2006 when the postman arrived with a brown envelope bearing bad news: they would have to pay business rates on the woodshed. It was a cruel twist in the seemingly endless battle with the planning authorities on Torridge Council,

The gentle, low-tech side of off-grid life.

and the subject of their next appeal. And it was another example of the advisability of seeking expert advice on-site. With the right advice, Marcus might have delayed putting up his shed, or made it smaller, or made it more of a lean-to than a fully fledged building.

While Marcus was staring blankly at his rates demand, the commune at Land Matters was putting up a fifty-foot barn. There are many differences in the rules for agricultural and woodland holdings. A barn called for prior notification to the council, but not a planning application. And being an agricultural building, it is not subject to rates. Land Matters' biggest advantage in their fight was that they sought advice from Simon Fairlie.

Simon is particularly in demand at appeals in front of planning inspectors, where his combination of in-depth knowledge – he can quote the byzantine regulations at the inspectors – and sturdy common sense has won many a hopeless case. 'I can't say I enjoy doing planning appeals,' he told me as we sat outside his scythe shop, 'it's just an endless series of deadlines. But the actual Public Enquiry itself is quite fun. You can pretend you're Perry Mason or something. I do have a great deal of respect for the public inquiry process. It's far better than the charade that goes on in council committee meetings. They don't have the time to do anything properly and the elected representatives don't have any understanding of the issues. But the inspectors are highly skilled, very committed people. If the planning system wasn't there then the whole of England would have turned into one huge suburb.' Naturally Simon doesn't want that, but nor does he want the planning regime to continue to 'keep the countryside for an elite'.

He learned most of what he knows while winning temporary permission for 'the Bubble'. He was by then being contacted daily by others wanting advice, and 'it just turned into an advice helpline from that'. Chapter 7, as the advice service is called, has published a manual, *DIY Planning Briefings*, on planning permission for affordable housing (I have drawn on it heavily for parts of this chapter). It is an important document if you are thinking of buying land or living in a van or in any way tangling with the planning authorities, although you need to make sure you have an up-to-date copy (see www.tlio.org.uk/chapter7). And you will still need your expert.

Simon is careful not to recommend just moving on to land in the hope of winning the battle in the end. 'I just put the evidence I know to people and let them make a decision,' he said. 'No doubt the chances of getting permission are greater if you just move on first, but it's not something I would advise. The main thing is to have a decent reason for being there. How you justify yourself – that is what the system wants to know most of all.'

Key points to beat the planners

Enforcement notices. Never ignore an enforcement notice. Remember, once the planners decide to issue one you are in the system and have only twenty-eight days to appeal. While I was talking to Simon he heard from someone whose wife committed suicide after they were fined £5,000 for disobeying an enforcement notice. They failed to appeal in time, and did not even hire a solicitor to represent them. A fine of that size from a magistrate is almost unheard of, but, Simon said, 'it would not have happened if he had appealed and hired a solicitor'.

Advisers. As you will recall, Roy Fountain had to wait ten years for his planning permission because he wrote in his planning application that the tumbledown cottage he wanted to convert into his home was being used as a shelter for livestock. If he had been advised to claim simply that it was an uninhabited cottage he might have received his permission straight away. Do at least run your application past an expert: a rural campaigner like Simon, a planning consultant or a solicitor. If you can't afford them your local Citizens Advice Bureau might be able to help. But your best bet might be to ask around and try to convince a solicitor or planning consultant that you are a deserving case for a little pro bono advice. Alternatively you could advertise on my off-grid website for someone in your local area who knows the ropes and is a supporter of off-grid living, perhaps someone who even does it themselves.

Social geography. Pay attention to the area where you are planning to go off-grid and tailor your behaviour to what is suitable and appropriate. If it is touristy, it may be easier to get away with a caravan in a field, though if too many others have been trying recently it may be harder. Up north, in former industrial landscapes, councils may be more lenient about a shack hidden among some trees than they would be in the Lake District. The Land Matters commune spent some time researching the history of their area to establish that although Allaleigh is a near-empty corner of England now, in previous centuries it had been a thriving community. One of their fields contained a derelict cottage which had been the home of a long-departed blacksmith. That does not give them the right to treat it as a residential property still, but it may be relevant during their appeal.

Local community. Genuine enhancement of the local community is a valid additional argument in planning battles. Job creation or the provision of skills that do not otherwise exist in the community are factors an inspector would consider at an appeal. But simply having a good relationship with the locals is not in itself an argument.

For Marcus Tribe and Sarah Harvey, planning issues were like giant brackets around their lives saying, 'Hold it right there, please. Normal life will resume one day, perhaps.' Although the original visit from the council came as the result of a complaint by a neighbour, their relationship with the community helped sustain them and gave them hope at times when they seemed to be losing their long battle, though it was unlikely to have been a major consideration for the inspectors. What may have carried more weight was that local goodwill towards them was reflected in support from their parish council. Marcus certainly thinks the parish council evidence to the inquiry was a decisive factor in their favour.

While Marcus had initially kept a low profile, hoping the authorities would leave well alone, Nigel Lowthrop immediately applied for planning permission for a low-impact dwelling in Hill Holt Wood. Where Marcus was hoping to live a low-cost, low-income life, Nigel and his wife Karen had much grander plans. Marcus was going back to nature, plain and simple; Nigel's approach was about management, and above all about involving the local community, as detailed in chapter 3. 'The first thing I did after we bought the place was to let everyone know they were welcome to visit and use the woods during the day,' he told me. 'At night the gate was closed, and that made the locals feel good about it as well, because they knew there wouldn't be any kids or drugs up there.' As soon as he could, Nigel formed a management committee made up of locals from the four parishes in the immediate area. That was a masterstroke, because not only did he co-opt precisely those who could have become the opposition, he also began to delegate the job of influencing the local council and even some of the work on the property.

Getting everybody on your side is certainly one way to lobby for planning permission. But even if you don't want to commit yourself to a lifetime of local meetings and good works, having the parish council on your side can help persuade the local ward councillor that you are a good thing. That's if you are trying to get planning permission from the local council, rather than assuming you won't win them over and focusing on winning the appeal.

The media. We've just seen how effective Jyoti Fernandes's pronouncement to the press was, and many I spoke to said they felt their courting of the media had helped win their case. This is for two reasons: locally elected officials are susceptible to local opinion; and property developers are a fairly secretive and cosy bunch who do a lot of business over liquid lunches with planners, so the last thing many planners want is to have their actions scrutinised in the media. They know that if they grant permission to someone who has started giving interviews to the local papers, then that person will go away.

The lawyer

The inspectors are, as Simon Fairlie indicated, a pretty clever bunch, and it would be unwise to lie to them, but there are numerous loopholes in the law. To find out more about them I went to see a planning barrister, the sort of person who is only brought in to the picture at an inspector's hearing or a higher court, when you want to exploit these loopholes to the full.

Lincoln's Inn Fields in Holborn, London, on a cloudless September day was as heart-stirring as any Devon valley. The huge square of Georgian terrace houses on two sides facing modern office buildings where bombs fell during World War Two has a large park in the middle with an excellent restaurant, tennis courts and, at 10.30 this weekday morning, a number of tramps sunning themselves on the benches or the neatly clipped lawn. Garden Court Chambers is a busy practice, and messengers were entering and leaving every minute as I waited for Stephen Cottle in an elegant lobby with an enormous fireplace. Stephen had been responsible for defeating the council at Peod over the attempted ousting of van and tipi dwellers from a local piece of land which had so upset Sandy Boulanger and which left the council with a massive legal bill (see chapter 6). He also helped Tony Wrench at Brith Dir Mawr over the years in his long-term fight to preserve his round-house, and led Emma Orbach's successful appeal against eviction from her dwelling on the adjacent piece of land.

I was expecting someone in a suit and a wig, but Stephen was wearing a black leather jacket and trainers. He appeared carrying mounds of books and papers to help me in my researches. Stephen specialises in gypsies and travellers, he told me as we sat down at a polished wooden table in a large meeting room. He was in the midst of preparing his case for a hearing in Pontypool the next day, where a group were about to be evicted from a council car-park. He was planning to use the Race Relations Amendment Act in their defence. He had only limited time, and as I furiously scribbled notes he rattled off a few pieces of advice he wanted me to pass on to off-grid communities everywhere.

Stephen's first piece of advice was to take the council's area development plan (see below) at face value and treat it far more seriously than others had suggested. He even recommended taking part in the political process and getting involved in the formulation of the plan to make sure it contained a genuine commitment to eco-dwelling. 'There's a whole world of consultation out there,' Stephen informed me, 'and you can make representations without being in any way a troublemaker.' But if you are trying to decide whether to move from city to country, and changing the development plan in your new home town is too long-winded, then find out in detail about the development plan of the areas you are considering, and choose the best one. If necessary, contact Friends of the Earth (www.foe.co.uk) or the Green Party for advice and suggestions.

Sure enough, the pile of papers Stephen gave me included a page from the 2004 Planning and Compulsory Purchase Act: 'if regard is to be had to the development plan for the purpose of any determination to be made under the planning Acts, the determination must be made in accordance with the plan . . .' When Stephen was fighting Emma Orbach's enforcement notice 'we managed to get an eighteen-month extension because the inspector was persuaded that the National Park was about to adopt a low-impact policy'. The new policy would have the same force as a new development plan from a local council and therefore altered the material circumstances of the case, Stephen explained. Perhaps his most important advice was this: 'It's a plan-led system.' When you are deciding how to handle the planning application you look at the plan and then decide whether you will say you are complying with the plan or argue instead that there are material considerations which justify not doing so.

This phrase 'material considerations' (MCs) was key to Stephen's next piece of advice. Section 38.6 of the 2004 Act says that the planning decision 'must be made in accordance with the plan, unless material considerations indicate otherwise'. Those MCs might be something as simple as complying with the national policy on sustainability, even if this local area has not taken it into account; it might be an argument based on affordable housing. However, no single MC can 'trump' planning controls. Inspectors and judges have to balance the weight of evidence – the whole 'basket of factors', as Stephen called it, including what would happen to you, the appellant, if you did not receive your permission. Would your children's lives be disrupted, or your livelihood be destroyed? These are legitimate considerations.

Returning to the principle of respect for the landowner to decide what happens on his land, which Stephen told me had been dropped from Labour's 1999 planning guidance, a series of cases had reinstated the principle into English law via the 1998 Human Rights Act. 'Article 1 of the first Protocol of the European Convention implies that planning departments have to balance the rights and freedoms of the whole community against their respect for the property owners' desires to do certain things on their own land,' Stephen told me. It all comes down to value judgements in the end, whether what you want to do with the property is appropriate in the circumstances. The key thing to bear in mind when deciding whether to attempt to live off-grid on a specific piece of land is the area's development plan. Whether you intend to shoehorn your project into that plan, or claim that there are other 'material considerations' which justify your living there – even if they merely amount to the fact that your sustainable dwelling is on your own land, and doing more good than harm to the environment – I would advise against quoting the Human Rights Act to an obscurantist planning official. But Article 1 is a useful weapon to have at a planning inquiry, or a High Court appeal beyond that. The problem is the mismatch between what off-gridders are trying to do with low-impact development and the policy framework which still does not, outside a few enlightened councils, contain provisions designed to allow this kind of development.

Stephen's third piece of advice was one we've already heard: choose the right adviser from the start. Stephen stressed its importance. 'You need someone who can meet you on the land and is aware of what's in the area planning framework as well as the local plan, who may have dealt with those planners before, and can give advice based on all those aspects simultaneously.'

Area development plans

If you don't want to work the land, Simon Fairlie told me, 'then you want to be on the edge of a village. Inside the village is unaffordable, but the planning system does allow for affordable housing within or adjacent to a village but outside the area allocated for development.'

All English councils are obliged to have an area development plan, comprising a number of development documents in which they state their policies about sustainable development, wildlife protection or renewable energy as well as defining the sort of redevelopment they are seeking or permitting in the area. Welsh councils have a similar scheme, although less complicated. In Scotland the system is more complicated, and each council has a development plan, a structure plan and a local plan. You could find conflicts between them, or reasons to support what you are doing in one of them but reasons to oppose it in another. In fact many councils are just paying lip service to national guidelines when they make these statements. 'They all say the same thing – they all give a nod to sustainability,' said Simon, and he doubts whether they mean it. However, when it comes to an appeal, it helps to be able to point to the council's own policy in support of your application.

Some villages have no area allocated for development. Housing development is concentrated on larger key villages, and when buying land you need to check if it is in a development area or somewhere likely to become a development area in the next review. In terms of affordability versus likelihood of getting planning permission, you are treading a thin line: the more likely it is that planning permission will be granted, the less affordable it is likely to be. 'On the edge of a village but not in an area allocated for development,' Simon concluded, 'is the most suitable place for people who want to build a house (off-grid) with a biggish garden, without actually working the land.'

Planning Policy Statements (PPSs)

Although some case law is involved, the planning process is not decided by reference to laws or rules, but to the policy guidance statements issued by the government from time to time. Within the overall framework of the Planning Acts, governments lay down vague guidelines called Planning Policy Statements (which are slowly replacing Planning Policy Guidances). The current government's four aims for sustainable development as specified in PPS1, *Creating Sustainable Communities* (ODPM, 2004), are:

1. Maintenance of high and stable economic growth and employment.
2. Social progress which recognises the needs of everyone.
3. Effective protection of the environment.
4. The prudent use of natural resources.

This is all too new to have been properly tested yet, but if you think of the case of a hypothetical community like Land Matters at Allaleigh, but where the roads are a little wider and the local populace have not worked themselves up into quite such a frenzy, then they ought to fulfil each of those criteria by, for a start, bringing employment and economic activity to an underpopulated part of the countryside. 'Social progress' is always an arguable concept, but permaculture methods, for example, are always going to be good for the environment, and clearly living in benders, closer to nature, is 'prudent' (no doubt Gordon Brown would heartily approve as they shiver through the winter).

Permitted Development (PD)

PD can apply to a wide range of buildings and outhouses. You are, for instance, allowed to put up a barn on a farm or a shed in a wood, and

Finished shelter with watchful eyes.

in some circumstances you can even stay in it for up to twenty-eight days a year. The phrase means that you do not need planning permission to make a change on your land, though you may still need to inform the council planning department of your actions.

There are dozens of specific items that are listed as permitted development. Anything incidental to the enjoyment of your house is one example; so if you park a caravan in the garden and use it as a spare room, that is PD (and you do not even need to inform the council). If your guest stayed a few months and the council got to know about it, they might ask you to apply for planning permission.

To qualify as PD on farmland, the building has to be 'reasonably necessary' for farming purposes. To qualify as PD in a wood, a building cannot be used as a dwelling, cannot be within twenty-five metres of a classified road, and must be 'reasonably necessary' for the purposes of forestry. Also, it must be designed for the purpose for which it is intended; so a forestry hut that looks sufficiently like a house, or is judged to be providing overnight shelter, is not allowed as PD.

So it must not look like a house. OK. Suppose it were a container (NB a container can sometimes be viewed as a structure requiring planning permission). Suppose it had a desk and a chair and a sofa in case you had to 'work' late. And you will need a phone, toilet facilities and somewhere to wash down after a day's forestry work in the woods harvesting all those trees. Assuming you do not have electricity or mains water in your forest, your cooking (essential to forestry work) will be on 'mobile/temporary catering equipment' run off butane, or the car battery, or the solar energy pack. The water will be harvested from the roof of the office. It would be a stretch to live like that full-time, but you may not want to; it may be enough to keep your things there and stay occasionally. The point is that this might count as permitted development. When I checked with Simon Fairlie, he was of the opinion that 'if you do that without appearing to take the mickey, it should not be classed as development at all and there would be no need to apply for change of use.'

In one 1997 appeal, a planning inspector waved through a sixty-foot-by-twenty-foot wooden building used for storing equipment, as a workspace for making fence posts and as an office with washroom facilities, all of which he deemed necessary for managing a twenty-one-hectare coppice woodland in Kent. You may need to prove you are running this operation as a business, with a business plan, but that should not be too difficult.

I double-checked by speaking to a few consultants, and the rules do suggest that a caravan for forestry purposes, such as for storage, as a shelter for workers or as an office, is OK. If the caravan is not a residence, it falls completely outside planning control, and there is no need even to ask the planning authority in advance. This is just one interpretation however, and different councils may have different approaches.

The Control of Development Act 1960, section 29, gives the legal definition of a caravan. Under this definition, there is no need for the caravan (or mobile home) to have wheels, as long as it is under the size limit (given on p. 262) and is capable of being moved in one piece along a road when assembled.

Almost any 'ancillary' building on farmland, up to 450 square feet, could be classed as permitted development, depending on the circumstances, the size of the landholding and its actual use. But to repeat and underline my earlier warning: if something is permitted development you have to inform the council you are doing it in order to give them a chance to disagree. If you do it without telling them and they find out about it, then you lose the right to have it treated as permitted development and you have to apply for planning permission in the normal way.

My place in Ecoburbia

I left Stephen Cottle's chambers determined to apply his way of think-ing to my own situation and those of the people I met. At Big Green I met dozens who wanted to quit the town or city and earn their living in the country. Writers like myself, artisans, clerical workers, every kind of person wanted to try country life, and there were a disproportionate number of self-employed. This is not surprising. It is the self-employed who have the freedom to set their own hours, and who can choose to reduce earnings in return for more free time. For us, the problem is how we can legally run our micro-businesses from a forest.

First we'd have to move in and build a room. Then there is the question of what that room is for. It could be an 'office', but only a forestry office, because as we know, you are not allowed to do primarily non-forestry work in a forest: the law says that any building (or track if you build one) must be for forestry and not primarily for leisure use (although it can be used for leisure as long as its primary use is for forestry). You could live in a forest if, like Marcus Tribe, it is essential to the work you are doing there; but basically, an office that manages the maintenance of your forest and the 'harvesting' of the trees is OK. According to a Chapter 7 briefing, in contrast to agricultural PD rights which are reduced for holdings of less than twelve acres (and are non-existent for less than one acre), there appear to be fewer restrictions on the size of the forestry building, no requirement that the forestry must be run as a trade or business (so amateur forestry is OK), and full PD rights apply to any size of forestry holding.

If working the land and/or managing an office is out of the question, then you have very little justification for building a home without permission unless you can claim it is affordable housing under PPS3 (sometimes called the 'rural exceptions policy'), which calls for affordable housing to remain affordable in the future. This affordability test sometimes means very strict conditions are placed on any planning permission to prevent resale, and this may become more common in the future. But for now, the PP53 strategy is likely to be reserved for housing associations and co-operatives with members local to the area, and there needs to be a survey to prove the local need for it.

As was mentioned in chapter 3, Paul and Susie are trying that route with a carefully laid plan that starts off by forming a housing co-operative comprising the two of them and some friends. Each has bought shares in the Future Roots Co-op, and it will own the land they are trying to buy. If any of them wants to sell, the remaining members will have first option. What they want to do there is exciting and imaginative, and it could be revolutionary, though it comes at a price. They need to raise between £80,000 and £100,000 to buy land before even considering the cost of building homes. Their co-operative is searching for that special kind of land on the edge of what is called the 'village envelope' – meaning it has not already been designated as being available for building in principle, but it adjoins land which has been so designated. Not just anyone can buy such land and expect to get planning permission; but a housing co-operative has special rights (and obligations).

From a community planning point of view, a housing co-op fulfils certain criteria that some councils are looking for in terms of providing affordable housing. As long as they can prove their members are from the area and there is a need for affordable housing in that area, they can expect to be granted permission.

For city dwellers considering a life off-grid, Paul's solution may be the most attractive in the long term because it does not require any commitment to working the land. And there is an extra twist in his plan, because Paul's design for caravan-sized eco-homes means his eco-village will be a housing association on a caravan site, thereby benefiting from caravan park planning permission, which is less stringent than for a normal housing development. It also means they do not have to conform to fully fledged building regulations.

Whatever you decide, it is best to spend only as much as seems proportionate to the level of certainty you have that you may eventually be given permission. To go back to the example of the forest office, it might be tempting fate to build one of Paul's caravans there; safer to erect a rough shed, built on old tyres, or some other sort of temporary foundation. Stephen Cottle thinks that if a case like this reached the inspector or the courts you would be expected to have talked to the planners in advance and attempted to negotiate an agreement with them, rather than just have built first and asked questions afterwards. It is exactly on points like this, he reminded me, that you need to seek advice from a local expert.

And if many start to take advantage of these loopholes, the whole planning system will be in danger of losing its credibility, which in turn will lead to new rules, or a tightening of the old ones. Simon Fairlie, for one, is afraid that the whole thing might get out of hand, leading to eco-houses mushrooming everywhere. Like Tom Jaine, but for different reasons, he abhors the suburbanisation of the countryside. He calls it Ecoburbia.

I am not so sure. After all, we have to live somewhere, and if large numbers wish to live off-grid in wide open countryside, which is currently under-farmed, under-populated and in many cases riddled with dying communities, why should they not be able to do so?

But this is something of a digression from my aim to learn from Stephen Cottle's approach, and work out a way to legally live off-grid in a wood or a field. I already knew it was easier to win planning permission if you were working the land. As Roy Fountain discovered, one test of working the land is that you have a sustainable business model, and he spent years submitting business models before the council accepted one. But that model does not have to produce results immediately. As with any business start-up, you can legitimately argue that it will take three years to break even, perhaps more.

And here's the key: you do not have to offer to work full-time in your field or forest. In fact, it can be advantageous not to. In Pembrokeshire, which is pioneering a new Welsh approach to sustainable development, my discussions with the planning office revealed that their presumption now is that you can live in a wood as long as you prove you are earning from the wood 75 per cent of the minimum wage you would need to survive. That is not 75 per cent of your total earnings, but 75 per cent of a subsistence income – a few thousand pounds a year. You might do this, for example, by cultivating truffles on the trees in the wood, and then selling them at the local farmers' market. In Simon Fairlie's opinion, the precedents show that you can win agricultural planning permission in that situation. Firstly, he explained, 'the guidance now allows for subsistence living – way below the minimum agricultural wage'. That means you do not have to be making a large profit in order to prove you have a sustainable business model. You can be a part-time agricultural worker and still be entitled to agricultural status, because the guidance says you must be 'mainly employed in' agriculture, not solely employed. And, crucially, it's the hours you spend, not how you make your money, that determine whether you are mainly employed in agriculture. So if you spend more time in the fields but make more money on the Internet or in town, you still qualify as an agricultural worker.

'There was an appeal about that,' Simon said, rustling through some papers in his tiny office, but failing to find the ones he wanted. He screwed up his eyes to recall the details. 'It was someone who was asking for the agricultural tie on an existing cottage to be removed, because he was a carpenter, making furniture. The council objected on the grounds that he was farming the woodland – selling Christmas trees in fact. Both sides agreed that he made more money from selling the Christmas trees he harvested in the wood, but he spent more time making his furniture. The inspector decided he was mainly employed making his furniture and therefore the agricultural tie would be removed.' But Simon stressed that the decision, though a precedent, did not have the status of case law. So, like everything about planning, there was only speculation, no certainty.

In Quicken Wood, Wealden, Sussex, Simon and Jyoti had a historic victory in December 2003 which *is* an important precedent for anyone wanting to live sustainably without working the land. They were representing two couples living in buses, with solar power and a composting loo. 'One was a nurse, one a mechanic, and I forget what else,' said Jyoti, 'but they also managed the land and had a goat and chickens.' The case had been turned down by a top barrister on the grounds that it was unwinnable, but the inspector decided in their favour. 'They had a right to live an ecological self-sufficient lifestyle,' the inspector said. 'And their underlying objective *was* to live a sustainable and self-sufficient life,' Jyoti continued. 'The holistic approach would be lost and could not be realised to the same degree by living in a conventional dwelling.' More rigidity in the ruling would have 'denied them the right to a lifestyle of sustainability which is now a fundamental part of current government planning policy'. The inspector added that they were 'not there just because it's a nice place to live'.

Jyoti is not sure if this decision is just a one-off, but a 2005 article in *Planning* magazine said it was part of a pattern of developments that were 'beginning to secure a significant level of support from planning officials'. It quoted the Countryside Agency (as it was then called) saying that developments like Quicken Wood 'make a limited but positive contribution to sustainable development in rural areas'. And there was more support for this approach from a surprising quarter. Robin Bryer, the planning inspector I'd spoken to, told me that he has supported 'farming couples who make that argument'. As long as you make a minimum agricultural wage from the forest then 'if you or your partner have income from elsewhere, lucky you'.

Ben Law, the woodsman who manages ten acres of permaculture woodland near Haslemere in Surrey, believes that far more people should be allowed to live in woods, and the planning rules should be loosened, permitting off-grid developments in 'plantation woodlands'. The rules would have to be strictly framed, though, Ben added, so that developers would not take advantage of them. 'And there does need to be some survey, some plan in place as to what they are going to do with that woodland, and some kind of criteria for the types of dwellings that might be built, and what from, and making sure they are off-grid.' Perhaps the most important criterion would be to limit car transport so that the countryside does not fall even further under the thrall of the car. Even better would be to make the rise of off-grid dwellings the trigger for a revival of rural public transport, with green travel plans and car pools; and it would happen because the group making it happen would have the best incentive: an affordable house in the countryside. Remember, the case Stephen Cottle won in Peod was opposed by locals on the grounds that the area was full of narrow lanes and the extra traffic was disrupting their life.

Simon Fairlie continues to campaign for reform to make off-grid living more accessible. 'I would like to see a two-tier planning system,' he said, 'one set of criteria for the development land which is all bought up and monopolised by the Barratts and Bellways, and another to encourage the small-time off-grid developers who come forward with very highly sustainable developments. It is unfair to make them compete for land which has been jacked up to a hundred times its value. We should provide an incentive for developers to come forward with innovative and sustainable projects.' The degree to which this would be allowed to happen would be up to planners, who could calibrate the developments they attracted with the stringency of the conditions they impose. 'Ultimately it would allow planning permission on land that cost only £4,000 an acre. It's a massive incentive for sustainability.'

Stephen Cottle's view is that the whole principle of being able to build off-grid developments in the countryside comes down to the issue of the right of a landowner to build on his own land. 'The planning authorities must respect the right to property,' he told me. 'And that means they should only interfere on objectively justifiable grounds, unless there is a pressing social need.' It is, however, hard to imagine what pressing social need could prevent the building of a low-profile, low-impact family home. It is easier to understand objections to a medium-sized settlement, mainly because of the extra road use that might result. As Stephen pointed out, planners can impose conditions on granting permission, and that may include restrictions on the number of cars a community like the one at Allaleigh could own between them. This, however, would reduce their ability to work, and at the moment not one of the Land Matters co-operative claims the dole or income support, though several have low-income tax credits.

Checklist for Planning

If after all this you are still planning to go off-grid on a piece of bare land, here is a checklist of things to make sure you consider. This is not a set of instructions, of course, and following them brings no guarantee that you will be successful.

The following advice is universally applicable.

❖   Be aware of planning control. Ignorance is widespread, but you have to take the whole thing seriously, respond to notices, and prepare for a planning battle even if one never happens.

❖   Before buying your land, find out what the local council policy is on sustainable development. Choose an area that seems favourable, where other off-grid schemes have succeeded in the recent past.

❖   Check out the area development plan's policies in your area. If appropriate, make representations to have the plan changed.

❖   Contact the local environmental and Agenda 21 departments of the council but not the planners at this stage. (Agenda 21 is a UN programme related to sustainable development, a comprehensive blueprint of action to be taken globally, nationally and locally by organisations of the UN, governments, and major groups in every area in which humans impact on the environment.)

❖ Find an adviser, preferably one who is local and who will stay on your team throughout the process.

❖ Prepare a management plan and a business plan.

❖ Prepare a planning application which either complies with the area development plan or explains what 'material considerations' prevent it from doing so.

The items below should not be regarded as my recommendations because I would not want to encourage anyone to follow them without knowing the specific circumstances. I have, however, listed them because they have been adopted by some I have met, to good effect. They are to be followed 'at your own risk' and depend on your specific circumstances and the degree to which you are prepared to stick your neck out.

❖ Decide whether to apply for planning first, or to move on and do it retrospectively.

❖ Begin work on the land, whatever your plan or business is.

❖ Move on under the twenty-eight-day rule in a caravan.

❖ If you go for a retrospective application, then move fast to get your permanent shelter built and yourself established as living and working there.

❖ If your new shelter is truly discreet and the council does not contact you for four years, then you are home free, as long as you can prove you lived there for those four years. To this end, invite your solicitor to your housewarming party.

8

Get Serious
Energy for Life

Now over these small hills, they have built the concrete
That trails black wire:
Pylons, those pillars
Bare like nude giant girls that have no secret

'The Pylons', Stephen Spender (1933)

DICK STRAWBRIDGE, the moustachioed star of the BBC2 series *It's Not Easy Being Green*, has a lovely family, and I thought his show, about the green makeover of their home in Cornwall, was tops. But interviewing him for the off-grid website was a disappointment. I asked him what he thought about the concept of living off-grid; could he imagine his beautiful eco-renovation, with its waterwheel and solar panels, going that way? 'I don't want to go back to the Stone Age,' he replied disparagingly. 'I want to serve my guests drinking water from the mains.' So, he did not want to live off-grid himself – that was his choice. Tony Marmont feels the same way, but Dick, unlike Tony, could see no place for off-grid living in today's society. But there is a truth we must all face: we cannot expect to sustain our present living standard indefinitely. Yes, there may yet be a series of scientific breakthroughs that extricate us from the problems confronting us (problems that led Dick to make his series in the first place), but this is unlikely to happen soon. Meanwhile, Dick's waterwheel may be picturesque, and good family entertainment, but it is also expensive to build and maintain. And not everyone has access to a charming detached home and garden in Cornwall in which to situate their renewable energy arrangements.

Tony, Dick and Donnachadh McCarthy, the former accounts clerk, are all examples of the way many more of us will live over the next few decades. They are off-grid ready. If the grid ever collapsed, Tony would be able to switch to his own power supply. His wide-ranging energy system, outlined in chapter 3, is detailed later in this chapter because although it is way over the top for any normal house, it provides useful guidance for anyone thinking of becoming off-grid ready. Even with a less lavish set-up than Tony's, there is no need to lose a single creature comfort if you switch to 100 per cent renewable power, although you will have to reduce your energy consumption. This is not to save the planet, it is to save you money and effort. The less power you use, the less often your batteries will go flat – or, to put it another way, the less you will need to spend on generating equipment. And as I said, if you live off-grid you can run a similar life to the one you have now. The difference is that you cannot run all your appliances at the same time, and the system will go down occasionally for lack of wind or sun or water, or because of a faulty part. Then again, the grid occasionally fails as well, especially in remote areas.

Solar, Hydro or Wind?

Dick Strawbridge had at least one thing right: if you are clever or lucky enough to have access to fast-flowing water then hydro power is the best option. Both PV (photovoltaic), otherwise known as solar panels, and wind power tend to cost about £3,000 per kW of energy they produce; hydro equipment costs about half that. But these figures fluctuate.

PV manufacturers are constantly trying to maximise the efficiency of their product to increase the electricity it can produce, but currently, if you have very low energy requirements – perhaps just a light, a computer, a mobile phone and an iPod – then your best bet may be solar power, even in poor weather. PV cells will last at least thirty years, with little maintenance, so you can just leave them in the sun and get on with your life, and take the power they produce for granted. Hydro turbines, while they can be more expensive to install (depending on the source of your water), will provide steady, reliable electricity as long as the water source does not dry up. Hydro schemes have a lifespan of twenty-five years and equipment for a small, domestic hydro power scheme can cost as little as £1,500 per kW – though the water supply must be tailored to work effectively with the hydro turbine. So, a micro-hydro set-up can provide enough electricity for your house and more, but a large and expensive wind turbine will be needed to achieve the same result, for wind turbines can be less efficient. If an average home uses between 3.5kW and 4.5kW at peak time, then a turbine providing that sort of electricity will need to have a considerable wing span of around five metres in diameter – not to mention windy conditions. If the wind is weak the turbine might work at only 50 per cent of its usual power, no matter how good it is.

A Scoraig turbine – one of dozens.

There are other forms of energy production, like ground source heat pumps, woodchip boilers and fuel cells (which we'll come to soon), but a word of warning: even though wind and water power are old technologies, renewable energy is still in its infancy. Like the Internet in 1995, things just do not work very well yet. They are slowly improving, but come back in a few years if you want a cheap, simple solution that meets all your needs and works straight out of the box.

Wind Turbines

It was a revelation to hear from Hugh Piggott, one of the leading figures in wind power in the UK (www.scoraigwind.co.uk), and the man who'd invited me to visit Scoraig, that the basic features of their design mean that small wind turbines will always have fundamental maintenance problems. On Scoraig he is surrounded by small turbines of many different designs, most of which he has erected for his neighbours over the years, and of course he relies on one for his own house, so he is closer to the problems than most renewable energy suppliers. It seems the smaller turbines are just not sturdy enough to withstand the buffeting they are subjected to in high and variable winds. They also need higher wind than a larger turbine to put out a useful amount of power.

'Small wind turbines are produced by small companies,' Hugh told me, 'working in a price-sensitive market. Big wind is intrinsically more competitively priced because of economies of scale. It is easier to devote huge resources to one machine if it produces a huge amount of energy.' Hugh said that turbines below 20kW (i.e. all turbines that houses or communities are likely to be dealing with) with built-in gear-

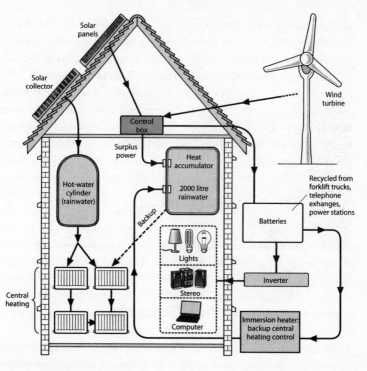

Hugh's Household Power System.

boxes are less reliable than ones with direct drives because there is more to go wrong.

The consensus among turbine-owners was that Proven is the best brand on the market. There were several in Scoraig, and Simon Marr-Johnson had one, as did Neil Hammond near Glenelg. The smaller Proven models, like the 600W or the 2.5kW, still suffer from the same drawbacks as other small turbines, but the 6kW and 15kW turbines are able to withstand winds of 150mph and can function trouble-free for years. They are not cheap, though: it costs at least £20,000 (before subsidies) to put one up. And they produce more electricity than is needed in a typical three-bedroom house, so they are best for groups of houses, communes, or for selling electricity to the grid.

One of the best small wind turbines if you are running a 12V system is the D400 (www.d400.co.uk). It costs about £900 and will produce power even in low wind, and up to 500W at higher speeds. Like the Proven, it has the latest kind of design: a direct drive instead of one with gears. It is designed for marine, camper or rooftop uses. It is exceptionally quiet and is available in low-visibility black to keep the neighbours from complaining. It is also available in a 24V version for use with an inverter in a 240V system. But be prepared for maintenance costs. If you can get together with some neighbours and buy a bigger turbine you might find that is the best value for money in the long term.

Solar Panels

There are three kinds of solar panel, as Tony Marmont explained to me, based on the way the silicon is cut. The first is monocrystalline. That is the most expensive and the most efficient (at 15 per cent) at converting the sun's rays into energy. The second is polycrystalline, which, as its name suggests, is the combination of more than one slice of crystal; it's 13 per cent efficient. And the least expensive and efficient (at 9 per cent) is called amorphous. There is an exception to this rule: in conditions of low sunlight, such as prevail in the UK for most of the year, amorphous is as efficient as monocrystalline. I would still recommend the more expensive panel, though, as it will charge your battery faster when it is sunny.

The active ingredient in solar panels, the cell that converts sunlight into electricity, is made from silicon, the second most common element after oxygen. Ironically, there will be a world shortage of solar cells (and, consequently, high prices) until at least 2008 due to production bottle-necks. Manufacturers like Nanosolar are developing new technologies that require less silicon by cutting silicon wafers more thinly, but that will not increase supply in the short term. Shell Solar has a different solution. It is banking on a variant based on copper indium di-selenide (CIS). By 2008, expect to see a new generation of solar panels which have mirrors to concentrate the sun's rays and are up to 25 per cent efficient.

For a basic 12V kit like the one on my bus, with one 50W panel, but two heavy-duty batteries so that you can always have one of them fully charged, the cost (as I write) would be as follows:

panel	£243.44
two batteries	£199
very basic regulator	£18.09
4mm copper cable	£50
two cigarette lighter sockets from Maplins	£3.98
cheap inverter (for occasional 240V use)	£30

(figures from Raisystems at Townhead, 11/2006)

So you can get started with a basic system that will power your phone charger, computer and car stereo most of the year for around £550. As you add more or bigger panels, and more batteries, the price, naturally, rises accordingly. Piet Defoe at Townhead reckons that a typical small domestic set-up for solar panels might be 4 × 85W panels costing £1,544.80 (including VAT) plus a regulator (£25 to £80) and an 800W pure sinewave inverter at £621.25. The installation, assuming a straightforward job, would cost about £400 and the batteries would be extra, perhaps £400 for four mid-range batteries. So, a total cost of about £3,000. This would provide power for lights, computers, TV and the like for nine months of the year, though it won't do washing

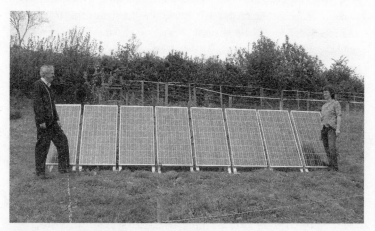

Andrew and Lizzie Purchase – happy solar days.

machines with heaters, storage heaters, electric kettles or immersion heaters. (For the coldest, darkest three months of the year, from early November to late January, a small wind turbine, or a micro hydro if you have flowing water, would be needed to supplement the solar.)

Once you have decided to go for a solar panel (or panels) you find the right site. You need to place it at the correct angle so as to maximise the solar power input, which will mean finding True South – not to be confused with Magnetic South (in Australia, replace 'South' with 'North'). The first thing you need is your latitude and longitude. I have a GPS reader on my Suunto watch but not a clue how to make it work, and the Suunto office were of little help when I asked them. But there is another way, if you have Internet access (I am grateful to Steve Spence of Green Trust for the following instructions). Go to www.astro.com/cgi-bin/atlw3/aq.cgi?lang=e, enter your country and town, or even district, and the calculator will give you your latitude and longitude. Now click over to www.geocities.com/senol_gulgonul/sun/, type in your longitude and latitude in the space provided, and this web tool will give you your solar noon time (which was 11.44 in the morning on the day I happened to try it). Go outside and hold a stick at a ninety-degree angle to the ground. The shadow cast by the stick at your solar noon is a direct line from True South to True North. This is the direction in which your panel should be pointing for maximum solar power.

Now you need to find out the angle of tilt required. Getting this right makes a huge difference through the year as the sun's angle to the earth changes wildly with the seasons. Click over to the Wattsun website, www.wattsun.com/resources/calculators/photovoltaic_tilt.html, and enter just your latitude number. You will get a table showing, each month, the sun's angle to the earth and the degree of tilt you need to maximise your solar absorption. You will have to adjust the tilt through the year, and you can also manually change the direction in which the panel is pointing through the day if you have time. The technology exists to change the tilt and track the sun automatically, but you end up dealing with fiddly machinery that itself needs electric power to run. Clive Menhenett from Magrec showed me a 'sun-tracker' at Big Green, and it worked fine, but in the end it may be simpler and easier just to move the panel yourself from time to time. It depends how busy or lazy you are and how crucial it is to maximise the efficiency of your panel.

For sun charts, declination maps and an inclinometer (complete kit), visit www.jshow.com/sunkit/listings/6.html.

Solar Thermal

At Townhead, some of the houses have old radiators painted black and fixed to their south-facing walls. This is the simplest form of DIY solar water heater. It works best if there is a sealed, pressurised hot water system to draw water through the solar heaters. The water from their well, or rainwater tanks on the roof, passes through the radiator, is heated by the sun, and then rises up through the system, perhaps passing through a conventional water heater run off Calor gas for further heating.

Even the most on-grid home should consider having solar water heating installed on the roof. A well-designed system should provide the majority (about 80 per cent) of hot water during summer months and make a useful contribution at other times, giving an overall saving of up to 60 per cent of the hot water bill.

Evacuated-tube solar water heaters are well established as the most efficient way to produce hot water from renewable energy. They work by passing the water through a row of ten or twenty tubes sealed inside a box. Each evacuated tube consists of two tubes made out of extremely strong glass. The outer tube is transparent, allowing light rays to pass through with minimal reflection; the inner tube has a special selective coating (Al-N/Al) that absorbs the sun's rays more efficiently than conventional flat plate collector systems. The tops of the two tubes are fused together and the air contained in the space between the two layers of glass is pumped out while exposing the tube to high temperatures. This 'evacuation' of the gases forms a vacuum.

A typical domestic system could use solar hot water collector array units covering four to five square metres. Ideally, panels should go on an unshaded slope or pitched roof facing south, although SE to SW is acceptable. A basic solar hot water system costs about £1,800, but it's difficult to estimate accurately as the price depends on the existing infrastructure and each household will have different requirements for hot water, which will govern the type of system chosen. If the house doesn't

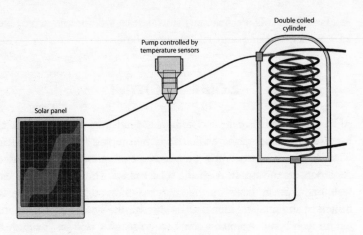

Townhead hot water (from a sketch by Scouse Martin).

have a hot water cylinder – for example if there is a combi boiler – then a cylinder would be required, and that might mean changing the gas boiler, which would increase costs. It all depends on how much needs changing. A more advanced system would be around £2,000 to £4,000.

Piet at Townhead says it is important to have a 'twin coiled water cylinder when incorporating solar hot water into an existing hot water system'. This is to keep the two methods of heating water separate. In a gravity-fed system there is no pump and the water moves as it heats up by convection. These systems are not pressurised. They have a header tank and a vent. Solar panel systems usually have a pump, and the water is at a different pressure.

Micro Hydro

The key to making hydro power work for you is to maximise the amount of energy you generate from the available water. At its peak in the 1920s, hydro was the main source of electricity in towns and villages all over the UK. The rise of cheap oil and gas led to mills and turbines falling into disrepair. Now interest is rising again: it's estimated that there are 20,000 historic micro hydro sites in the UK lying dormant, just waiting to be tapped. These vary from mountainous regions with fast-flowing streams to wide rivers in lowland areas. The advantage of historic sites is that water flow is likely to be assured (although the watercourse may have been diverted since), and it's likely that you will be able to use some of the existing infrastructure, thus saving on installation costs and reducing the impact on the environment.

When he moved onto the Bolton Abbey Estate in 1990, David Allender installed a small wind turbine, a diesel generator and a battery to store the generated power. But the turbine did not produce the plentiful electricity he expected. 'It was surprising to find how many windless days there are in January, even at a thousand feet above sea level in the Pennines,' he remarked. So he installed a micro hydro electricity generator powered by a nearby stream. 'The basic principle of hydro electricity is that if water can be piped from one level to a lower level, the resulting water pressure can be converted into electrical energy,' said Allender. The water is passed though narrow jets which increases the pressure and therefore the speed at which it hits the turbine, forcing it to turn.

With a decent water supply you can generate huge amounts of electricity – up to 10kW or more. The amount of power from a system depends on two factors: the amount of water flowing (flow) and the vertical distance over which it falls (head). Most systems are 'run-of-river', with heads of only a few metres. Run-of-river supplies do not require a reservoir; they just use the water and return it to the watercourse downstream, extracting nothing but energy from the river. The river will have a reduced flow between the point of intake and the location of the turbine, but if you are careful there will be no adverse effects on the local economy.

An advantage of hydro power over wind and solar is that average rainfall is highly predictable and therefore output is reliable. Plus flow doesn't fluctuate from minute to minute like the wind; it changes only gradually from day to day, and the variation in flow generally matches the energy demands – i.e. the more rain there is, the more energy can be produced when it's needed most (in winter).

Judy of the Woods had a sophisticated hydro-power set-up. As she'd decided not to site her dwelling near the river at the bottom of her land, it was not the right choice as a power source. 'The cable run would have been too long for twelve-volt,' she told me. She learned anyway that the 'head' on the river water, i.e. the force with which the water moves, would not have generated enough power to create viable amounts of electricity. Had she used the river, she might have been able to install an Ampair submersible generator, which sits on the riverbed and generates power from the current, but it would have required too much engineering work to make the water flow fast enough (like a Venturi water-powered suction pump). She would also have needed 'a way to stop fish from getting hurt' as they passed the turbine, something similar to the fine-mesh device used by Tony Marmont on his hydro turbine. She could perhaps have constructed a waterfall, but the area is also an SSSI and a site of European importance, and is patrolled by bailiffs who would have reported her activities to the local office of the Environment Agency. The rules have been toughened since Judy set up her system. Since November 2003, any water extraction activity from a river requires a licence. Also, the river can flood very quickly, and debris such as tree-trunks, which frequently wash downstream, would smash the turbine in no time.

Since Judy had springs up on a hillside she knew she would be able to trap the water in large containers – she ended up using 500-litre orange juice barrels collected free from a shipper who would otherwise have junked them – and then let it run down the hillside to the generator. The water hits a little paddle inside the generator which spins a disc with magnets that passes by copper wires to create power. The generator, the charmingly named Waterbaby, was installed by a friend she met on the Internet, a micro hydro expert from British Columbia in Canada who flew in for a two-week stay – a perfect example of the work-life balance but not good for his carbon footprint. The spring is 150 feet higher than the turbine, to ensure there is enough pressure. A control panel tells her what power is leaving the generator and entering the batteries. The water flow can be adjusted to stay in line with the amount coming into the old orange juice containers. So, if there are three litres per minute flowing into the tank, and four litres per minute leaving it, then the net outflow is one litre per minute, meaning it will take 500 minutes, or eight hours, to empty the containers. Since Judy usually has the generator running only a few hours at a time, that is plenty in the summer. In the winter she needs more power, but there is much more water.

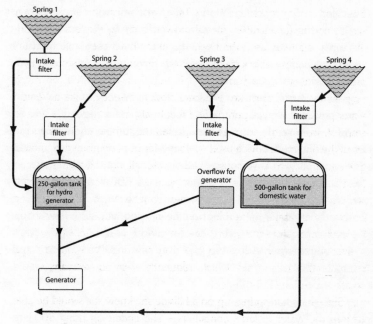

Judy's micro-hydro power system.

Judy spent most of last summer working on her water system. There are still complications: the size of the pipe, for instance, is a little smaller than optimal, and as a result the friction of the water moving along the pipe slows it down slightly so it is not producing all the power it could. After I departed she would take the two 500-litre containers she was using higher up the hill (having emptied them first, of course) so they would have more pressure and be more effective at creating power.

Despite Judy's reservations, some experts will tell you that your turbine can be located up to several kilometres from where you need the power, as it will travel through relatively modest cables without great transmission losses. This is nonsense. The closer you are to the source, the more cost-efficient your system will be. And anything more than 500 metres will result in an unacceptable loss of power and cabling expense. If you are relying on outside help the first thing you need is a pre-feasibility study for around £100 which will tell you if your scheme is practical in terms of output and planning. A more detailed study may cost around £1,000, and will map out exactly what you need to do, including dams and waterfalls. In all cases some form of environmental assessment is essential to obtain planning permission, so it's advisable to work closely with the Environment Agency and your local planning authority too.

With permission from the Environment Agency to create a water store or reservoir, you can control the speed and amount of water that hits the turbine. This doesn't need to be a major feat of engineering. In fact, there's no bottom limit to the amount of power you can produce. PowerPal (www.powerpal.co.uk) sell systems that don't require any extraction of water at all, producing from 200W upwards – easily enough to charge batteries and provide lighting needs. The systems cost around £1,400 for the turbine and the all-important water-flow shaping components; from there costs can rise sharply as the size of the system (and output) rises. Additional pipework and installation costs can be prohibitive.

Hydro pros and cons

Pros
- ❖ Power produced at fairly constant rate compared to other renewables
- ❖ Adaptable, simple, robust technology, and cost-effective
- ❖ Can be very competitive on price
- ❖ Low maintenance costs
- ❖ No carbon emissions, little noise

Cons
- ❖ Site specific
- ❖ Power and expansion limitations
- ❖ Weather-dependent without reservoir
- ❖ High costs up front
- ❖ Has a low-level impact on watercourse

For more information, contact the British Hydropower Association (www.british-hydro.org).

Batteries

Having decided which is the best source of energy for your particular circumstances, the next question is how to store it. If solar panels and wind turbines produced the power we needed when we needed it, there would be no place for batteries, but the sun and wind are un-reliable. And even a steady source of energy like water power cannot cope with peaks in demand around family dinner- and bathtime. So the energy has to be stored somewhere until it is needed. Batteries are a necessary evil, what Clive from Magrec called 'the essential, unpleasant side of the standalone system'.

In a nutshell, batteries are an outdated technology, too low in capacity, too heavy, and much too expensive. Although there are new technologies around the corner, including vanadium batteries from VRB in Vancouver, and fuel cells, this section is about lead/acid batteries, like a car battery only heavier and more powerful. These are still the ones everybody uses to keep their off-grid household powered up, partly because of price. They are made of nasty, polluting lead and plastic, but 97 per cent of all batteries are recycled, according to industry figures, so they are not particularly harmful to the environment. Nickel-cadmium (NiCd) batteries are a step up from lead/acid, but 'are a bit scary', Clive told me. 'You have to charge them exactly right. If you overcharge, they will get hot and burst into flames. The lead/acid battery is more tolerant of a little bit of abuse, and easier to regulate.'

Lead/acid batteries are largely *not* designed to be run until they are flat; most are meant to remain topped up to at least 50 per cent of their full charge all the time. Clive stressed the importance of regular battery maintenance, ensuring that each cell is full of battery acid and each battery is fully charged. 'I top all my batteries up at least once a month because they self-discharge and that is not good for them. Don't ever leave them flat.' Many battery salespeople will still tell you to discharge your lead/acid batteries completely before recharging them. If you follow their advice your batteries will not last more than two years. A battery that is completely dead for more than twelve hours begins to corrode, and this shortens its life. After twenty-four hours with zero power, a full year of life can be lost. So a fully discharged battery should be recharged as soon as possible.

The thickness of the metal plates is the best guide to the quality of a battery. The thicker the plates and the heavier the battery, the more charge it will store and the longer it will take to corrode if the battery sits around uncharged. A good battery should also have a large capacity (measured in amperes; 110 amps is optimal), meaning it can store a lot of energy. It should be capable of being charged, used and recharged many times over. This is called a cycle. You should try to get a battery capable of at least 500 cycles.

On my travels I saw lead/acid batteries that had been requisitioned from many sources: fork-lift trucks, power stations, telephone exchanges, even submarines. They, you may recall, belonged to Tony Marmont – going for the top-end solution as always. Ben Law also had ex-sub batteries. They are very heavy, robust and expensive, though they can be free if they are being disposed of second-hand, and they can be refurbished, though not to an as-new state.

There are three kinds of lead/acid batteries: car batteries, including big lorry or tractor batteries; leisure or RV (recreational vehicle) batteries; and deep cycle batteries. Car batteries are designed to remain permanently fairly fully charged, and do not react well to being drained of power. They are also designed to put out a lot of energy quickly (during engine starting). They are not suitable for the sort of long, slow discharge needed for a low-wattage light bulb. Marine batteries have the same capabilities as car batteries. The so-called leisure batteries sold in shops like Halfords are really just repurposed truck batteries and are designed for caravans and smaller applications. Proper leisure batteries (sometimes called solar batteries), by contrast, are designed to put out a medium amount of power steadily. They discharge at only half the rate of car batteries, so they will last twice as long if they are fully charged. They are not right for power tools or other power-hungry machines, but they are fine for low-energy devices such as phone chargers, computers, small sound systems and small TVs. (Many of these also run off small AA batteries.)

Deep cycle batteries have the thickest plates, giving a longer, slower discharge for lighting or a water pump, for example. If it does not say 'Deep Cycle' on the battery, then it is not a deep cycle battery. A deep cycle battery that is recharged immediately after use should last up to ten years if it is regularly maintained in this way. The rule of thumb is

Hugh and his second-hand batteries.

that you need to charge a battery for as long as it has been discharging. You can discharge up to 80 per cent of the best batteries but then need to recharge them as quickly as possible. The manufacturer's instructions will tell you how many times a battery can be cycled, but that partly depends on how flat they have been allowed to get. The instructions might say they can be cycled, for example, a thousand times at 50 per cent discharge, but only 500 times at 80 per cent discharge. Lithium-ion batteries are the only ones that do not mind being left uncharged or half-charged for long periods. However, they are more expensive.

The most expensive lead/acid battery is the Rolls, made by the Canadian company Surrette: it weighs over 200lb and costs over £500. The consensus among off-grid electricians favours the Elecsol brand of lead/acid batteries for small 12V systems. They have triple the life of a typical deep cycle battery and a top-of-the-range 220-amp 12V example costs about £225 plus VAT. They would not have the capacity of a Rolls, but at less than half the weight (50kg) and less than half the price, Piet Defoe thinks they are good value. He has used, and sold, loads of Elecsol batteries and systems for years. 'They come with guarantees and work fine,' he said. 'They use a sort of carbon lead mat which increases the surface area of lead available to the acid electrolyte and also helps prevent electrode disintegration (shredding) which happens when batteries are deeply discharged.' For a big domestic system, Clive Menhenett prefers to use a set of 2V traction (or forklift) batteries. 'They are built to be cycled every day,' he explained.

Dump load

Batteries can also be damaged by being overcharged, at which point they can overheat and the acid starts bubbling. To prevent this you need a box to monitor the charge and switch off the power when they are full. However, unless you happen to be watching the system at the time, your solar panel or turbine will still be producing power once the batteries are full, and that power needs to go somewhere. This could be to a water heater, which can then store the excess power temporarily by heating the water.

The simplest form of dump load looks like a heavy-duty one-bar electric fire. When I encountered one (at Brith Dir Mawr) I knew that I had found the solution to my search for a simple way of heating my cold hut in Majorca when I am not there, so that it's not damp when I am. A wind turbine will be connected to a battery and a dump load, and once the battery is full, the fire will come on and stay on as long as the windmill is turning.

There is a detailed set of instructions, together with a video showing how to maintain your batteries, on the Trojan website (www.trojanbattery.com/Tech-Support/BatteryMaintenance.aspx). Cadex is another battery brand with a helpful site: www.battery university.com. For advice on household batteries, visit www.michael bluejay.com/batteries/.

12V Versus 240V

And now, having decided which is the best source of energy for your particular circumstances, and how to store it, you need to decide on what voltage to use around your house. If you go for 240V you will be able to use the same equipment as any normal house, but you will need to invest in a variety of expensive gadgets to make your 240V system work. You or your installer will need to decide whether to generate the power as 12V, 24V or 48V DC (direct current) before it is converted into 240V AC (alternating current).

A 12V system is the cheapest, simplest way of switching on the power, just as it comes out of the battery. A car stereo, a small fridge, a phone charger – many devices can be found in a 12V version, thanks mainly to auto and marine supply stores. And if there is something you vitally need to run at 240V, you can always buy a small, cheap inverter (see next section). There's also a wide range of low-energy, low-cost 12V bulbs and lights, both halogen and LED, which throw out a cold light but are fine for reading. Again they can be found at auto parts shops as well as on the Internet. And at Townhead I was introduced to the National Luna, a South African medical fridge which costs £800 but uses little energy. At Land Matters, Richard Brain, known as Brains, runs a complex sound system from his 12V supply. Brains and his partner Maren live in a bender separated by a hedge from the rest of the commune, with a neat picket fence around it, and an air of suburban tranquillity. He works part-time as a DJ and keeps his mobile equipment running on twelve volts both at home and when out on a job. He has a typical solar panel set-up, with the panels feeding into batteries, but the difference is he does not need an inverter to take the power from 12V to 240V. Even laptop computers will charge at 12V if you buy a different transformer to the one supplied.

One important precaution for a 12V system is a thick power cable and a large fuse to connect the batteries to the regulator – the black box that sits between the power source (solar panels, for example) and the batteries and prevents overcharging. This is because the current (measured in amps) is much higher in 12V systems and can melt the wires if they are not thick enough.

Woodsman Ben Law runs virtually his entire woodland set-up on 12V. He has two large wind turbines and two small ones, as well as several solar panels, all feeding into six big submarine batteries. Almost all his electrical devices are 12V, although he does have a small inverter to run a central heating pump and a food blender for his new baby.

Another factor in your choice between 12V and 240V is what kit you already own, and what friends happen to donate when you are starting up. I would recommend 12V for a small system and 240V for a larger one. Whether you go for 12V or 240V will depend on how much of a normal life you want to lead, what gadgets you already own, and whether you have children, among other considerations.

There is a valuable Internet discussion group for living on 12V systems at http://groups.yahoo.com/group/12VDC_Power/.

Inverters

You use an inverter when you want to run normal 240V items, like a hairdryer or a toaster. (Inverters are not to be confused with transformers. The latter turn 110V alternating current into 240V, or the other way around. Inverters turn 12V direct current into 240V alternating current.) The bigger and more expensive your inverter, the more items you can run simultaneously. The cheapest inverter costs £30 from a camping shop and will handle one appliance at a time.

But to run a 240V system with multiple appliances plugged in off a 12V, 24V or 48V battery requires a more sophisticated kind of inverter which can handle numerous appliances, monitor the health of the battery and monitor the incoming power simultaneously. The most sophisticated inverters lose less power as they convert from DC to AC and can also switch incoming power from one battery to another, or automatically switch on a diesel generator if there is too little power coming in from solar panels or wind turbines. They can cost from a few hundred to a couple of thousand pounds. The top-of-the-range inverters used in most professionally installed home systems are the Xantrex (formerly Trace) and Sunny Island range of Sunny Boy inverters.

A pure sinewave inverter is recommended if you are running sound equipment, because it eliminates the slight buzz you hear when it is running off a normal inverter. Computers are also safer on a pure sinewave inverter.

Generators

When you run out of renewable power you need a generator to keep you going. Over half the homes I visited had a back-up generator somewhere in the garden for use when the power consumption outstripped the supply – whether because of an extended period of low wind, or little sun, or problems with the renewable energy equipment itself. One of them had only a generator. (Annette Potter, the horse breeder, was the only person I visited who had no batteries at all; she simply turned the generator on whenever she needed to run a light, or her daughter's computer. But Annette uses a petrol generator, which is very expensive and pumps far more hydrocarbons into the atmosphere than the alternatives.)

The main requirements of a generator are reliability and efficient fuel consumption. Most of the generators I saw were the big, heavy, ultra-reliable Lister diesel engines with alternators fitted – cast-iron monuments to Britain's manufacturing heyday. The old ones are based on a design from early last century, so they are simple, have no electronics and can be fixed easily. The engine gives out a reassuring low throbbing sound, and the weight of the chassis means they do not rattle. So compared with a modern gennie like the Subaru I have in Majorca, they are far less intrusive.

Farmers used to power their electrics this way, running the 'gennie' on red diesel, which is reserved for agricultural uses. (In January 2007, red diesel was being taxed at 7.69p/litre, compared to bio-diesel at 28.35p, ultra low sulphur diesel at 48.35p, and ordinary diesel at 54.52p. Like a diesel car engine, a generator can also run on vegetable oil, but it would not make economic sense as red diesel costs less than veggie oil at retail prices.) But Lister engines are dying out now. Although I saw a range of them housed in a variety of sheds, I don't recommend buying an antique unless you have a neighbour who enjoys tinkering with farming memorabilia. A skills shortage means they can be difficult to have serviced if you live remotely. Lister-Petter, which made the superb generators for almost a century, went into receivership a couple of years ago, and emerged a different company with little interest in off-grid client service. It still makes high-quality generators, but its network of engineers has been disbanded, and it is focusing on large industrial orders overseas, which is where the money is.

Remember, you can always use the car engine as a generator. Although that is not a long-term solution, it is what I do in Majorca with hire cars, whose engines and batteries may suffer as a result. That leaves the options of maintaining an old generator yourself, or buying a noisy, new, low-maintenance machine like my Subaru for a few hundred pounds and scrapping it when it goes wrong. I saw the Honda EB5000X generator recommended on an Internet discussion group (http://groups.google.com/group/alt.energy.homepower), but I cannot vouch for it.

Whatever generator you choose, noise will be an issue, and the Internet is full of advice on how to reduce it.

Nine ways to hush your generator

Since off-grid locations are likely to be isolated, a quiet generator is important to avoid sound pollution every time you need to boost the batteries. When coupled with a sophisticated inverter, generators can be rigged up to switch on automatically when the batteries are low. This can mean they start up in the middle of the night, which will make quite a racket in most off-grid locations.

1 If you haven't bought your engine yet, the easiest thing to do is to go for a 'silent' generator. These do tend to be a few hundred pounds more expensive than regular engines, but depending on your needs, it might be worth it. At www.myrak.com you can get a Mosa GE6000 super silent diesel generator c/w Yanmar L100 engine 6kVA, 4.8kW, on trolley, 110/240V, for £1,699. A cheaper alternative can be found at www.thegreenreaper.co.uk: the Kipor Storm Force KDE6700T silent diesel generator 4.5kVA for £649.99.

2 If you already have a generator and don't fancy buying a new one, you can invest in a ready-made sound shield, which costs something in the region of £950 for a 3.5kW to 5kW model; they are available at www.soundstop.com. The Super-Silencer sound shield is a 'flexible, flame-resistant noise suppressor – a composite of fibreglass batting faced with a tough, reinforced, quilted vinyl film laminated to a vinyl noise barrier'.

3 If a ready-made sound shield does not fit your dimensions, you may have to make one (the website www.supersoundproofing.com has a great forum where you can find all sorts of tips on how to soundproof effectively). You'll need to build an enclosure for your generator out of an appropriate material. Wood is not an option as it transmits sound easily. Instead, use something called 'soundboard', or 'homasote', or MDF (medium-density fibreboard). You can also use aluminium. The box needs to be made up of three separate boxes. You can check out a price list for materials that can be used to soundproof your generator box at www.customaudiodesigns.co.uk (see Enclosure/Duct Soundproofing Products). Of course you may decide to soundproof the engine room rather than the generator. This means that other noisy equipment can be set up in the room, and money spent soundproofing the walls (and possibly the ceiling), and laying a heavy carpet on the floor, is spread over more than one noise source.

4   Keep the generator box as small as practical to reduce 'drum' effect, and if possible, locate the box so that there are also barriers such as walls in the way. If located next to a wall, sound reflection from the box to or through the wall can be reduced by covering the wall around the generator with thin absorbent mat.

5   If you are worried about the temperature inside your box and unsure whether or not you need fans, you can use a meat thermometer inserted through a hole drilled in the box to monitor temperature. Check with the manufacturer to find the temperature tolerance of your noise source.

6   Small computer power supply box fans move a lot of air, are cheap, and can run on 12V DC or 110V AC. To prevent noise escaping from the enclosure via the inlet and outlet air ducts you can construct baffles composed of mass loaded vinyl (MLV), a tough, wear-resistant material that can also be placed on or under hard floors to reduce sound reflection and transfer dramatically, or inside walls and ceilings. You can buy it at www.soundproofing.org, but it and other materials like it will cost £1 per square foot plus delivery. For baffles you can use cheap eight-by-twelve-inch cake pans with one end cut out to make a form for attaching the vinyl.

7 To isolate the noise source from the floor, 'vibration pads' can be used. These can also be bought from www.sound-proofing.org for approximately 60p per two-inch pad, depending on the size of your box. However, they are not needed if your floor is concrete.

8 Wrapping the pump or motor is an additional way of reducing the sound emitted by it, leaving the ends open, if needed, for ventilation. You can use lead or MLV, and tie it in place with wire or nylon 'tie wraps'.

9 Something else to consider when managing noise is standing waves, the result of soundwaves bouncing off parallel walls to form an extra wave of sound in the middle. So that no standing waves are formed, no two walls of your soundproofing material should be parallel. Any time you're going to use a second layer of material, *don't* create a parallel plane. You can build walls using a third canted panel between ('I \ I'), which are soundproof.

For more tricks that are generator-specific, check out 'Hushing Up Your Generator' on the www.passagemaker.com forum.

Combined Systems

Hugh Piggott, David Boon and Sandy Boulanger all have systems that combine solar panels with wind power and solar water heaters. This is expensive, but it results in more reliable power when you cannot count on either wind or sun being there when you need it. Theirs are top-of-the-range renewable energy systems, designed to allow you to live as closely as possible to a normal grid-connected existence.

The most sophisticated is Hugh Piggott's in Scoraig. Hugh has power coming in from a turbine, solar panels and a solar water collector (see p. 313). Occasionally, if he is doing some building work, Hugh might wheel a gennie into place for a few days, but normally he manages without. The solar panels and the wind turbine feed power into a control box which sends it out to his mix of second-hand heavy-duty batteries. When the batteries are full, a second charge control box dumps the excess electricity into a hot water cylinder which supplies the family with its hot water. The cylinder is also heated directly by the solar collector so there is always plenty of hot water in the Piggott household. Once that water is hot, excess electricity is sent to another 'heat accumulator', a 2,000-litre water tank which will run the full central heating system Hugh was installing when I visited him.

The Boons' set-up also has a mix of wind turbine and solar panel, but theirs is more an example of how not to go off-grid – a useful reality check for what they never tell you about renewable power. Whatever can go wrong has gone wrong for David and Anne and their two French bulldogs Louis and Jim. 'From being very passionate and excited and thrilled by it all, I'm very, very disillusioned,' David told me. 'When you are running your own power station, you can't neglect it. You've got to be here virtually all the time, aware of it, aware of the wind, of the fact it's all going to need replacing one day.' David taught me that unless you are Hugh Piggott, able to devote yourself to the equipment, you must keep it simple to avoid extra work and worry.

Are You Off-Grid Ready?

Tony Marmont's complex energy system is a testbed to learn what is possible with different kinds of renewable energy systems. West Beacon Farm's energy technologies use, according to the website www.beaconenergy.co.uk,

❖ two 25kW two-bladed wind turbines (now seventeen years old);
❖ three interlinked 1kW photovoltaic arrays;
❖ 6kW fixed photovoltaic arrays (now twenty years old);
❖ hydrogen energy storage;

❖ water conservation (no mains water connection, rainwater-only source);
❖ hydro power;
❖ and sustainable transportation (electric and hybrid cars).

Tony is more than a scientific oddity, he is off-grid ready. He is connected to the grid but, in the event of a temporary or prolonged brown-out of the power or water system, he will have all the electricity and water he needs to keep going as if nothing had happened, almost at the flick of a switch.

For the vast majority of readers, being off-grid ready, even in just one room of your home, may be the closest you will come to the full experience. The only obstacle is the power companies' insistence that if you connect to the grid to sell them power, you have to automatically stop generating in the event the grid shuts down for any reason. 'This is not sensible,' said Tony. 'When one power station goes down, do we have to close all the others? It is not the case in other parts of the world.' I spoke to green electricity company Good Energy. Their boss, Juliette Davenport, confirmed that intelligent systems exist to automatically and safely switch over to batteries and micro-generation if power to our homes is cut off. However, government regulations currently forbid this because utility workers don't want to be fixing a downed connection when micro-generators are pumping out power. 'I think it is another lever used by the utilities to try to stop distributed generation,' Tony added darkly. Was there not some way round this? I asked. After all, part of the point of investing in renewable energy if you already have a grid connection is to reduce your reliance on the grid. It's not much use if you have to switch your power off when the grid goes down. 'You should be able to fit an isolator,' Juliette pointed out, which is a simple switch that would disconnect home-generation equipment from the grid in the event of a blackout.

After he moved in to the farm, Tony's first move was to replace his oil-fired boiler with a ground source heat pump (GSHP) system, an energy-efficient alternative to conventional central heating. The US Department of Energy website (www.eere.energy.gov) carries a clear explanation of how heat pumps work. Like your refrigerator, heat pumps use electricity to move heat from a cool space into a warm one, making the cool space cooler and the warm space warmer. During the winter, heat pumps move heat from the cool outdoors into your warm house; during the summer season, they move heat from your cool house into the warm outdoors. Because they move heat rather than generate it, heat pumps can provide around four times the amount of electrical energy they consume.

The most common type of heat pump is the air source heat pump, which transfers heat between your house and the outside air. 'If you heat with electricity, a heat pump can trim the amount of electricity you use for heating by as much as 30% to 40%,' claims the US website. A heat pump can be used for hot water as well as heating the air. Geothermal (ground source or water source) heat pumps are more efficient than air source, but more expensive to install. They transfer heat between your house and the ground or a nearby water source. In the US, about 40,000 geothermal heat pumps are installed each year, but in the UK the number is only a few hundred, largely because the market here is not big enough to bring the price down. Tony's AB Thermis system makes use of the reasonably stable temperature of the water in his man-made two-acre lake to transfer the heat to a well-insulated thermal water storage tank. He then uses the heat in the tank to heat the house as well as the hot water (supplemented by a bank of Thermomax evacuated-tube solar collectors mounted on the garage roof).

A GSHP needs electricity to work. That does not rule it out in off-grid situations, but it does need a reliable source of power. When it was installed, Tony powered his GSHP with mains electricity. Shortly after the heat pump was up and running, in about 1986, he installed a 4kW wind turbine and a 3kW array of solar panels to provide the electricity required to make the heat pump a self-sufficient system powered entirely by renewable energy. Tony is exchanging one unit of high-quality electricity for three to four units of low-grade heat, so a GSHP is only for those with plenty of spare power.

Tony also added insulation to the farmhouse soon after he arrived. The original walls consisted of a brick outer leaf and concrete breeze-block inner leaf with an air cavity between. The wall cavities were filled with blown insulation. The windows are the original timber-framed double-glazed units.

The largest generators of energy at West Beacon Farm are two fixed-pitch two-bladed wind turbines. These are rated at 25kW each and were installed in 1990 at a cost of £60,000. Over a typical year, these turbines will generate between 40MWh and 50MWh of electricity – enough for about 160 energy-efficient homes. The second-largest electricity generators are two sets of solar panels: one row of fifty-four monocrystalline cells made by a company called ARCO, and one row of eighty-one polycrystalline cells made by Solarex, generating approximately 4.5MWh of electricity a year between them since their installation twenty years ago, with no decline in performance. A team from the University of Loughborough recently examined the panels and found no degradation. There aren't many twenty-year-old panels still in service, and the popular supposition is that they degrade, though according to Tony that's no longer true. 'They are making better ones now than they were then. The manufacturing process has advanced. I went down to British Aerospace at Filton. They built geographic satellites with solar panels to make the electricity for the communications, and recently the shuttle recovered some satellites to bring them back to earth for inspection and repair. They were staggered to find that the panels were still producing full power. So nowadays they put on the exact size they want instead of making them much larger than needed, like they used to.'

Operating on the principle of multiple redundancy also favoured by David Allender at Bolton Abbey, Tony has a conventional central heating system and radiators in the farmhouse to back up his GSHP. (A wood-burning stove in the lounge is another source of supplementary heating – fallen wood from the planted trees is used as fuel – although it is mainly for aesthetic purposes.) He only uses it when he can't get enough power from renewables – about an hour a day in winter, but never in summer. Rather than a standard oil- or natural gas-fuelled boiler, however, he fitted a Biklim TOTEM combined heat and power (CHP) unit fuelled by Calor gas. These units work by generating electricity, and then the excess heat produced at the same time is captured and stored, usually in the form of hot water. Tony explained the principle of the CHP to me. 'With traditional separate generation the energy is created in a power station, and the additional heat used to create the electricity is lost [as steam], and as a result the traditional power station is only about 35 per cent efficient. The CHP unit is approximately 90 per cent fuel efficient, and although propane is a fossil fuel, it burns cleaner than standard fuels, with relatively low emissions of greenhouse gases. The unit also allows for the possibility of using gas from a biomass gasifier or hydrogen from an electrolyser.' CHP is the standard for heating in Denmark, Sweden and the Netherlands, Manhattan, and much of central Paris and Berlin. The heat is transmitted down pre-insulated pipes into apartment buildings. The UK decided to pipe gas into each individual home (see chapter 2). 'My contention would be that it is better to do it as a community than as an individual,' said Michael King of the Combined Heat and Power Association (www.chpa.co.uk). 'You have far more bargaining power and there are economies of scale.'

Even on a cloudy day the air in the house is heated by solar energy. A system of automatic fans and shutters controls the ducted flow of this air into the main house, for passive solar heating in winter and ventilation. The heat pump system also runs through the duct which enhances its own heating/cooling performance.

Tony and the control hub of his energy network.

All in all, Tony's energy-generating equipment, excluding his fuel cells, cost £250,000. 'When you lead with stuff you can't go out and buy bog-standard kit,' he pointed out, half embarrassed at his extravagance but just as proud. 'You have to have it made specially. When steam engines and cars were invented the early pioneers had to pay a fortune. It cost a lot of money, but I don't regret spending it. What good is it to me when I'm dead? We've only got ten years, then it's irreversible. What good is the payback then? If you can stop your grand-children from dying, it doesn't matter what it cost.' Recently, of course, Tony added a new engineering plant room and garage at a cost of another £250,000 so that he could start producing hydrogen for fuel cells. Angela, his wife, was not happy with this new industrial addition to their home, so he added a conservatory on top of the plant room. The hydrogen production technology cost another £250,000. Tony seems to talk in units of £250,000.

Daylight is brought into the darker areas of Tony's farmhouse using monodraught lightpipes. These sealed, highly reflective ducts transfer daylight from a clear dome on the roof to enclosed areas such as the cloakrooms and hallways. Low-energy compact fluorescent lights are used elsewhere in the house. You can buy energy-efficient light bulbs to replace traditional ones, which waste energy by turning it into heat. They work in the same way as fluorescent bulbs, which have a gas inside them. When an electric current is passed through the tube of gas it makes the tube's coating glow. These bulbs last on average twelve times longer than ordinary ones, so although they cost around £3.50 compared with 50p for a regular bulb, they do save money in the long run. Lightbulbs Direct has an energy-saving calculator on its website (www.lightbulbs-direct.com/article_view.asp?ArticleID=4). Another way to reduce energy is to install low-energy light fittings. These use a transformer fitted into the base of the light fitting which controls the supply of electricity to the bulb, allowing for a small surge of power for a millisecond to light the bulb and then reducing the electricity flow to a very low level. Low-energy fittings require a pin-based energy-saving bulb (a different fitting to a conventional bulb).

Past the lake adjacent to Tony's house, at the bottom of the next field, sits a building constructed out of local stone containing two water turbine systems. The larger, which uses the flow of water between the turbine house and the lake, powers a 2.2kW generator which sends out power to the back-up batteries. The smaller turbine is powered by the water flowing in a stream outside the building, and generates up to 850W after rainfall in the summer, and more constantly during the winter. To prevent wildlife or debris from the stream falling into the turbine, the water passes over a Coanda effect water filter, a vertical bank of horizontal steel wires. Any solid matter falls by gravity over the wires and back into the stream. The lake is topped up by rainfall and by a natural spring fifty metres below ground. The power to pump the water to the surface is supplied by three interlinked 1kW solar panels which use a sun-tracking system that increases their output by 61 per cent. The water is pumped from below ground when the sun shines – approximately 4,000 gallons each day during the summer, delivered via a fountain jet, and 2,000 gallons in the winter.

Storage is the big problem when it comes to renewable energy generation. Batteries are an old and wasteful technology. But renewable power is irregular because it depends on the weather, and demand for electricity varies depending on the time of day and year. To meet the demand for electricity constantly and reliably with renewable energy, the energy has to be stored in some more reliable form than even the most advanced batteries.

Batteries are used for small-scale energy storage, as discussed earlier. For longer-term, larger-scale storage, hydrogen is the best, but it is only Tony and a few others like him who are in a position to produce it. He uses his surplus electricity to power a process called electrolysis which divides water into its constituent parts, hydrogen and oxygen; the gas is then stored in pressurised tanks. To use the hydrogen to produce electricity, it is fed into a fuel cell where it recombines with oxygen and as a result generates electricity and hot water. So fuel cells are not a source of energy. The hydrogen is the energy source; the cells simply use that hydrogen to produce electricity. A hydrogen storage system makes it possible to store energy created from renewable sources to give a constant and reliable supply of power with zero CO_2 emissions. They may be the next generation of batteries as soon as the leading-edge companies racing to complete their products work out how hydrogen can be made and stored safely in ordinary domestic situations.

Future Trends

In a way, the fuel cell is an indicator that we as a society are looking for the wrong answer, or trying to solve the wrong problem. The issue at stake is our giant urge to consume; the fuel cell simply enables us to keep consuming more. Investors are circling the area like buzzards; new fuel cell companies are announced almost weekly. In the UK, the industry leader Ceres Power claims to be nearing the launch of its first mass-market fuel cells. I rang Ceres' chief executive, Peter Bance, who is working with BOC (now Linde Group) on fuel cell devices that supplement conventional cylinder gases such as LPG, propane or butane. These devices could provide power to remote locations in the UK or elsewhere, which means off-grid homes could have a source of electricity for the price of a tank of Calor gas. Ceres is also working with British Gas on devices that can power ordinary domestic heating and hot water, as well as household electricity, by incorporating the fuel cell into a boiler. This will give households low-cost electricity without substantially increasing their gas bill. First demonstrations of Ceres devices are expected during 2008.

Meanwhile, there is a whole other industry developing on the back of our consumption of carbon – the renewable certificates industry. As a result of government regulations, the energy you generate at home qualifies for tiny payments from the government as it goes towards fulfilling their Kyoto commitments. This is good news for off-gridders as they generate only renewable energy, and they use very little energy. If personal carbon allowances are ever introduced, off-gridders would have a surplus they could sell to city bankers.

The forty-eight hydrogen storage cylinders on Tony Marmont's farm can produce enough electricity to provide all the power required at the farm for three weeks (around 4MWh). Before the hydrogen store was established, of course, the surplus power generated at the farm was exported and sold to the national grid. From 1990 to 1999, 317MWh of wind-generated power was sold; this produced an income of almost £35,000. All generators of renewable energy, whether on- or off-grid, earn ROCs, renewable obligation certificates, a payment whose value, whether or not it is sold, varies according to the carbon offset on the open market. Good Energy has hundreds of customers generating renewable energy, some of them on the grid selling the power they create to the company, and just twenty of them off-grid simply claiming the ROCs via Good Energy, which acts as the middle man and aggregator. There are two options for selling your renewable energy back to your electricity supplier. Using the first option, 'net metering', it's possible to earn the same per unit exported as you pay for it, but this involves a *lot* of paperwork. The second, and easier, option pays less per unit generated, but it is also less hassle. If you expect to produce thousands of pounds-worth of surplus electricity, you'll want to set up a net-metering arrangement. This means that your energy supplier will pay you a decent price for every spare kW of electricity generated that you don't need yourself. It does mean that you'll need to get an OFGEM-approved export meter, but your supplier may be able to help. You also get to keep your ROC entitlements with this option.

Juliette explained the system to me. First the householder creating the energy has to be accredited with OFGEM, the power industry regulator, by filling in some forms and in some cases undergoing an inspection. Next he installs an accredited meter for £50 (it is sensible to install this meter at the same time as the renewable system). Once a year he sends in a meter reading to OFGEM and receives his ROCs credit – typically £30 to £40 per year. Good Energy then pays the customer for the renewables generated and claims the money back from the government. Technically, the electricity supply licence holders, such as Good Energy or EDF, are buying the electricity from the house-holder and selling it back without it ever leaving their home. 'They sell the electricity they generate to a supply company under a sell-and-buy-back agreement,' Juliette explained. Good Energy has 250 micro-generators (producing an average of 1.5MWh per annum), 'which we think is between 10 and 15 per cent of the market'. But their research only includes work done by government-accredited installers. Most of the people I met had not used approved installers to do their work. 'This government is very good at putting new policies forward and putting new legislation in place but appalling at implementing it,' Juliette added. 'The administration on ROCs for micro-generators is still very complex and hard work. They were meant to be coming out with new guidelines a year ago but still haven't done it.'

A DEFRA spokeswoman said that small communities and communes can apply to the DTI's Low Carbon Buildings Programme, which provides micro-generation grants for solar PV, solar water heating, wind turbines, micro hydro, ground/water/air source heat pumps, biomass (including biomass boilers and room heaters/stoves) and micro combined heat and power (including fuel cells). Grants are up to a maximum of £30,000, or 50 per cent of the capital and installation cost of the micro-generation technologies installed. The programme is managed on the government's behalf by the Energy Savings Trust. Full details at www.lowcarbonbuildings.org.uk.

The problem is that the programme requires consumers to use an accredited installer. These installers charge more than non-accredited but industry-certificated installers, and as a result it is often cheaper, or no more expensive, to install renewables without any grant. And as Tony Marmont made clear, the electricity companies still insist that in the event of a power failure on the grid, all grid-connected energy generation has to cease for safety reasons. One could fit an isolator, as Juliette Davenport advised, but UK electricity companies do not currently offer to supply them. Other countries, like Canada, do not have this problem.

DEFRA also has an Environmental Action Fund for voluntary and community groups in England. Grants, requiring 50 per cent matched funding, are from £25,000 to £250,000 per year (£75,000 and £750,000 over the three-year grant period). The full funding for the three-year period 2005–2008 has been allocated, and DEFRA said they hope the fund will run for 2008–2011 as well. But true to form, they had had not made any announcement by mid-November 2007. Funds are awarded on a competitive basis, with all applications judged against agreed criteria. Further information on the fund is available from www.defra.gov.uk/environment/eaf/index.htm.

There are no specific grants for off-grid energy generation, and there seems to be little chance of this happening, unless Thomas Homer-Dixon's predictions come true and we move into a long-term crisis sparked off by events such as a shortage of Russian gas supplies or serious damage caused by climate change.

Postscript

Relax, Feel at Home – Embracing the Off-Grid World

Two roads diverged in a wood and I –
I took the one less travelled by,
And that has made all the difference.

The Road Not Taken, Robert Frost

THE CRISIS, if it happens, may not be on a scale that has the likes of Hector Christie reaching for his crossbow and hiding food around the estate. But doom-laden forecasts continue to echo across the media, and my consciousness. In darker moments I wonder what I would do if the system breaks down. How would I protect my family? I imagine us alone in winter during an energy crisis. The Bus runs out of petrol on a deserted B-road. The normal concerns of life recede, and the battle for survival is on.

Then my natural optimism reasserts itself. I push aside the feelings of fear and remember that the crisis may never happen. In any case, I did not set out to explore off-grid living out of a sense of fear or self-preservation. Off-grid is about looking outwards, creating a more open society. A sense of freedom and control over my own life that comes with the unplugging, is what makes it worth the effort. I went into this for the joy, not because of some inward-looking end-of-the world scenario.

And anyway, surviving in the wild need not prove a negative experience. It's a battle the human species have been winning for centuries. My recent off-grid immersion, and a beginners' course in bushcraft, has hardly equipped me to handle any hardship life could throw at me, but with Fiona there to bail me out when my common sense fails to kick in, it might even be fun (at least for a while). We would have with us the contents of the small Crisis Bag (as detailed in chapter 5). Though that is more of a summer kit.

I contacted Robin at Land Matters for further advice on survival. He told me that he and half a dozen advanced bushcraft classmates spend evenings around the campfire discussing national crisis scenarios and strategies for coping with it. 'You would probably head for the coast,' he told me, which was useful. Before this conversation I would instinctively have headed inland, looking for a national park. (That would only work if you were a squirrel, Robin pointed out, with a stock of food put aside for the months when there is none to be found.) No, what I wanted was coastal woodland. There I would have shelter, plus access to sea-fishing and many varieties of edible plant in winter that cannot be found elsewhere: sea kale, wild cabbage, sea beet (also known as wild spinach) 'and loads of edible seaweeds like bladderwrack and dabberlocks'. A wood by the sea would give me the best chance of surviving in style rather than merely making do.

The crisis scenario is what Robin and his classmates are waiting, perhaps almost hoping, for. It would justify their critique of consumer society, and they expect to survive in relative comfort, so attuned are they to the rhythm of nature. I liked the extremism of Robin's approach, and admired even more the glorious unworldliness of Emma Orbach on her subsection of Brith Dir Mawr. Environment Secretary David Miliband has suggested we should all have to live with personal carbon allowances (PCAs) which we can choose to spend on fuel or air flights, and then buy more PCAs once we exceed our limit. That would be a bonus to Emma and Robin who would not need their full allowance.

But off-grid success and happiness can be found in different ways. Brith Dir Mawr is off the map of possibilities for me personally. I want to stay in touch with the city, at least some of the time; to flit between worlds, and enjoy the best that each has to offer. During my journey, I discovered I would be happy to join a community (not a commune), a group of households drawn together by a desire to live a certain way, one that has a reason for existing that binds disparate residents together. We all need an alliance to fall back on when we are under threat, whether from the council planning department, angry nimbys or marauding foragers looking for free food. In more normal times a group is a skills bank and a buying co-operative, bringing economies of scale for everything from food to renewable energy.

Community life is not the only way, of course; Marcus Tribe and Sarah Harvey in their yurt and Renee Vaughan Sutherland in her boat prove that. But I could not be a hermit. A community feels natural to me. It leaves each member free to pursue the things that most interest him or her, and also free to leave home for a few days or a few months without imperilling the crops or overall security. I like the idea of a group of friends buying a wood together, perhaps sharing whatever shelter they are allowed to build. And as these ideas catch hold I expect to see hamlets, small villages and suburban streets becoming off-grid ready, like Tony Marmont and Donnachadh McCarthy – sharing the cost of a borehole, setting up their own microgrid, being capable of living off-grid at any moment but choosing not to do so, or at least not all the time. As cars trek between woodland and townhouse, or we sidestep the effects of a cloudy, windless week by turning on the generator, this may not be a full solution to global warming and over-consumption, but it's a giant step in the right direction.

Double Standards?

I had been warned by Professor Offer that I might be merely exchanging one grid for another: the roads, the mobile phone and the Internet become more important as my use of mains power and water declines. And now that mobile technologies and renewable energy are quickly becoming more sophisticated and widespread, it is harder to define where the grid begins and ends. Merlin Howse waiting at the bottom of the track to Steward Wood for his washing to be delivered in a 4×4; the residents of Townhead commuting to work and dropping their children off at school; Patrick Scott the former close protection officer and his near industrial-scale bartering – are these contradictions really anything to be concerned about?

I don't think so. They may seem to raise wider issues but in the end they are just personal choices. Rural communities have always depended on barter, and Patrick does pay tax on his main earnings, as well as council tax and VAT. Do we want to create a society where Patrick would have to declare his earnings from fishing and gathering mushrooms? And why should Merlin not use part of his (so far notional) carbon allowance on his mother-in-law's washing machine if that is what he prefers? I sympathise with the Townhead commuters as they struggle back to the land at a time when there is no longer an agricultural community for them to be part of. What about Reuben the wood-carver, now receiving legal aid to fight the council's charge of non-compliance with his enforcement notice? He may not pay any income tax at the moment, but in this country we accept the principle that everyone has access to the law, not just the rich. It may be slightly unfair that Reuben ends up with a house on the cheap – we'd all like a nice house in a wood overlooking a valley. But he has worked hard for it, and if he was forced to demolish it the council would have to re-house him in any case.

Are Reuben's double standards any less acceptable than Roger Wilson's whenever he has a Tesco van trundle up the five miles to his house rather than support his local shops? How do Tony Marmont's eco-beliefs square with the frequent helicopter rides he takes? They don't, but that is no reason for Tony to stop enjoying himself (doing, after all, what many of us would like to do if we were in his position). Does it matter that Renee is earning good money at the council and ducking and diving to avoid the need to pay rent or council tax, or that Jyoti Fernandes has an EU grant for her food-processing barn while insisting that she be allowed to live on her farm because she cannot afford a house in the area? The Land Matters collective is setting up a society independent of the excesses of modern civilisation, but their homes are built out of the waste products of the very society they criticise. Robin's answer, given to me by phone as he drove to the pub one Sunday lunchtime, was, 'We are living in the community, using the pubs and the buses and the village shops. I'd like to pay council tax, but they won't let me. We have community-supported farming – allowing local people to grow their food on our land. In [nearby] Salcombe 40 to 80 per cent of the houses are second homes. The owners contribute nothing and are destroying the local communities.'

Yes, you could accuse them all of double standards, of isolating themselves from society, flouting convention and criticising the materialism and high consumption of the straight world on the one hand, but on the other of claiming dole, or paying tax, of sending their kids to the school and the doctor, and of applying for grants from the Lottery Fund. They probably are guilty of such contradictions, but aren't we all? Double standards are one of the things we British excel at. Perhaps it's an unavoidable part of being such a law-abiding society: we draw firm lines and then transgress them. Hypocrisy is deep in the fabric of our way of life. Look at the behaviour tolerated among public figures: mega-bonuses to CEOs of failing companies; jackpot pension schemes for senior BBC executives; cocaine-snorting models; wife-beating footballers; large fees for the Prime Minister's wife to talk about life at

Number Ten; loans for honours . . . Unless we have decided to raise the moral bar far higher for off-gridders, I choose to believe that none of the examples I have given really matters much, if at all. I think it is more important that our society should allow people like Renee and Judy the freedom to live on their boats or in their woods. They and all the others I met on my journey are adding to the diversity of our society and the richness of our culture.

Whether you agree with Thomas Homer-Dixon that a sizeable off-grid population improves our 'resilience' in the event of a crisis brought on by a trade war or global warming or terrorism, or you simply believe that every person living off-grid is one less demand on our scarce housing stock, off-grid living is good for society, even without invoking the ecological argument in its favour. At the moment just a few thousand people a year are moving to live off-grid, but there seems to be a much larger demand for it, and people now want to integrate their off-grid existence into mainstream working lives. Does that alter the moral situation? I do not believe so.

Success Unplugged

When I set off to do this research I was still wondering whether the off-grid life was hopelessly marginal. Had I entered a tiny subculture that was speaking only to itself? Thinking about it back at my desk, I realised it was Scoraig and Hill Holt Wood that convinced me I was on to something.

Nigel Lowthrop and his wife Karen have built an inspirational organisation out of nothing, and have successfully integrated their work with their life. Nigel's ambition is boundless, and now he has the ear of government. Much as I enjoyed visiting Marcus and Sarah in Nomansland, and envied their quiet, gentle existence, with a turnover one fiftieth of Nigel's, I feel more inspired to emulate Nigel's achievement. I should like to create a community where none had existed previously and show how off-grid principles can turn around an entire area.

I do not underestimate the effort that has gone into Hill Holt Wood; it was years of slog with no guaranteed return. But gradually something lasting and replicable emerged. The team of policy advisers and forestry bigwigs sent by the Environment Minister later commissioned a research project on Hill Holt Wood which led to policy recommendations, which in turn led to a visit by Sir Brian Bender, the Permanent Secretary. 'It's all about a different way of doing business in the climate-change era,' Nigel said to me. And that is the message he took to a meeting with Tony Blair in Downing Street in November 2006, along with a few other social enterprise leaders. And whatever Blair made of this meeting, the local council and the Forestry Commission have 'taken on board the rangers living on site and off-grid', Nigel said. The same month he was handed another much larger forest to play with. The Forestry Commission is devolving over a thousand acres of nearby Stapleford Wood to a replication on a grand scale of what Nigel has achieved at Hill Holt. 'It's a development that does not add carbon,' Nigel told me on a visit to London, enthusiastic as always. 'It will sweep away the idea that you cannot have development in woodland. The wildlife will live there if you provide the right conditions, the feeding areas.' He will not be retraining problem children in Stapleford Wood, but he will apply the same principles of mixing off-grid living and working, woodland reclamation, community involvement and commercial sense. 'It's pretty scabby but it will need to make £300,000-a-year profit.' Nigel plans to build 10,000 square metres of green office space to pay for the rest of the development of the site. It will cost millions, so he needs to involve a major property company. 'It will be gold standard on green construction, use local timber to power the site, and facilitate local landowners to grow energy crops. We will sell the power and the heat on site to our cornerstone tenant. One idea we have is a leisure centre with an outdoor swimming pool, a natural pool that will look like a reed-bed lake . . .' Nigel was off again. And I bet he makes a huge success of Stapleford Wood.

It is the opposite of the principles at work in Scoraig, where the founding fathers insisted each household should be a self-contained unit. Hugh Piggott has a business model that others could follow thanks to the Internet – a tiny but global enterprise offering a quality niche product (i.e. wind turbines, plus books and consultancy). He did it by taking something he needed to do in his own village (build a turbine) and offering it to the rest of the world. The same idea could work for organic sausages, or hand-knitted clothes, or hundreds of other products and services.

Scoraig's success comes down to its population of steady, kind, responsible, resourceful men and women who have contributed over the years. Scoraig proves that off-grid living can work for non-ideological folk. All it takes is a hands-off approach from the local authorities, who leave Scoraig alone to get on with it.

Coincidentally, Scoraig has a similar social structure to that on my Majorcan mountain: neighbours are near enough to overhear as they talk at night around the fire but far enough away that I can maintain the illusion of being in a private space cut off from the world. In Majorca, we all come together twice a year to maintain the road, but other than that the 'community' aspect comprises gossiping when we meet and helping one another out of difficulties.

Hector Christie's stately home is another model of the way forward. Hector has the same idealistic exuberance as Nigel. He is hemmed in, weighed down, by the obligations of ownership and his semi-aristocratic inheritance, and his role as the top dog at Tapeley is certainly different to Scoraig's series of independent self-managing households, or Townhead's highly communal decision-making process, or Allaleigh's workers' co-op constitution. But if Hector succeeds in taking Tapeley off-grid then who is to say which model is better or worse? The only thing lacking in Hector's set-up is long-term stability and security for everyone other than Hector. But if he could solve that problem, and adopt a slightly more democratic structure, he might have the best of all possible worlds.

You Can Free Yourself

After my trek around the UK, I still cannot be sure what the fullest possible off-grid life consists of. Is it about pulling completely out of the system, like Emma Orbach? Not as far as Nigel Lowthrop is concerned: he is making off-grid as mainstream as he can. Is it about building a powerful renewable energy system like Judy of the Woods? Not if you want to include Annette Potter and her family horse-breeding business, powered by a single generator. Is there a right way and a wrong way to be off-grid? Does it have to be a moral choice in the end, or is it OK to simply want to be free?

Although living off-grid is superficially about energy and water arrangements and the mundane details of toilets and shovels, turbines and solar panels, in fact it is more interesting and important than that. It offers freedom from utility bills, sure, and the low outgoings of the off-gridders I met freed them from the need to work hard, if at all. But it goes deeper than that, to a more meaningful kind of freedom, as I attempted to express in the opening chapter of this book. On balance, the lives of the majority of the people I spent time with, from Jyoti Fernandes and Marcus Tribe to Annette Potter and Judy of the Woods, were tough. Most of them had no money. But money just does not seem to matter. 'What's important,' Emma Orbach maintained, 'is to concentrate on dreaming a beautiful future.' In *Walden, or Life in the Woods*, Henry Thoreau expressed a similar sentiment: 'If one advances confidently in the direction of his dreams, and endeavours to live the life which he has imagined, he will meet with a success. In proportion as he simplifies his life, the laws of the universe will appear less complex, and solitude will not be solitude, nor poverty poverty, nor weakness weakness.'

Live more simply, and improve your life. Live a high-income, high-stress life, and feel isolated, trapped by your commitments, and as nothing compared to the person a few rungs below on the ladder. It is not a new message, and it will not dissolve the problems of our complex modern lives, but it's a start. Living off-grid remains a financial choice for some, a moral choice for others, a survival option for a third group. To me, it just feels right.

My search for a UK hideaway is progressing slowly. I have put the word out for coastal mixed-use woodland, discreet yet accessible, cheap yet elegant in appearance. A few properties have come my way, but as yet none of them is right. Price is a major consideration when buying your fourth home (after Hoxton, Majorca and the Bus), especially when you know you may not be using it often. Perhaps I shall choose not to buy an off-grid home or piece of land or woodland in the UK. For now, I shall continue to explore the van-dwelling life, with Fiona and Caitlin some of the time, or alone, as our family's advance scout in a continuing search for the ideal off-grid existence. I shall revisit the places I have already been to, because they moved me the first time. I want to know them well enough that they all feel like home. Once I feel at home everywhere, I may not need a home anywhere.

That may be where my travels lead, but being realistic, I doubt it. In the UK, owning property is the only way to control your destiny. I have been here before, twenty years ago, when I lived in a squat in central London and told myself I would never need to buy a home. Who would have expected then that London would become the world's most expensive city? Now I have been mugged by reality, and forced to become a property owner, or else leave the capital. And in just the same way, the rise in land prices, the city bonuses spent on snapping up small farms, the relentless sale of useless patches of forest to speculators, all mean that soon enough you won't even be able to afford a yurt in this country unless your parents help you buy it.

But I want to see the countryside become vibrant again, used to the full rather than preserved for the few. As I said at the outset of this postscript, to me off-grid is about looking outwards, creating a more open society, not looking inwards towards self-preservation. I also want to see our cities become more diverse. Existing buildings will not be taken off-grid unless there is a major crisis, but there are still huge tracts of land in and around cities that could be given over to off-grid homes.

There are two reforms that would enable tens of thousands who are currently prevented from doing so to take up this harmless lifestyle. The first I have touched upon throughout this book – bringing off-grid within the planning system. The other is to find a way to allow anyone to stay on farmland and common land for a week or two if they behave responsibly. Just as continuous cruisers are allowed to moor along the canals for up to a fortnight, I would like to see areas of private non-farming land made over to temporary, casual public use. Any holding of more than a thousand acres should be obligated to put aside a few of those acres for camper vans or tents or yurts, on the understanding they can be moved on instantly if they abuse the privilege. Think of off-gridding as a lifestyle to dip into, occasionally, for a few months at a time but more likely just for a weekend or at most a few weeks. Yes, there would be all sorts of unintended and unexpected problems, but wouldn't it be worth it to turn our thousands of miles of empty hedgerows into living communities once more?

If we do not make that choice for positive reasons now, it may be forced on us by crisis later. Whichever way it happens, I know that is the direction in which my own future lies.

Afterword

When I started writing this book, the idea of living off-grid was not on the cultural radar. Nothing earth-shattering has changed since, just a steady drip-drip of climate change events: melting ice-caps, weird weather, Al Gore, and the growing clamour of celebrities, broadcasters and mega-corporations jumping on the green bandwagon. But the media has slowly warmed to the idea of off-grid living. Since the first edition was published in June 2007, the *Grand Designs* TV series started using the word 'off-grid'; Jyoti Fernandes did a deal with the *River Cottage* TV series; BBC *Breakfast Time* featured Nigel Lowthrop in his social enterprise wood in Lincolnshire; the *Sunday Times* put Off-Grid in their weekly 'Going Up' trend monitor, with the words 'Free yourself from bills and the chains of corporate enslavement'; and even the *Sunday Express* property section devoted a feature to the money you could save from buying an off-grid home.

The media's more general infatuation with all things eco can only be a move in the right direction, but inevitably most of the coverage is designed to make us feel that if only we used a few more low-energy light-bulbs, turned the thermostat down a notch, saved water and recycled, we could go on living pretty much as before. We can't, but it will take something pretty nasty in the way of a natural catastrophe to make this sink in.

The summer of 2007 was no scorcher, in fact it was rather wet; we even had the irony of a flood causing a water shortage in parts of the country. There was no panic-inducing moment that persuaded large numbers they had better take the off-grid lifestyle seriously, but the indicators kept ticking towards a time when living off-grid will seem a sensible, mainstream choice. The price of oil crept towards $100 a barrel; sales of wood-burning stoves reached their highest point since the introduction of gas central heating; and house prices cooled, though they remained unaffordable to vast swathes of first-time buyers.

In July 2007 Tony Wrench was yet again refused planning permission by Pembrokeshire Council for his roundhouse; yet to their own and everyone else's surprise the residents of Land Matters in Devon received temporary planning permission in August. The public inquiry pitted Simon Fairlie against the financial resources of the local residents and their lawyers. The planning inspector indicated that one of the reasons for finding in favour of the bender community was that living off-grid coincided with so much current Government policy: lowering carbon emissions, bringing life and employment back to the countryside, and above all creating affordable housing. There was also good news from Marcus Tribe, who told me that the rates on his woodland workshop had been reduced from a thousand pounds a year to a couple of hundred.

I kept looking for my own off-grid place, and now I think I have found it – a piece of woodland which does not conform to every one of my criteria, but is beautiful and tranquil. And I am extremely fortunate that I did not have to buy it: I have it on a long-term loan from someone who read this book and contacted me via the off-grid website, which has become a place where people can meet others who are thinking of making the move off-grid, and find like-minded souls in their area.

In September 2007 Baroness Miller of Chilthorne Domer, a Lib Dem peer, raised a series of parliamentary questions, and they led to some useful answers which will be of help in terms of future planning appeals to people who want to live off-grid. Baroness Miller asked whether the Government would be introducing 'a planning category for low-impact, low-density housing that is not connected to national distribution networks for water and electricity'. Baroness Andrews, Parliamentary Under-Secretary of State, Department for Communities and Local Government, replied, 'Local planning authorities should encourage applicants to bring forward sustainable and environmentally friendly new development, and consider locations for housing where it can readily and viably draw its energy supply from decentralised energy supply systems based on renewable and low-carbon forms of energy supply, or where there is clear potential for this to be realised.' It remains for this answer to be tested in a public enquiry, but the suggestion is that the government is moving towards a presumption in favour of off-grid homes. Another written answer to Baroness Miller, this time from Lord Rooker, announced that there were 'around 50,000 private water supplies, serving 0.6 per cent of the population'. That means a total of roughly 360,000 people are off the water grid in the UK. But, as is so often the case, the Government sent out mixed signals. Lord Rooker went on to make it clear that the department in charge of climate change and environment is not currently concerned with promoting the energy-saving lifestyle of off-grid living. 'Defra does not hold statistics for the number of houses off the electricity grid and has made no estimate of the average energy efficiency or carbon dioxide emissions from homes unconnected to mains electricity supply. The Government do not provide incentives for householders to manage their own energy needs.'

The Government is looking into the numbers of people living off-grid, but not in normal houses; as they put it in another parliamentary exchange, only 'in boats, caravans, camper vans, tipis, yurts, tree-houses, benders, or other forms of unconventional accommodation'. The Office of National Statistics has offered a figure of '47,359 families' living in 'caravan or other mobile or temporary structures', which is considerably higher than my own estimate of 25,000 households in total living off-grid. The Government figure excludes those living off-grid in fixed structures such as houses, so assuming another 5,000 families live in houses, the new 'official' figure for the number of people (not families) living off-grid all year round is probably closer to 100,000 than the estimate of 75,000 in the first edition of this book.

In July 2007 Gordon Brown announced that he intended to pave the way for five new eco-towns of 5,000 to 20,000 homes which would be exemplar 'green' developments. 'They will be designed to meet the highest standards of sustainability, including zero-carbon technologies and good public transport, as well as lead the way in design, facilities and services, jobs, health and community involvement.' Baroness Andrews told Baroness Miller, 'We expect the developments to be planned in a way which supports low-carbon living, and this includes minimising carbon emissions from transport. There should also be the opportunity for the community to own and manage assets and to have a greater say in the running of their community.' I hope these 'assets' can include power, water and sewage facilities, run by locals for locals.

By September 2007 the Government had announced that they intended to build not five but ten eco-towns around Britain. Again, the reasoning was partly environmental, but it was also aimed at boosting the overall rate of new housebuilding. Whether any of these eco-towns will be off-grid remains to be seen. My view is that if they are not off-grid then they cannot be accurately described as eco-towns.

Whatever happens with this or that Government initiative, I feel sure that the overall political agenda is moving in favour of off-grid living, and technology is making it near inevitable. Perhaps one of the key moments will come when the price of batteries, solar panels and wind turbines drops (or the price of electricity rises) to the point where it costs the same for a typical household to get its power off-grid. With solar panel production due to double in 2008 and redouble in 2009, forecasters say this moment is not far away.

But more important than economics or technology is the growing understanding among planners and the public that with a more relaxed planning regime we would be free to live in beautiful places at a price most of us can truly afford.

Bibliography

Building and architecture

Khan, Lloyd (ed.), *Shelter*, Shelter Publications, 1973
Reynolds, Michael, *Earthship*, Solar Survival Press, 1993
Schmitz-Gunter, Thomas; Fisher, Thomas; Abraham, Loren,
   Living Spaces – Ecological Building and Design, Konemann, 1999
Pearson, David, *Yurts, Tipis and Benders*, Gaia Books, 2001
Living in Motion, Vitra Design Museum, 2002
Matthews, Robert, *All About Self-build*, Blackberry Books, 2002
Roaf, Sue, *Ecohouse* 2, Elsevier, 2003
Seymour, John, *The New Complete Book of Self-sufficiency*,
   Dorling Kindersley, 2003
Bruegmann, Robert, *Sprawl: A Compact History*,
   University of Chicago Press, 2005
The Green Building Bible, Green Building Press, 2005
Pearson, David, *Designing Your Natural Home*, Gaia Books, 2005
Anderson, Will, *Diary of an Eco-Builder*, Green Books, 2006

Energy and water

Allen, Paul, *Off the Grid*, CAT Publications, 1995
Solar Power in 12V Systems, El Morcon, Spain, 1998
Davis, Scott, *Micro Hydro*, New Society, 2003
Thomas, David, *Frozen Oceans: The Floating World of Pack Ice*,
   Natural History Museum, 2004
Brende, Eric, *Better Off – Flipping the Switch on Technology*,
   HarperCollins, 2005
Kemp, William, *The Renewable Energy Handbook*, Aztext Press, 2005
The Humanure Handbook, obtainable from Green Books, 2005

Monbiot, George, *Heat: How to Stop the Planet Burning*, Allen Lane, 2006
Pearce, Fred, *When the Rivers Run Dry*, Eden Project Books, 2006

Food

Atterbury, Stella, *Leave it to Cook*, Penguin, 1968
Edwards, Pat, *Cheap Eating*, Upper Access Books, 1993
Spooner, Brian, *Mushrooms and Toadstools*, Collins Wild Guide, 1996
Mabey, Richard, *Food for Free*, Collins, 2001

General

The Countryman's Weekend Book, Seeley Service & Co., 1944
Saunders, Nicholas, *Alternative England and Wales*, self-published, 1975
Callenback, Ernest, *Ecotopian Encyclopaedia*, And/Or Press, 1980
Holford, Patrick and Cass, Hyla, *Chill – 25 Ways to Relax and Beat Stress*, Piatkus, 2003
Bush, Alan, *Escape to Scorraig*, self-published, 2004
Hill Holt Wood Social Audit Report, 2004–2005, Hill Holt Wood, 2005
Hodgkinson, Tom, *How to Be Free*, Penguin, 2006

Going mobile

Wilkinson, Gerald, *Woodland Walks in South West England*, Webb & Bower, 1986
Botting, Douglas, *Wild Britain*, Interlink Books, 1999
Belsey, Valerie, *Discovering Green Lanes*, Green Books, 2001
The Green Holiday Guide, Great Britain and Northern Ireland, European Centre for Ecological and Agricultural Tourism, Green Books, 2002
Trant, Kate (ed.), *Home Away From Home*, Black Dog Publishing, 2005
Knight, Jonathan, *Cool Camping*, Punk Publishing, 2006

History

Mais, S. P. B., 'A Plain Man's Guide to England' in *Britain and the Beast* (ed. William Clough Ellis), J. M. Dent, 1937

Rowland, John, *Progress in Power: The Contribution of Charles Merz and His Associates to Sixty Years of Electrical Development, 1899–1959*, Newman Neame (privately published on behalf of Merz & McLellan), 1960

Byatt, I. C. R., *The British Electrical Industry, 1875–1914*, Oxford University Press, 1979

Hannah, Leslie, *Electricity Before Nationalisation*, Johns Hopkins University Press, 1979

Williams, Trevor I., *A History of the British Gas Industry*, Oxford University Press, 1981

Hannah, Leslie, *Engineers, Managers, and Politicians: The First Fifteen Years of Nationalised Electricity Supply in Britain*, Johns Hopkins University Press, 1982

Hughes, Thomas P., *Networks of Power: Electrification in Western Society, 1880–1930*, Johns Hopkins University Press, 1984

Luckin, Bill, *Questions of Power: Electricity and Environment in Inter-war Britain*, Manchester University Press, c. 1990

Hamlin, Christopher, *A Science of Impurity: Water Analysis in the Nineteenth Century*, University of California Press, 1990

Off-grid ready

Siegle, Lucy, *Green Living in the Urban Jungle*, Green Books, 2001

Decentralising Power, Greenpeace, 2005

Prasad, Deo and Snow, Mark, *Designing with Solar Power*, Images Publishing, 2005

Kemp, William, *Smart Power*, Aztext Press, 2006

Waddington, Paul, *The 21st-Century Smallholder*, Eden Books, 2006

Philosophy

Gladwell, Malcolm, *Tipping Point*, Little, Brown, 2000

Lane, John, *Timeless Simplicity*, Green Books, 2001

Grayling, A. C., *What is Good?*, Phoenix, 2004

Honore, Carl, *In Praise of Slow*, Orion, 2004

Homer-Dixon, Thomas, *The Upside of Down*, Random House, 2006

Lovelock, James, *The Revenge of Gaia*, Allen Lane, 2006

Planning permission

Fairlie, Simon, *Low Impact Development: Planning and People in a Sustainable Countryside*, Jon Carpenter, 1996

Ward, Colin and Hardy, Dennis, *Arcadia for All – the Legacy of a Makeshift Landscape*, J. M. Dent, 2003

Planning Policy Statement 1: Delivering Sustainable Development, ODPM, 2004

DIY Planning Briefings, 3rd edition, Chapter 7, 2005

Survival

Mears, Ray, *The Outdoor Survival Handbook: A Guide to the Resources and Materials Available in the Wild and How to Use Them for Food, Shelter, Warmth and Navigation*, St Martin's Press, 1993

Wiseman, John, *SAS Survival Guide*, Collins Gem, 2004

Woodland

Law, Ben, *The Woodland Way*, Permanent Publications, 2001

Moffat, Andy J., 'The State of Britain's Forests at the Beginning of the 21st Century' in *International Forestry Review* 4(3), 2002

Magazines

British

Building for a Future
Permaculture
Planning
The Ecologist
The Idler
The Land

American

Budget Living
Budget Travel
Homepower
Mother Earth News
Outside
The Tightwad Gazette

Acknowledgements

In the course of my researching this book, many people invited me into their off-grid homes, be they boats, vans, yurts, benders, cabins or even brick buildings. Thanks for giving so generously of your personal space and your time, both when I visited and in subsequent phone calls, especially Dylan Evans, who is writing his own book, and who shared his thoughts on the potential chaos facing our society as we sat in his yurt.

I am also grateful to Stephen Cottle and Simon Fairlie for their help and suggestions on planning permission. It is a complex subject, and any mistakes that remain are mine, not theirs. Thanks also to Simon Chambers for his filming assistance and wise words about permaculture; Piet at Raisystems for answering so many questions about renewable energy systems; Giles Elgood, who told me the word; and Paul Allen (of CAT), who was one of the first in this country to spot the importance of living off-grid. Particular thanks to Michael Edge, whose encouragement kept me going; Keith at Pendragon Framers, who made sure the van came to no harm; Alex Aylesbury of Agency 23 for his work on the website; Ivan Mulcahy, who advised on an early draft; Felix Unger-Hamilton, who maintained and monitored the video-tapes as I travelled around the country; and Bridget Smith for the nice photo of me.

I lucked into editor Susanna Wadeson, a model of enthusiasm and level-headed advice, and brilliant copy editor Daniel Balado. Jonathan Winkler was invaluable on the historical research, and Elena Andreicheva scoured the Internet for useful tips and fact-checked on scores of topics.

Text and Ilustration Acknowledgements

The author and publisher are grateful to the following sources for permission to reproduce extracts: lines from *The Anticipation of the Reaction of Mechanical and Scientific Progress Upon Human Life and Thought* copyright © 1902 by permission of A P Watt on behalf of the Literary Executors of the Estate of H G Wells; extract from *Portable Houses* by Irene Rawlings and Mary Abel, copyright © 2004, published by Gibbs Smith, Publisher, 2004; 'The Tree Hoose Song' by Barnie McCormack copyright © 2001, by permission of Barnie McCormack; extract from *Low Impact Development* by Simon Fairlie, copyright © 1996, published by Jon Carpenter Publishing; 'Pylons' from *New Collected Poems* by Stephen Spender © 2004, reprinted by kind permission of the Estate of Sir Stephen Spender; 'The Road Not Taken' from *The Poetry of Robert Frost*, edited by Edward Connery Lathem, published by Jonathan Cape, reprinted by permission of The Random House Group.

Illustrations on pages 8, 187, 233, 309, 317 © 2007 H L Studios.
Illustration on page 314 © 2007 Scouse Martin

All photographs are copyright © Nick Rosen, except for the following: photograph of Jyoti Fernandes © Venetia Dearden (p.177); photograph of Julienne Dolphin Wilding and her container © Monika Zanolin (p.208).

Every effort has been made to obtain the necessary permissions with reference to copyright material, both illustrative and quoted. We apologise for any omissions in this respect and will be pleased to make the appropriate acknowledgements in any future edition.